The Distinctive Identity of the Church

The Distinctive Identity of the Church

A Constructive Study of the Post-Christendom Theologies of Lesslie Newbigin and John Howard Yoder

Jeppe Bach Nikolajsen

PICKWICK *Publications* • Eugene, Oregon

THE DISTINCTIVE IDENTITY OF THE CHURCH
A Constructive Study of the Post-Christendom Theologies of Lesslie Newbigin and John Howard Yoder

Copyright © 2015 Jeppe Bach Nikolajsen. All rights reserved. Except for brief quotations in critical publications or reviews, no part of this book may be reproduced in any manner without prior written permission from the publisher. Write: Permissions. Wipf and Stock Publishers, 199 W. 8th Ave., Suite 3, Eugene, OR 97401.

Pickwick Publications
An Imprint of Wipf and Stock Publishers
199 W. 8th Ave., Suite 3
Eugene, OR 97401

www.wipfandstock.com

ISBN 13: 978-1-4982-0207-7

Cataloguing-in-Publication Data

Nikolajsen, Jeppe Bach

    The distinctive identity of the church : a constructive study of the post-Christendom theologies of Lesslie Newbigin and John Howard Yoder / Jeppe Bach Nikolajsen.

    x + 220 p. ; 23 cm. Includes bibliographical references and index(es).

    ISBN 13: 978-1-4982-0207-7

    1. Church. 2. Yoder, John Howard. 3. Newbigin, Lesslie. I. Title.

BR162.3 .N55 2015

Manufactured in the U.S.A.   03/19/2015

Parts of this book have been published before. This book is published with permission from *Swedish Missiological Themes, International Review of Mission, Missiology: An International Review, Exchange: A Journal for Ecumenical and Missiological Research*, and Kolon Press.

Unlesss otherwise indicated, Scripture quotations are taken from New Revised Standard Version Bible, copyright © 1989 the Division of Christian Education of the National Council of the Churches of Christ in the United States of America. Used by permission. All rights reserved.

Contents

Preface | ix

Part I: Introduction

1 Post-Christendom Ecclesiology | 3
   1.1 The Problem | 3
   1.2 The Material | 11
   1.3 The Method | 15
   1.4 The Process | 18
   1.5 The Ambition | 19

Part II: Lesslie Newbigin

2 Sent by Christ to the World | 23
   2.1 Introduction | 23
   2.2 Christendom | 25
      2.2.1 Newbigin's Theological Project and Christendom | 25
      2.2.2 Newbigin's Evaluation of Christendom | 26
   2.3 Ecclesiology | 33
      2.3.1 Election and Salvation History | 33
      2.3.2 Election and Necessity | 38
      2.3.3 Election and Ecclesiology | 40
   2.4 Missiology | 41
      2.4.1 Church and Mission in the Ecumenical Movement | 42
      2.4.2 Church and Mission in the Theology of Newbigin | 46
      2.4.3 Church and Mission in Light of a Trinitarian Perspective | 48
      2.4.4 Missiology and Ecclesiology | 52
   2.5 Eschatology | 54
      2.5.1 The Old Age | 54
      2.5.2 The New Age | 56
      2.5.3 The Church as Sign, Instrument and Foretaste | 58

2.5.4 Eschatology and Ecclesiology | 61
2.6 Social Ethics | 62
    2.6.1 The Church as a Distinct Social Order | 62
    2.6.2 The Church as a Servant Community | 64
    2.6.3 Ethics and Ecclesiology | 66
2.7 Epistemology | 67
    2.7.1 Two Traditions | 67
    2.7.2 The Rationalistic Humanist Tradition | 70
    2.7.3 The Christian Tradition | 73
    2.7.4 The Rationalistic Humanist and the Christian Tradition | 77
    2.7.5 Epistemology and Ecclesiology | 79
2.8 Conclusion | 80
    2.8.1 The Distinctive Identity of the Church | 80
    2.8.2 The Role of the Church in a Post-Christendom Society | 84
        The Church as a Minority in a Post-Christendom Society | 84
        The Church in a Diverse Post-Christendom Society | 85
        The Church Shaping Various Areas of a Post-Christendom Society | 87

Part III: John Howard Yoder

3 Following the Way of Christ in the World | 95
    3.1 Introduction | 95
    3.2 Constantinianism | 98
        3.2.1 Constantinianism and the Theological Project of Yoder | 98
        3.2.2 Consequences of Constantinianism | 101
        3.2.3 Constantinianism and Modern Western History | 103
    3.3 Ecclesiology | 105
        3.3.1 The Diasporic Existence of the People of God | 105
        3.3.2 Believers' Church | 112
        3.3.3 Five Practices of the Early Church | 113
        3.3.4 The Visibility of the Church | 116
        3.3.5 The Marks of the Church | 117
        3.3.6 The Church Is the Mission | 118
        3.3.7 Ecclesiology | 121
    3.4 Social Ethics | 122

3.4.1 The Disassociation of Ethics From Jesus | 122
3.4.2 Christology and Social Ethics | 124
3.4.3 The Politics of Jesus | 125
3.4.4 Revolutionary Subordination | 128
3.4.5 Suffering Like Jesus | 130
3.4.6 Jesus Was a Pacifist | 131
3.4.7 Social Ethics and Ecclesiology | 140

3.5 Eschatology | 141
3.5.1 The Two Ages | 141
3.5.2 The Creation of the World | 142
3.5.3 The Rebellion against God | 142
3.5.4 The Salvation of Christ | 146
3.5.5 The Lordship of Christ | 148
3.5.6 Eschatology and Ecclesiology | 150

3.6 Conclusion | 154
3.6.1 The Distinctive Identity of the Church | 154
3.6.2 The Role of the Church in a Post-Christendom Society | 158
The Church as a Minority in a Post-Christendom Society | 158
The Church in a Diverse Post-Christendom Society | 159
The Church and State in a Post-Christendom Society | 160

Part IV: Toward a Post-Christendom Ecclesiology

4 Beyond Sectarianism | 163
4.1 Introduction | 163
4.2 Sent by a Missionary God | 166
4.3 The Church as Community | 172
4.4 The Church as Servant | 176
4.5 The Church as Prophet | 180
4.6 Oriented to the Kingdom of God | 185
4.7 Conclusion | 186

Part V: Conclusion

5 Corpus Christianum or Corpus Christi? | 191

Bibliography | 197

Index | 213

Preface

THE IDEA FOR THIS book was born in the late summer of 2006, when I studied at Fuller Theological Seminary. It was there that Veli-Matti Kärkkäinen encouraged me to begin reading Lesslie Newbigin. During the following summer, I had the possibility to visit Michael W. Goheen in Vancouver. This was an excellent opportunity for me to converse about the incipient design of this book. It was Goheen who encouraged me to compare Lesslie Newbigin and John Howard Yoder's so-called countercultural theologies.

Thus, the bigger lines of this book were sketched. I was then enrolled at the doctoral program of MF Norwegian School of Theology in Oslo in 2007. Here my supervisor, Tormod Engelsviken, and also Jan-Olav Henriksen, helped me sharpen my research problem and methodological approach and the whole design of the project. Thus, this book is a revised edition of the dissertation I defended at MF Norwegian School of Theology in Oslo.

Doing research in St. Paul in 2009 and 2010, I had several inspiring conversations with Pat Taylor Ellison, and Patrick Keifert at Luther Seminary, and also with William Cavanaugh working at that time at University of St. Thomas, during a period in which this work began to take shape rapidly. Toward the end of this process Michael W. Goheen and Arne Rasmusson read some of the chapters, and gave me many helpful comments.

The past years, Keld Dahlmann, Mogens S. Mogensen, and Viggo Mortensen have often encouraged me, and I also had many inspiring conversations with my colleagues at Lutheran School of Theology in Aarhus. Andreas Ø. Nielsen, Klaus Vibe, and Morten H. Jensen have been, from beginning to end, inspiring conversation partners. I would also like to thank my colleagues at MF Norwegian School of Theology in Oslo, Vija Herefoss, Kristin Norseth, Knud Jørgensen, and Roar Fotland. All the persons mentioned above have influenced my work with the book that I hereby present.

I would also like to thank the Mikkelsen Foundation, the Erichsen Foundation, the Areopagos Foundation, the Oticon Foundation, the Danish Mission Council, and the Danish Council of Churches for supporting my trips to the World Council of Churches' archives in Geneva and the John Howard Yoder Archives in Goshen, Indiana, and for supporting my participation in conferences and trips to Luther Seminary, Fuller Theological Seminary, Boston University School of Theology, the Department of Theology at Notre Dame University, and Yale Divinity School.

I believe the future demands that Christians continuously reflect on the church's relation to the rest of society. Hopefully, this book will provide helpful reflections on the identity of the church and its role in increasingly pluralistic Western societies. It is my hope that this book will help churches discern faithful ways of being the body of Christ in the world.

—Jeppe Bach Nikolajsen

Aarhus, Denmark

August 2014

PART I
Introduction

1

Post-Christendom Ecclesiology

1.1 The Problem

THE RELATIONSHIP BETWEEN CHRISTIANITY and culture is a classic theological hurdle and has, throughout history, been the subject of numerous discussions.¹ Due to significant cultural and religious changes in the Western world, an intriguing discussion has emerged within this classic theological debate. An increasing number of theologians assert that the Western world has moved from, or is currently in transition from, an era of Christendom to one of post-Christendom, the magnitude and significance of which has been discussed in a number of books.²

Darrell L. Guder believes that there exist at least six key problems in this time of transition, claiming that the church in the era of Christendom was responsible for theological reductionism in terms of soteriology, eschatology, Pneumatology, Christology, missiology, and ecclesiology.³ Ac-

---

1. In his book *Christ and Culture*, H. Richard Niebuhr exemplifies the variety of theological positions in the Christian tradition with respect to this issue. It is important to note the omission of the church in Niebuhr's discussion of the relation between Christ and culture. This can also be said about Robert C. Kimball and Paul Tillich's book *Theology of Culture*, and Charles H. Kraft's book *Christianity in Culture*. In this book, I will allow ecclesiology to serve as a perspective on the relationship between Christ and culture.

2. Minor parts of this chapter have been published in my articles "Missional Folk Church" and "Beyond Christendom." Also, parts of this chapter have been presented in Danish in my article "Kirkens konstantinske fangenskab."

3. Guder presents strong critique of the theology developed in the era of Christendom. According to Guder, Christendom generated several theological reductionisms. For example, the gospel was reduced to the "benefits that accrue to the individual believer," and had a one-sided focus on individualistic salvation (soteriology). The church also lost "confidence in God's promised future which invests our present life and ministry with hope and which gives our witness energy" and was reduced "to an apocalyptic sense of the future" (eschatology). Furthermore, the church made a false "separation between the Saviorhood and the Lordship of Christ" (Christology). According to Guder, the impact of these theological reductionisms upon Western

cording to Guder, it is important to come to terms with this theological reductionism. As it would not serve the purpose of this book to discuss all of these contentions at length, I will instead focus on one of these six key problems and present a discussion of the transition from the era of Christendom to post-Christendom, with special attention paid to the ecclesiological consequences of this shift.[4]

In an increasing number of books, this transition is discussed from the basis of historical, systematic theological, and practical theological perspectives. A common thread throughout these portrayals is that Western church history is divided into three eras: the pre-Christendom era, the Christendom era, and the post-Christendom era.[5]

The term "pre-Christendom" describes a specific relationship between the Christian church and its surrounding society in the period from the first century to the fourth century. During this period, the Christian church did not benefit from any societal privileges and had no notable political influence, being a persecuted church. In the beginning of the fourth century, the Roman Emperor Constantine, who controlled the Western provinces in the Roman Empire, defeated another Western Roman Emperor, Maxentius, thereby gaining sovereignty over the sole *Western* Roman Empire.[6] The Roman Emperor Licinius, after a victory over the Roman Emperor Maximinus II in 313 AD, gained sovereignty over the entire *Eastern* Roman empire. The two emperors, Licinius and

---

theologizing led to "the very serious loss of a missional dynamic which places the theological disciplines within and in support of our shared apostolic vocation" (missiology). These propositional and abstract approaches to "Scripture obscure the way in which the Bible, through the Holy Spirit, works formatively in the witnessing community" (Pneumatology). Finally, "the community called to witness to God's breaking reign in Christ becomes the church that receives, contains, and serves saved souls (. . .). In Christendom, these processes constitute in reality a reductionism of the church to a partner of the state and thus a cultural agency captive to its environment" (ecclesiology). See Guder, "Missional Hermeneutics," 112–13.

4. It is not possible to separate ecclesiology from soteriology, eschatology, missiology, Christology, and Pneumatology. Ecclesiology is always, consciously or unconsciously, woven into a bigger theological framework. In this section I attempt, however, to frame a specifically ecclesiological research problem for the purposes of this book. How this ecclesiological research problem is woven into a greater theological framework will be demonstrated later.

5. However, I do not wish to go into depth with these historical analyses. Rather, my intention is to frame the greater historical picture and then, from these analyses, to frame a systematic theological research problem which will be the starting point for this book.

6. Murray, *Post-Christendom*, 25.

Constantine, now lived side by side: Licinius in the East and Constantine in the West. In 324 AD, a war broke out between them, a war that Constantine won, which consequently led Constantine to become the sole Emperor of the Roman Empire.[7]

Previous to this, Constantine had for some time shown interest in the Christian religion and, after his "conversion" to Christianity, he became known as the first Christian Emperor of the Roman Empire.[8] In 313 AD, Licinius and Constantine announced the Edict of Milan, in which the Christian religion was legalized and made equal with other religions in the Roman Empire. Hereby, the conditions for the church's position in society were changed significantly, with two hundred and fifty years of persecution of the Christian church coming to an end.[9] Constantine continued to show favoritism to the Christian church. For example, he issued "laws favouring the churches, lavished privileges and resources on them, [and] sought the counsel of bishops."[10] He was baptized on his deathbed, and then buried in the Church of the Twelve Apostles in Constantinople.[11] The Constantinian endorsement of Christianity culminated in the Christian religion becoming the official religion of the Roman Empire in 380 AD, after the death of Constantine.[12] Later, in 391 AD pagan worship was condemned.

With the aforementioned announcements of 313 AD and 380 AD, the so-called era of Christendom began.[13] The church was now officially accepted and over time its wealth increased, it obtained political influence, and it became an important factor in society. As a result of Christianity becoming a politically and culturally established religion, the distinctions between church and society were weakened. Thus, in contrast to the pre-Christendom era, by the fourth century, Christians

---

7. Pohlsander, *The Emperor Constantine*, 24, 42.

8. Historians have for a long time debated whether Constantine truly did convert. How did he influence the church and its theology? Did he become a Christian? Or did he just use the church to foster his political agendas? See, for example, Baynes, *Constantine the Great and the Christian Church*; Barnes, *Constantine and Eusebius*; Kee, *Constantine versus Christ*; among others.

9. Cf. Nissen, "Folkekirken—sendt til det danske folk," 90.

10. Murray, *Post-Christendom*, 25.

11. Ibid., 26.

12. Cf. Nissen, "Folkekirken—sendt til det danske folk," 90.

13. Herrin states that, already by the early third century, a notion of a Christian age was established. See *The Formation of Christendom*, 4.

did not seem to be distinct. Robert A. Markus concludes that, already by the middle of the fourth century, very little separated a Christian from his pagan counterpart in the Roman Empire.[14] Charlemagne, king of the Franks from 768 AD, and Emperor of the Romans from 800 AD until his death in 814 AD, identified his empire and its population as Christendom, and "[t]he terms *Franci* and *christiani* became almost identical as terms for his subjects. Baptism was a prerequisite for both. His wars of conquest were holy wars, and the conquered not only saw their territory incorporated into his empire but were also forced to become Christians. Conquest and Christianization went together and the preachers of the gospel worked in the service of the Frankish rulers."[15] In this way, the church and European society fused together as a single cultural, political and religious entity.[16] As Michael W. Goheen describes the development: "The church moved from a marginal position to a dominant institution in society; from being socially, politically, and intellectually inferior to being in a position of power and superiority; from being economically weak and poor to being in a position of immense wealth; from being an oppressed minority to being the oppressive majority; from being a *religio illicita* to becoming the only religion in the civic community; from being resident aliens in a pagan environment to being an established church in a professedly Christian state."[17]

The Middle Ages were similarly marked by a close relationship between the church and the European states represented by the Emperor, kings and princes of the European kingdoms. This led to power struggles. Could the Emperor be crowned without the Pope's approval? Could the Pope take office without the Emperor's approval? Could the kings and the Emperor appoint bishops? Regardless of these clashes, the close relationship between the church and the European states continued to express a synthesis between Christianity and culture, church and state.[18] Thus, in the medieval period, the state was often viewed as the protector of the church. A clear expression of this can be seen during the Reformation in the German regions where the German princes, who in many cases were also

---

14. Markus, *The End of Ancient Christianity*, 27.
15. Bredero, *Christendom and Christianity in the Middle Ages*, 17.
16. Herrin, *The Formation of Christendom*, 4.
17. Goheen, *As the Father Has Sent Me*, 2–3.
18. Nissen, *En gammel folkekirke i en ny tid*, 24.

bishops, protected the German national church.[19] Hence, Arne Rasmusson refers to the medieval Christian world as the paradigmatic example of Christendom.[20] The medieval fusion of church and society into a cultural, political, and religious unity is also referred to as *corpus Christianum*.[21]

A clear example of Christendom can also be found during the Reformation in my own country, Denmark, when Lutheranism became the state religion. In 1536, the Danish king took over the bishops' property and their right to receive the church's tithes, promising to both protect the country against outside attack and to be the supreme guarantor of the Evangelical Lutheran Church of Denmark. Until 1849, all citizens in Denmark were obliged to be members of the Lutheran Church of Denmark.[22] They were also forced to be baptized and to attend services, and the authorities sought to control the morality of the people.[23]

In many ways, the close relationship between church and state still exists in Denmark. Today, the Danish king or queen is considered the head of the so-called Danish Folk Church according to Danish law and, consequently, the regent authorizes the liturgy, the rituals, the bible translation and the book of hymns of the church.[24] Also, Danish politicians to a great extent impact the policies of the church. Moreover, around 80 percent of the Danish population are members of the Danish Folk Church, even though less than 2 percent of the population attends church services on a given Sunday. Furthermore, the Danish Folk Church is responsible for the national registration of citizens.

As a radical example of the vision for a Christendom society, Douglas John Hall refers to a book published by English E. Griffith-Jones in 1926, which states: "The distinction between the secular and the sacred will disappear from human life, for all that is secular will be sanctified. When this ideal state will be realized, the world will once more be God's world, and his 'will be done on earth as it is in heaven.'"[25] Accordingly, a Christendom society expresses a close relationship between church and

---

19. Grane, *Evangeliet for folket*, 91.

20. Rasmusson, "Christendom," 97.

21. See, for example, Harvey, *Another City*, 81.

22. However, in the 1680s, the few Jews, Baptists, and Reformed Christians in the country were allowed not to have their infants baptized.

23. Lausten, *Danmarks kirkehistorie*, 175, 239.

24. Nissen, "Missional kirke: En kirke sendt til det danske folk," 98.

25. Hall refers to Griffith-Jones, *The Dominion of Man*, 311; cf. Hall, *The End of Christendom*, 14.

society with the church obtaining an influential position, and Christian values being important elements in legislation. In this way, Christendom not only refers to the medieval Christian world, but also "refers to later forms of politically and culturally established Christianity."[26] I have given Denmark as an example of this, but many other examples could also have been given.[27]

Today, as mentioned, a number of theologians claim that the Western world is in transition from Christendom to post-Christendom, some of whom even claim that we have long ago left the era of Christendom. Stuart Murray defines the term "post-Christendom" as follows: "Post-Christendom is the culture that emerges as the Christian faith loses coherence within a society that has been definitively shaped by the Christian story and as the institutions that have been developed to express Christian convictions decline in influence."[28] Thus, when theologians refer to Western culture's transition from Christendom to post-Christendom, they mean that the larger societal institutions, the most important cultural, political, and educational institutions, no longer consider themselves to be Christian. This means that the church gradually loses its central and influential position in society, and that Christianity can no longer be considered as a mainstay in Western society.

When one attempts to analyze such a complex history, one often runs the risk of drawing oversimplified conclusions. Hence, clarifications of the discussion have been presented. Anton Wessels has shown that noticeable paganism and syncretism were apparent in medieval Europe.[29] Despite this, he does not question that the church played a significant role in European societies. Jean Delumeau concludes, along the same lines as Wessels, that the Christianization of Europe at the time of the Reformation in many ways was superficial.[30] Building on this, Murray states that it is misleading to use the term "post-Christendom" synonymously with

26. Rasmusson, "Christendom," 97.

27. For example, the preamble to the Constitution of Ireland states: "In the Name of the Most Holy Trinity, from Whom is all authority and to Whom, as our final end, all actions both of men and States must be referred, We, the people of Éire, Humbly acknowledging all our obligations to our Divine Lord, Jesus Christ (. . .). Do hereby adopt, enact, and give to ourselves this Constitution." See *The Constitution of Ireland*, 8. The preambles to the Constitution of Poland, Greece, Germany, and Slovakia also refer to God, the Christian church or Christianity.

28. Murray, *Post-Christendom*, 19.

29. See, for example, Wessels, *Europe: Was it Ever Really Christian?*, 149–60.

30. Delumeau, *Le catholicisme entre Luther et Voltaire*, 227–55.

"post-Christian." This can lead to the idea that the difference between the Christendom and post-Christendom is a transition from a Christian society to a post-Christian society. As Wessels, Delumeau and others have shown, Europe was to a great extent marked by paganism in the Middle Ages. Instead, the difference between the Christendom era and the post-Christendom era is, first and foremost, the loss of the church's central and influential position in society.

A post-Christendom society also cannot be equated with a thoroughgoing secular society according to Murray. People in a post-Christendom society will be incessantly preoccupied with religiosity. A post-Christendom society may merely be understood as a pluralistic, multireligious society. However, most people will not consider themselves Christian.[31]

Few doubt the overall interpretation that church history has contained two major shifts. The first shift encompasses the church's movement from being marginalized to having an influential position in society; the second shift embodies how the church is now losing its influential position and again is becoming marginalized. According to a number of theologians, we have been experiencing this last major shift since the time of the Enlightenment, a shift which gained momentum with the secularization of Western society in the twentieth century.[32]

In the debate concerning the significance of the transition from Christendom to post-Christendom, *the distinctiveness of the church* is a recurrent theme. On the one hand, it is argued that the era of Christendom is not over or that the legacy of Christendom still impacts the churches in the West.[33] A number of theologians argue that the synthesis between church and society present in Christendom is in conflict with the nature of the church, arguing that the nature of the church is to be

31. Murray, *Post-Christendom*, 4–12.

32. As I have shown, many helpful and clarifying contributions to this specific debate have already been presented. However, in my mind, current research still lacks further qualification of central concepts, more historical research and clarification of various systematic theological positions. It would also be helpful to clarify how the transition from Christendom to post-Christendom has developed differently in various geographical areas in the Western world, since every country has its own history; some articles with reference to Ireland, England, the Netherlands, Germany, and France have, however, been presented. See McLeod and Ustorf, *The Decline of Christendom in Western Europe*.

33. Hall, *The End of Christendom*, 1–18; Frost, *Exiles*, 3–8; Clapp, *A Peculiar People*, 29; Harvey, *Another City*, 93.

a chosen people, a people living amidst other people, and a community living among other communities. This sentiment implies that the church must differ from society. Without such a difference between church and society, the church cannot make a difference in society. It is argued that the distinctive character of the church is a fundamental aspect of the church's identity that it must never lose and, owing to the fact that the church in the era of Christendom lost its distinctive character, the church must today re-appropriate this distinctiveness.[34] On the other hand, it is argued that the era of Christendom is over, and that the previously central place of the Christian church in society is now challenged and, therefore, the self-understanding of the Western church is now threatened.[35] The Christian church is marginalized and its distinctiveness is becoming more and more evident, thus, it is important for the church to understand its distinctive identity and its role under these new cultural conditions.[36]

Although the distinctiveness of the church is a recurrent theme in the discussion of the transition from an era of Christendom to post-Christendom, we have not yet seen any coherent theological investigation into how we ought to understand the distinctive identity of the church. Rather, it is again and again presupposed in the debate. Therefore, I see good reasons for making this an object of investigation, as it seems an important and necessary task to disclose and examine this fundamental presupposition concerning the ongoing development of a post-Christendom ecclesiology. This book will, therefore, attempt to present a qualified answer to the following question: How are we to understand the distinctive identity of the church, with special reference to its role in a post-Christendom society?

It quickly becomes apparent that important problems are connected to such a survey. Stephen B. Bevans points out three important dangers related to such an investigation. First, the distinctive identity of the church can be emphasized to such an extent that the church may

---

34. See, for example, Harvey, *Another City*, 14–15, 23, 59; Kenneson, *Beyond Sectarianism*, 91; Hauerwas and Willimon, *Resident Aliens*, 46, 93–94; Hall, *The End of Christendom*, 36.

35. Kenneson, *Beyond Sectarianism*, 1. It is also worth noting the titles of the following books: Guroian, *Ethics after Christendom*; Bader-Saye, *Church and Israel after Christendom*; Smith, *Mission after Christendom*; Schuurman, *Vocation after Christendom*; Murray, *Church after Christendom*; Bartley, *Faith and Politics after Christendom*; Stone, *Evangelism after Christendom*.

36. Kenneson, *Beyond Sectarianism*, 2; Hall, *The End of Christendom*, 6–7; Guroian, *Ethics after Christendom*, 3.

be in danger of becoming "monocultural," a strong emphasis on the distinctiveness of the church leading to the tendency to create *one* specific culture in contrast to other cultures. Second, the distinctive identity of the church can be emphasized to such an extent that the church may be in danger of becoming "anticultural," leading the church to condemn society as wicked and evil. Third, the distinctive identity of the church can be emphasized to the point that the church may be in danger of becoming "sectarian," leading to the church cutting itself off from other people.[37] There are many dangers in developing an understanding of the church's distinctive identity.[38] At the end of this book I will discuss this last and, in my opinion, most important critique.[39]

1.2 The Material

Relevant theological sources must be considered in order to present a qualified theological analysis and discussion of the distinctive identity of the church. For the purposes of this book, I have chosen to make use of the writings of English theologian James Edward Lesslie Newbigin, and American theologian John Howard Yoder. This is due to several factors.

I find it relevant to analyze the writings of Newbigin, as the distinctive identity of the church plays an important role in his theology.[40] Newbigin asserts that the church is a "chosen people," "a peculiar people," "a particular people," and that the church "is always in a colonial situation." In addition to this, he also reflects on the church's role in a

---

37. For a clarification on the concept of "sectarianism" and a review of the role of this concept in newer theological debates, see Rasmusson, *Church as Polis*, 230–47. Also, Bevans clearly understands sectarianism with respect to society and not to other churches or Christians.

38. The danger of becoming monocultural, anticultural, and sectarian is obtained from Bevans's *Models of Contextual Theology*, 124–27. In this book, Bevans outlines a "countercultural contextualization model," in which these three dangers are presented. The subjects of study in this book, Lesslie Newbigin and John Howard Yoder, are both presented as exponents for this countercultural contextualization model. However, I describe these dangers slightly differently than does Bevans.

39. The Christendom debate that has been going on in recent years is very closely related to the discussion concerning "political theology" versus "theological politics." Cf. Rasmusson, *Church as Polis*. The research question of this book is related to this debate, but I have tried to frame the Christendom debate from a different angle.

40. Cf. Bevans, *Models of Contextual Theology*, 175.

post-Christendom society.⁴¹ Furthermore, I find it relevant to analyze the writings of Newbigin because of his reputation as an esteemed and influential theologian.⁴² In the past several years, Newbigin's theology has been the subject of much research in the form of essays, articles, monographs and dissertations completed in Finland, Holland, Switzerland, Italy, Scotland, England, Canada and the USA. These previous major engagements with his writings have dealt with themes such as election and cultural plurality;⁴³ mission and eschatology;⁴⁴ mission and ecclesiology;⁴⁵ and mission, pluralism and dialogue, among others.⁴⁶ Considering this breadth of material, it is notable that we have not yet seen an exhaustive or coherent analysis of the distinctive identity of the church in the writings of Newbigin, even though this plays an important role in his theology. Finally, I find it relevant to analyze the writings of Newbigin because he is a key missiologist in the twentieth century. Owing to the fact that there is a demand for a development of a post-Christendom ecclesiology, especially within the discipline of missiology, it is reasonable to choose a theologian from within this discipline. Thus, there are numerous compelling reasons to make use of the writings of Lesslie Newbigin as research material for this project.

I also find it relevant to analyze the writings of John Howard Yoder, as the distinctive identity of the church plays an important role in his theology as well. Yoder asserts that the church is a "different kind of community" and links expressions like "distinctiveness," "peculiarity" and "particularity" to his understanding of the church. The relevance of Yoder's writings lies also in the fact that he is one of the key ethicists of the twentieth century and, like Newbigin, is regarded as an esteemed and influential theologian. In contrast to Newbigin, Yoder is Mennonite, and is regarded as the theologian who has evoked broad interest in Anabaptist

---

41. Goheen, *As the Father Has Sent Me*, 58.

42. Newbigin has been characterized as an outstanding leader in the twentieth century: see Shenk, "Lesslie Newbigin's Contribution to the Theology of Mission," 59; he has been compared with the Church Fathers of early Christianity: see Wainwright, *Lesslie Newbigin*, 390; he has been compared with the early Karl Barth: see Ramachandra, *The Recovery of Mission*, 144.

43. Hunsberger, "The Missionary Significance of the Biblical Doctrine of Election."

44. Schuster, *Christian Mission in Eschatological Perspective*.

45. Goheen, *As the Father Has Sent Me*.

46. For a long list of dissertations written on theology of Newbigin, see Nikolajsen, *Redefining the Identity of the Church*, 14–15.

theology within Protestant circles.[47] The Anabaptist tradition is, among other things, known for challenging the concept of Christendom. During recent years, Yoder's theology has also been subject of numerous essays, articles, monographs and dissertations completed in South Africa, Italy, England, Canada, and the USA. The previous major engagements with his writings have dealt with themes such as church, mission, and social order;[48] post-Christendom political theology;[49] and the eschatological aspects of Yoder's critique of Constantinianism,[50] among others.[51] Thus, as with Newbigin, it is notable that we have not yet seen an exhaustive or coherent analysis of the distinctive identity of the church in Yoder's writings. For these reasons, I believe that there is good logic in employing the writings of Yoder alongside Newbigin's.

I believe that it is interesting to highlight two notable ecclesiological traditions within contemporary Protestant theology. The first tradition, which can be called *the missional church tradition*, originated in the ecumenical movement in the beginning of the twentieth century and was then furthered by Lesslie Newbigin and a North American academic network, the Gospel and Our Culture Network.[52] The second tradition is sometimes collectively known as *the free church tradition*, and finds a strong expression in the Anabaptist tradition as exemplified by Mennonite John Howard Yoder. That Newbigin and Yoder work so consistently within these traditions, so as to almost typify them, gives even further reason for choosing the writings of these two figures.

A final dimension of interest in making use of the writings of both theologians is the notable differences and similarities between them: both place a strong emphasis on the distinctiveness of the church and can be regarded as pioneers in developing a post-Christendom ecclesiology;

---

47. For example, Webber and Clapp say, "almost singlehandedly, Yoder has caused the theological world to take seriously the Anabaptist ecclesiology and social ethics." See *People of the Truth*, 133.

48. Wright, *Disavowing Constantine*.

49. Doerksen, *Beyond Suspicion*.

50. LeMasters, *The Import of Eschatology*.

51. For a long list of dissertations written on theology of Yoder, see Nikolajsen, *Redefining the Identity of the Church*, 16.

52. In my article "Missional Church: A Historical and Theological Analysis of an Ecclesiological Tradition" I present a historical and theological analysis of this three-part ecclesiological tradition. I also show that both Newbigin and the Gospel and Our Culture Network have a strong notion of the church as a contrast-community. See also Roxburgh, *What is the Missional Church?*; and Goheen, "The Missional Church," 484.

both are Protestant theologians from the twentieth century and are inspired by Karl Barth;[53] both are engaged in ecumenical affairs and are engaged in efforts outside the academic world; both had great influence not only on their own ecclesial tradition, but also beyond them; and for both of them, Christology is an important source of their theological reflections. However, even though we find obvious similarities between Newbigin and Yoder, there are also clear differences: while Newbigin is from England, Yoder is from the USA;[54] and while Newbigin is a Reformed theologian and inspired by the ecumenical movement, Yoder is a Mennonite theologian and inspired by the Anabaptist tradition.

It is in these similarities and differences between the writings of Newbigin and Yoder that I believe the benefit of my analysis, as well as discussions concerning the distinctive identity of the church and its role in a post-Christendom society, will lie.[55]

---

53. Newbigin was a Reformed theologian and Yoder studied under Barth and was a very able interpreter of Barth. Newbigin was, however, influenced by Barth to a lesser extent than Yoder. I will qualify the statement above in chapters 2 and 3.

54. It seems to me that there exists a tendency to be more one-sidedly critical of Christendom ecclesiology in North America, while many in Europe have a more pragmatic take on Christendom ecclesiology. For example, the archbishop in the Anglican Church, Rowan Williams, has introduced the expression "mixed economies," which expresses a strategy of making financial investments in established churches with roots in Christendom, on the one hand, and in so-called fresh expressions of the church, on the other hand. However, in the USA, one can also observe various emphases in the critique of the Christendom legacy. For example, Stanley Hauerwas has pointed out that he and Yoder come from different theological backgrounds and therefore have different ecclesiological emphases. See Hauerwas, "Reading Yoder Down Under," 173. The post-Christendom theologians do not represent a common position. Hopefully, this book will be able to contribute clarification of two important positions.

55. It could also be relevant to include Dietrich Bonhoeffer as a central interlocutor in this book. Employing the writings of Bonhoeffer, Newbigin and Yoder, I would have three theologians, representing Germany, England, and the USA respectively, each influenced by Karl Barth, pursuing a christologically informed theology, and preoccupied with ecclesiology. Bonhoeffer is not only left out in order to limit the focus of this study, but also because he is not dealing with "die konstantinische Epoche" or "die konstantinische Kirche." Therefore, I will focus on the writings of Newbigin and Yoder being more suitable because they use Christendom as a historical framework for many of their theological reflections. It could also be relevant to include Stanley Hauerwas as a central interlocutor in the book. However, Hauerwas's position lies too close to that of Yoder and therefore he has been excluded. For example, Hauerwas has said that he agrees with everything Yoder believed, which is, nevertheless, not the case; cf. Hovey, "The Public Ethics of John Howard Yoder and Stanley Hauerwas," 205. See also n54 above.

1.3 The Method

The method of the survey can be classified as a systematic theological methodology. What this means can be expounded in several ways. First, I will present three important aspects of my hermeneutical-analytical reading of Newbigin and Yoder's writing.

Text: My reading of Newbigin and Yoder's writing aims to display central themes which shed light on their thinking about the distinctive identity of the church, with special reference to the church's role in a post-Christendom society. To do this, a hermeneutical-analytical reading will be applied to the research material, disclosing fundamental theological arguments for, and perspectives on, the distinctive identity of the church, as well as describing which pragmatic consequences, according to Newbigin and Yoder, these arguments and perspectives must have. The hermeneutical-analytical reading attempts, first and foremost, to present their thoughts about the distinctive identity of the church and its role in a post-Christendom society based on their own conditions, with their own terminology and with the aim of making clear how they themselves understand this. Here I will also consider how well my hermeneutical reading matches each of their theological projects, and consider to what extent I am trying to read their writings based on premises differing from their own.

My hermeneutical reading aims to reconstruct their writings from the perspective of my basic research question, which I believe is of crucial importance to their theologies. What I place at the centre of my hermeneutics is important, as everything is structured based on this decision. Therefore, it is important to make clear what is actually understood by "church" and "distinctive identity." Hence, I first and foremost understand the term "church" as an expression of an actually existing local group of people situated in history. Following this, "distinctive" will be used "almost synonymously with the term 'identity.' Inspired by Paul Ricoeur, distinctiveness can be understood in two different, yet compatible, ways: first, the distinctiveness of the church can be captured or qualified as something intrinsic—from inside, rooted in the very being of the church (the church's *ipse-identity*). Second, the distinctiveness of the church may also be qualified in relation to something which is not the church, and in this way elucidate the distinction between the church and the world. Since the church is not just distinct, but is distinct in relation to something else, identity may be understood not in an isolated manner, but as a concept of relationality (the *idem*-identity of the church). These two aspects of the distinctiveness of the church cannot be disassociated. Rather, there is an interdependence and dialectic between the *ipse*-identity and the *idem*-identity of the church. Therefore, when I refer to 'the distinctiveness of the church', it is hard not to use such phrases without some ambiguity."[56] Also, in my mind, the church as a distinct social entity is inescapably a part of society, that is, an extended network between various social groups—economic and political—organized most often within a nation-state. The question here is therefore how we are to interpret the life of the church in such a society with theological terminology.

Context: This book aims first of all to analyze the writings of Newbigin and Yoder so as to demonstrate the fundamental *theological* preconditions for their thinking on the distinctive identity of the church and its role in a post-Christendom society. This will, however, not exclude taking *historical* conditions into account at times. In some cases, the historical context may constitute an important condition for their theological reflections. To establish an understanding of the writings of Newbigin and Yoder, it may be important to understand them not only on the basis of their theological considerations, but also on the basis of their historical contexts. In some cases, I will therefore probe how the conclusions they draw can be explained on the basis of both their historical context and theological tradition.

Intertext: The validity of Newbigin and Yoder's interpretations of their interlocutors will be discussed to a lesser extent and I will only refer to these interpretations to illustrate their own thinking, and only in exceptional cases will their interlocutor's literature be drawn into my hermeneutical-analytical reading. Present research on the writings of Newbigin and Yoder, although less relevant to the research problem of this book, will be used when I find it appropriate. At some points, it may also be helpful to let statements of other theologians shed light on Newbigin and Yoder's viewpoints.

I will now present three criteria that shed light on my evaluation of Newbigin and Yoder's thinking.

Authenticity: Theology must, in my mind, be committed to the divine revelation in Christ, as testified to in the Bible. Drawing on various sources, systematic theology must be a topical exposition of the Christian

---

56. Nikolajsen, "The Formative Power of Liturgy," 167. The concept of identity is much debated. For the purpose of my survey, I have limited myself to present a few clarifications inspired by Ricoeur, *Oneself as Another*.

message, and may not contradict elementary truths of the Christian faith. This means that new theological assertions sustain a burden of legitimization, to prove their Christian authenticity.[57] In my evaluation of the writings of Newbigin and Yoder, however, I will only to a lesser extent consider if what they express can be regarded as authentically Christian.[58] Such a criterion can be determined in many ways, and I believe establishing such a standard to be very difficult and unattainable.[59] To deal with such a question in a well-argued manner is beyond the scope of this work. Instead, I will focus on the extent to which they present a comprehensive position, that is, taking into consideration sufficient theological perspectives, or if they in fact fail to consider certain important perspectives.[60]

Consistency: I will also, to some extent, consider the consistency and coherence of Newbigin and Yoder's thinking about the distinctive identity of the church and its role in a post-Christendom society. Does their individual thought represent an inner coherence? Do they contradict themselves? To deal with questions like these thoroughly, however, also goes beyond the limitations of this book. Thus, I will not construct a comprehensive evaluation of the consistency of their positions, but will instead allow my criterion of consistency to inform my ongoing evaluation of their thinking.[61]

---

57. Gregersen, *Teologi og kultur*, 237.

58. In his book *Teologi og kultur*, Gregersen lists three criteria in relation to the discipline of systematic theology. He names these criteria as a criterion of authenticity, a criterion of consistency and a criterion of coherence. My understanding of the criterion of authenticity and the criterion of consistency is based on the work of Gregersen. However, while Gregersen's criterion of coherence explains that theological assertions must correspond with reality, my criterion of pragmatism explains that systematic theology should avoid unfortunate pragmatic consequences. See ibid., 227–39. Thiemann has outlined three similar criteria, which he terms "intelligibility," "Christian aptness" and "warranted assertability." See his *Revelation and Theology*, 92. Also, Lindbeck talks about a criterion of faithfulness, applicability, and intelligibility. See his *The Nature of Doctrine*, 112–38.

59. Søvik refers to various theories that suggest Jesus to be an alien, the last Pharaoh or Julius Caesar, and the Holy Spirit to be a space ship. In light of these suggestions, such a criterion seems relevant. See *The Power of God and the Problem of Evil*, 96.

60. Pannenberg has presented an impressive work on theological methods in relation to systematic theology. He also develops a criterion of authenticity. See *Systematische Theologie 1*, especially chapters 1 and 4. See also Pannenberg, *Wissenschaftstheorie und Theologie*.

61. Rescher develops a similar criterion in his *Philosophical Reasoning*, 142–50. For Gregersen's understanding of this criterion, see Gregersen, *Teologi og kultur*, 229–31.

Pragmatism: All theology has pragmatic consequences; some theological notions tend to have unfortunate consequences. I have already pointed out that there exist several potential pragmatic dangers in developing a strong notion of the distinctiveness of the church, pointing out the danger of the church becoming monocultural, anticultural, and sectarian. I will limit myself to evaluating the extent to which it is possible, on the background of Newbigin and Yoder's positions, to develop an ecclesiology that is able to withstand the critique that a strong notion of the distinctive identity of the church is equivalent to sectarianism. This will be taken into consideration at the end of this book.

Finally, on the basis of this hermeneutical-analytical reading of Newbigin's and Yoder's writings, I will apply a synthetic-constructive method, implying that the possibility of engaging in a comparative analysis between the two will be utilized very sparsely. The intention in using this method is to outline a discussion concerning the danger of sectarianism when developing an ecclesiology with a strong notion of distinctiveness. My evaluation of Newbigin and Yoder's positions will not only be evident in the hermeneutical-analytical reading of their writings, but will also play an important role in outlining the contours of my own constructive contribution to the development of a post-Christendom ecclesiology. In connection with this, new concepts will be established in order better to express central aspects of the church's distinctive identity. Both the analyses of Newbigin and of Yoder, as well as the outline of my discussion of sectarianism, will focus on presenting a constructive contribution to the ongoing debate concerning post-Christendom ecclesiology.[62]

1.4 The Process

The book as a whole is divided into five chapters. In this first chapter, the basic design of the book has been outlined. The second chapter addresses the distinctiveness of the church, with special reference to its role in a post-Christendom society, according to Lesslie Newbigin's theology. The third chapter addresses the same issue from the perspective of John Howard Yoder's writing. On the basis of these two chapters, I seek in the fourth chapter to develop a constructive contribution to our understanding of the distinctive identity of the church and its role in a post-Christendom society. The fifth chapter presents a concluding summation

---

62. See 1.1 above.

of the results of the analyses and also presents three consequences of the ecclesiological position, which I outline in the fourth chapter.

1.5 The Ambition

The main theme of this book is the distinctive identity of the church, the significance of which is to be understood in relation to the discussion that is going on in light of the fact that the church seems to be increasingly marginalized and losing influence in the Western world. As a result, a number of theologians have suggested that we recognize the distinctive identity of the church, which will help it to gain a better understanding of itself under these new cultural conditions. As Philip D. Kenneson states, "the church in this post-Christendom era will need different models for conceptualizing its own identity and its relation to the rest of society," and the future "will undoubtedly require that Christians continue to debate rigorously what Christ's church should look like and how it should understand itself and its mission."[63] The purpose of this book is to contribute to a better understanding of the role of the church in a post-Christendom society. Hopefully, this book will help churches in the twenty-first century Western context to better respond to the challenges and the opportunities with which they are being confronted.

63. Kenneson, *Beyond Sectarianism*, 2–4.

PART II
Lesslie Newbigin

2

Sent by Christ to the World

THE CHURCH OCCUPIES A prominent place in Lesslie Newbigin's theology, with all of his many theological reflections returning in one way or another to the church. George Vandervelde remarks that the "Christian community is the golden thread throughout all Newbigin's writings."[1] In this chapter, I will give an introduction to the life and works of Newbigin, analyze his evaluation of the rise of Western Christendom and then clarify his understanding of the distinctive identity of the church with special reference to its role in a post-Christendom society. My reading of Newbigin's writings discloses five central themes in which the distinctiveness of the church becomes apparent: ecclesiology, missiology, eschatology, ethics, and epistemology. However, because Newbigin's thoughts do not allow one to segregate his theology into such different domains, the five themes will be interrelated in the analysis. At the end of this chapter I will sum up and clarify his position.[2]

2.1 Introduction

James Edward Lesslie Newbigin was born on December 8, 1909. In 1928, Newbigin gained entrance to Queens College in Cambridge, where he began to study economics. Soon after, he experienced a desire to participate in Christian world mission. Therefore, after finishing his studies at Queens College, he began to study theology at Westminster College, also in Cambridge.

In 1936, Newbigin traveled to India to become a missionary. At the age of thirty-eight, he became bishop over Madurai and Ramnad in the Church of South India and later he also became bishop over Madras. His time in India was interspersed by periods in which he held positions in

---

1. Vandervelde, *The Church as Missionary Community*, 10.
2. A part of this chapter has been published in my article "Beyond Christendom."

the International Mission Council and the Commission for World Mission and Evangelism of the World Council of Churches. In 1974, Newbigin returned to England, where he was a pastor in a Reformed church and taught missiology and ecumenism at Selly Oak College in Birmingham.[3]

Newbigin was one of the leading missiological thinkers in the twentieth century. Some of his interpreters laud him even further: Wilbert R. Shenk characterizes him as an outstanding Christian leader in the twentieth century,[4] Geoffrey Wainwright compares him with the fathers of the early church,[5] and Vinoth Ramachandra compares his challenging of the Western church with the works of the early Karl Barth.[6]

He lectured at leading universities all over the world and published hundreds of articles and more than thirty books, these works leading to the establishment of academic networks in New Zealand, England, and North America. Broadly speaking, Newbigin made two major contributions to the discipline of Missiology: His early writings (prior to 1974) were a significant factor in the development of a missional ecclesiology, and his later writings (from 1974 to 1998) furthered this contribution in a development of a missiology of Western culture.

The first contribution of Newbigin to the advancement of a missional ecclesiology should be seen as a reaction to the modern missionary movement, which led to a disintegration of church and mission. In simplified terms, "mission" and "church" became two different entities, responsible for two different tasks, the former responsible for the proclamation of the gospel in foreign countries, while the later entity supported the mission in foreign countries, but was primarily responsible for maintaining the church in the Christian West. The early to mid-twentieth century, however, witnessed a theological reintegration of church and mission, to which Newbigin contributed significantly.[7]

Newbigin's second contribution to Western missiology can be seen in light of the de-christianization of the Western world. In 1974, Newbigin returned to a changed and—to his thinking—neopagan England. Thus, in the last twenty-four years of his life, he was preoccupied with

3. For a more detailed presentation of Newbigin's life and work, see Wainwright, *Lesslie Newbigin*, 3–28.

4. Shenk, "Lesslie Newbigin's Contribution to Mission Theology," 59.

5. Wainwright, *Lesslie Newbigin*, 390.

6. Ramachandra, *The Recovery of Mission*, 144.

7. Cf. Nikolajsen, "Missional Church." I will expand this analysis later. See 2.4 below.

reflections on mission, not in relation to the global south, but in relation to the Western world. Newbigin's missiological thinking about Western culture became the subject of much debate in the 1970s, 1980s, and 1990s and led to the establishment of three academic networks collectively known as the Gospel and Our Culture movement.[8]

Lesslie Newbigin died on January 30, 1998. To the very end of his life, Newbigin remained preoccupied with missiological challenges. Even when his eyes gave way, books were read aloud to him so that he could stay updated on current research. Writing until the end of his life, it is especially in these later works that Newbigin points out major challenges to the church in Western culture.[9] Thus, I will now show how he evaluates the consequences of the rise of Western Christendom.

2.2 Christendom

2.2.1 Newbigin's Theological Project and Christendom

As I have pointed out above, Newbigin's early writings can be regarded as an important contribution to the development of a missional ecclesiology, and his later writings to a development of a missiology of Western culture.[10] One could argue that both developments are a logical consequence of the disestablishment of Western Christendom. Due to the dissolution of the old Christendom, the church in the West now finds itself in a situation where it must witness to a society which can no longer be formally regarded as Christian. This shift has led to a renewed understanding of the church as a missionary community. It is difficult to argue explicitly that Newbigin's writings, in their entirety, can be regarded as a deliberate critique of Christendom, as Newbigin does not consistently develop his theology in response to Christendom. Often, the disestablishment or critique of Western Christendom remains an unspoken backdrop for his theological project. However, Newbigin also explicitly challenges the Christendom settlement throughout major portions of his writings.[11] Hence, the distinctive identity of the church, and its role in a

---

8. Nikolajsen, "Missional ekklesiologi," 24.
9. Cf. Nikolajsen, "Lesslie Newbigins udfordringer til den vestlige kirke."
10. See 2.1 above.
11. In his early years, Newbigin was not preoccupied with a critique of Christendom, but in the early 1940s we find the first examples of this central motif in his theology. Goheen says, "As evidenced by his first ecclesiological reflections in the decade

post-Christendom society, plays an important role in Newbigin's writings. One might say that Newbigin, in his early writings, develops a missional ecclesiology on the basis of his critique of Christendom ecclesiology, and that in his later writings he reflects on the mission of the church in a Western, post-Christendom society.

2.2.2 Newbigin's Evaluation of Christendom

Newbigin is primarily preoccupied with the implications of the disestablishment of Christendom for the Christian church, and for Christian theology. However, in some cases he is not making any terminological distinction between Christendom and Constantinianism. For example, Newbigin varies between expressions such as "the Christendom era" and "the Constantinian era."[12] Unfortunately, one never gets a clear impression of what precisely he means by "Constantinianism."[13]

However, Newbigin believes that when "the Christian Church was first launched into the life of the eastern Roman Empire it found itself surrounded by many religious societies which claimed to offer personal salvation to their members through a variety of teachings and disciplines."[14] While these religious societies enjoyed the protection of the state, and were described with Greek words such as *thiasos* and *heranos*, the early church, however, deliberately chose the name *ecclesia* to describe itself.[15] As Newbigin states, the early church did not see itself as a private religious society, but as a public assembly, "a movement launched into the public life of the world, challenging the *cultus publicus* of the Empire, claiming the allegiance of all without exception."[16] He further argues that

---

of the 1940s, his ecclesiology is shaped in the traditional Christendom mould. The terminology of a missionary church briefly appears but is not developed consistently." See *As the Father Has Sent Me*, 58.

12. See, for example, Newbigin, *Your Kingdom Come*, 28–30, 34–35. For examples of the use of terms like *pre-Constantinianism*, *Constantinianism* and *post-Constantinianism*, see Newbigin, *Priorities For A New Decade*, 5–6; Newbigin, *Your Kingdom Come*, 11, 28–30, 34–35; Newbigin, *Foolishness to the Greeks*, 99–102. See also Newbigin, *Honest Religion for Secular Man*, 102–8.

13. Bretherton defines Constantinianism as "the alignment of the Church with political power for solely temporal purposes." See "Constantinianism," 113.

14. Newbigin, *Your Kingdom Come*, 27.

15. Ibid.

16. Ibid., 28.

it was a matter of course, albeit implicit, for the pre-Christendom church to understand itself as a missionary community.[17]

Newbigin interprets Constantine's conversion and baptism as the inauguration of a new era in the history of Christianity asserting: "We are painfully aware of the consequences of that conversion; for centuries the Church was allied with the established power, sanctioned and even wielded the sword, [and] lost its critical relation to the ruling authorities."[18] Now the church accepted a role as the "protected and well decorated chaplaincy in the camp of the dominant power"[19] and became "the spiritual arm of the establishment."[20] Within Western Christendom "[t]he whole community was baptized" and the pagan world outside of this Western culture was left out of sight.[21] As Newbigin suggests, "the sense that the Church is a body sent into all the world, a body on the move and existing for the sake of those beyond its own borders, no longer played an effective part in men's thinking."[22] In this way, Christendom resulted in the church ceasing to understand itself as a missionary community. This development is the most central critique of Christendom in the writings of Newbigin. Consequently, this loss of a missionary identity led to a deficient understanding of four other realities: The sacraments, ministry, ecumenism, and ecclesiology.[23] Below, I will present a brief summary of these five negative aspects, which stem from Newbigin's own evaluation of the rise of Western Christendom.

First, Newbigin believes that it was natural for the pre-Christendom church to understand itself as a missionary community. He believes that "the New Testament assumes a missionary situation in which the Church is a small evangelizing movement in a pagan society."[24] However, in the era of Christendom, all were baptized, society was presumed to

17. Newbigin, *Honest Religion for Secular Man*, 104.
18. Newbigin, *Your Kingdom Come*, 28.
19. Newbigin, "Christ, Kingdom, and Church," 4.
20. Newbigin, *Your Kingdom Come*, 28.
21. Newbigin, *Honest Religion for Secular Man*, 106.
22. Newbigin, *A Faith for This One World?*, 110.
23. Goheen identifies similar themes in Newbigin's critique of Christendom, which I rely on. See *As the Father Has Sent Me*, 192–97. Goheen says that Newbigin also believes that Christendom led to a loss of eschatology. Newbigin expresses this in very few places, never developing it in any notable way; therefore, I am refraining from outlining it as an important theme in Newbigin's critique of Christendom.
24. Newbigin, "How Should We Understand Sacraments and Ministry?," 1.

be Christian and, consequently, the church ceased to understand itself as a missionary community.[25] According to Newbigin, all of this had serious consequences for Reformation theologies: "They are set not in a missionary situation but in this situation in which Christendom is taken for granted. This means that in their doctrines of the Church they are defining their position over against one another *within* the context of the *corpus Christianum*. They are not defining the Church as over and against a pagan world. It is not necessary to point out how profoundly this affects the structures of their thinking."[26] However, the collapse of Christendom has now led to "a recovery of a biblical doctrine of the Church as a missionary community."[27]

As to Newbigin's second critique, he writes that it was natural for the pre-Christendom church to understand the sacraments in light of their witness to their surrounding society. They understood baptism as an initiation into a community, which is sent to the world. Newbigin says, baptism "is our incorporation into the one baptism which is for the salvation of the world. To accept baptism, therefore, is to be committed to be with Christ in his ministry for all men."[28] A few times, Newbigin also expresses an understanding of communion in light of the mission of the church. When Christians share bread and wine, they are sharing in the body and blood of Christ; they are "made partakers of his dying and his risen life, consecrated afresh to the Father in and through him, and sent out into the world."[29] This participation in Christ meant, for the early church, a renewal in its participation in Christ's mission to the world.[30]

---

25. Ibid.

26. Newbigin, *The Household of God*, 1–2; italics original. Goheen believes that Newbigin's early writings express a shift from a Christendom ecclesiology to a missional ecclesiology. According to Goheen, this shift was the result of two important factors: "First, his missionary experience in India as a district missionary in Kanchipuram (1939–1947) and as a bishop in the newly formed Church of South India (1947–1959) challenged a Christendom understanding of the church that had been formed in Europe. Numerous elements of a missionary church emerged in the context of this missionary work. Second, Newbigin was heavily involved in the ecumenical movement during a time when a missionary ecclesiology was forming." See *As the Father Has Sent Me*, 58–59.

27. Newbigin, *Honest Religion for Secular Man*, 104.

28. Newbigin, "The Future of Missions and Missionaries," 217.

29. Newbigin, *The Open Secret*, 54; see also Newbigin, "Presiding at the Lord's Supper," 1.

30. Newbigin, *The Household of God*, 167.

Newbigin adds that the "true means of grace will precisely be in and for the discharge of this missionary task."[31] With the establishment of Western Christendom, the sacraments were no longer understood as a sign of mission as, for example, when baptism became a *rite de passage* into a settled institution.[32] In the era of Christendom, the individual believer became "a passive recipient of the means of grace," of which it was the business of the church to administer.[33]

Third, Newbigin believes that the self-understanding of the pre-Christendom church as a missionary community fundamentally impacted the early church's ministry, which was primarily leadership in mission. With the establishment of Christendom, ministry became "primarily pastoral care of established communities."[34] As Newbigin states: "The question has to be asked—and is repeatedly asked—whether the traditional forms of the ministry which have been inherited from the 'Christendom' period are fully compatible with the faith that the Church is called to be a missionary community."[35] In a lecture given in New York, Newbigin challenged three fundamental ministerial axioms shaped by Christendom: "(1) That the ministry is a paid profession, a full-time profession; (2) that it is composed of people who have an academic education comparable to that of the ministry in Britain or Germany; and (3) that the ministry should be supported by the giving of the people."[36] None of these axioms, according to Newbigin, are derived from the New Testament, and thus should be disqualified.

Fourth, Newbigin believes that when the church is in a missionary situation, which was the case for the pre-Christendom church, it will consider Christian disunity as an intolerable anomaly.[37] The early church understood that the reconciled work of Christ "is one, and we cannot be His ambassadors reconciling the world to God, if we have not ourselves been willing to be reconciled to one another."[38] In contrast to this, the rise of Western Christendom led to numerous theological controversies.

---

31. Ibid.
32. See Goheen, *As the Father Has Sent Me*, 268.
33. Newbigin, *The Household of God*, 167.
34. Newbigin, "How Should We Understand Sacraments and Ministry?," 1.
35. Newbigin, "Developments During 1962," 8.
36. Newbigin, "Missions and the Work of the Holy Spirit," 24.
37. Newbigin, *The Household of God*, 8.
38. Ibid., 9.

Newbigin rightly points out the paradoxical fact that the church fell apart in the assumed unity of Christendom. This is, according to Newbigin, the result of the church not being confronted by a pagan world, leading the church to instead concentrate on internal, rival interpretations of various issues. Today, as the church in Western culture finds itself once again in a missionary situation, there is fresh awareness of ecumenism and common dependency.[39]

Finally, Newbigin believes that it was natural for the pre-Christendom church to understand itself as a distinct community that in many ways was in contrast to the society in which it lived, another thing which changed with the transition to the Christendom era. Now, the church became allied with the established power, and lost its prophetical-critical stance towards society,[40] accepting a role as the "protected and well-decorated chaplaincy in the camp of the dominant power."[41] Thus, the church became "the religious department of European society," rather than a people among other people elected and appointed for a mission to its surrounding society.[42]

In summary, Newbigin's critique of Christendom is essentially that the church ceased to understand itself as a missionary community, all other perspectives of his critique of Christendom in one way or another deriving from this. Michael W. Goheen rightly points out that, "Newbigin does not only elaborate the *negative* consequences of Christendom; there is also a positive dimension. He believed that the church was right in taking responsibility for the cultural, social, and political life of early medieval Europe."[43] As Newbigin himself remarks,

> Much has been written about the harm done to the cause of the gospel when Constantine accepted baptism, and it is not difficult to expatiate on this theme. But could any other choice have been made? When the ancient classical world, which had seemed so brilliant and so all-conquering, ran out of spiritual fuel and turned to the church as the one society that could hold a disintegrating world together, should the church have refused the appeal and washed its hands of responsibility for the political order? It could not do so if it was to be faithful to

---

39. Ibid.
40. Newbigin, *Your Kingdom Come*, 28.
41. Newbigin, "Christ, Kingdom, and Church," 4.
42. Newbigin, *Honest Religion for Secular Man*, 103.
43. Goheen, *As the Father Has Sent Me*, 195; italics original.

its origins in Israel and the ministry of Jesus. It is easy to see with hindsight how quickly the church fell into the temptations of worldly power. It is easy to see with hindsight how quickly the church fell into the temptations of worldly power. It is easy to point (. . .) to the glaring contradictions between the Jesus of the Gospels and his followers occupying the seats of power and wealth. And yet we have to ask, would God's purpose as it is revealed in Scripture have been better served, if the church had refused all political responsibility, if there had never been a 'Christian' Europe, if all the churches for the past two thousand years had lived as persecuted minorities (. . .)? I find it hard to think so.[44]

Hence, a basic dialectic remains in Newbigin's discussion of Christendom.[45] On the one hand, Christendom led to the church ceasing to understand itself as a missionary community, having, as we have seen, negative consequences for the understanding of the sacraments, ministry, ecumenism, and ecclesiology. On the other hand, the Constantinian settlement was "the first great attempt to translate the universal claim of Christ into political terms."[46] Therefore, the church in the fourth century was faithful in taking responsibility for the social, cultural, and political life of Europe. Christ is Lord of both the church and the world, and thus, the church rightly took advantage of expressing this in the social, cultural and political life of the whole society. In this way, the church was faithful to the gospel's message concerning the universal reign of God.[47] Therefore, Newbigin believes that there do exist certain religio-political situations where the Christendom arrangement remains suitable: "There are some places in the world—not many—where this pattern is still valid, in some of the South Pacific islands, for example, where church and society are coterminous, a single *corpus Christianum*."[48] Accordingly, Murray insinuates that Newbigin never managed to fully liberate himself from the theological presuppositions which created Western Christendom.[49] Jürgen Schuster, in contrast, remarks that Newbigin never became a theolo-

---

44. Newbigin, *Foolishness to the Greeks*, 100–101.

45. Goheen talks about a basic tension in Newbigin's discussion of Christendom; see *As the Father Has Sent Me*, 420.

46. Newbigin, *Your Kingdom Come*, 28.

47. Newbigin, *The Other Side of 1984*, 102.

48. Newbigin, *Honest Religion for Secular Man*, 106.

49. Stuart Murray, *Post-Christendom*, 102–3.

gian endorsing Christendom due to his "awareness of the eschatological, provisional character of the Christian involvement in the public sphere."[50] I will further discuss this dialectic in Newbigin's evaluation of the rise of Western Christendom in the concluding section of this chapter.[51]

In truth, Newbigin believes that the time of Christendom is definitively over. In the last three centuries the church has left the Christendom era behind and "has moved into a new situation. A new ideology has replaced the Christian vision as the *cultus publicus* of western Christendom. It is the vision which dawned in that remarkable experience which those who shared it called 'the enlightenment.'"[52] Therefore, the Western church now exists under new cultural premises: On the one hand, Newbigin believes that the church cannot go back to a pre-Christendom innocence, just as the church, on the other hand, should not try to establish a new Christendom.[53] Newbigin is clear that the church cannot, like the pre-Christendom church, "treat all powers as evil and to wash our hands of responsibility for the realities of political power"[54] and neither can the church, as in Christendom, become allied with the established power, and see church and nation as a single entity. The task for the church, according to Newbigin, is to witness to the Lordship of Christ over all life, yet without falling into the Constantinian trap.[55]

In his analysis of Newbigin's critique of Christendom, Goheen emphasizes, with good reason, the missiological aspects. However, we can also see in Newbigin's critique of Christendom an understanding of the church as a distinct social entity. This sentiment is a common thread throughout the writings of Newbigin, and is developed in various ways: At times the distinctiveness of the church is contrasted with Christendom, while at other times this is not the case. In the following five sections, I will expand on the themes of ecclesiology, missiology, eschatology, social ethics, and epistemology, all of which shed light on Newbigin's understanding of the distinctive identity of the church.

---

50. Schuster, *Christian Mission in Eschatological*, 206.

51. See 2.8 below.

52. Newbigin, *Your Kingdom Come*, 29.

53. Newbigin, *Foolishness to the Greeks*, 101–2; see also Newbigin, "The Cultural Captivity of Western Christianity," 73; Newbigin, "Evangelism in the Context of Secularization," 157; Newbigin, *The Gospel in a Pluralist Society*, 224, 232.

54. Newbigin, *Foolishness to the Greeks*, 102.

55. Goheen, *As the Father Has Sent Me*, 197.

2.3 Ecclesiology

The church is a chosen people. This is, according to Newbigin, the most fundamental statement we can make about the church. Consequently, election composes the very heart of Newbigin's ecclesiology.[56] Thus, it seems fair to begin an investigation of the distinctive identity of the church here. While Newbigin's ecclesiology contains many aspects, I will here concentrate only on his understanding of election, which makes up the center of his ecclesiology.[57]

2.3.1 Election and Salvation History

The Christian faith states that God is the creator of all things and that humankind "is fallen from his true estate and involved in a common sin against the creator."[58] Thus, Newbigin states, "what God is doing in Christ is the culmination of a plan which begins with the choosing of a people to be his own people, to be his witnesses and the agents of his purpose for the world."[59] Newbigin believes that the greater part of the biblical story can be regarded as a story about election, an election first of Israel, subsequently of Christ, and finally of the church.[60] Highlighting election as a consistent theme in the Bible which is difficult to neglect,

---

56. Cf. Newbigin, *The Household of God*, 112; cf. also Hunsberger, *Bearing the Witness of the Spirit*, 51.

57. Hunsberger has examined what role election plays in various stages of Newbigin's writings and, in doing this, sketches out three periods. The first period includes the late 1940s, and most of the 1950s, when Newbigin was bishop over Madura and Ramnad in India. In this period, Newbigin develops the most essential aspects of his understanding of election. The second period includes the 1960s and runs into the 1970s, when Newbigin had returned to the West for a short time. Election does not play an important role in this period of his writings, with only indirect references to the doctrine of election. The third period includes the late 1970s, 1980s, and 1990s, when Newbigin lived in England and was confronted with a secular and pluralistic England. During this time, once again, election plays an important role in his writings, and becomes the fundamental rationale for Newbigin's understanding of the gospel's encounter with modern, Western culture. In addition, election plays an important role in Newbigin's primer on missiology, *The Open Secret*, although he adds nothing substantial to his understanding of election, other than expanding his point of view. Still, we may conclude, with Hunsberger, that election is a dominant and consistent idea in Newbigin's theology. See Hunsberger, *Bearing the Witness of the Spirit*, 45–81.

58. Newbigin, *A Faith for This One World?*, 61.

59. Ibid.

60. Ibid., 77.

Newbigin states: "Throughout the Bible we find it repeatedly stated that God has chosen certain individuals and groups, out of the general mass of their fellow-men, for some purpose of His. There is no escaping the fact of election in the Bible."[61] As the mission of God emerges into view in the Old Testament, it does so in terms of the election of Israel as God's people. Here, Newbigin is not excluding the individual aspects of election, but is asserting that the election of individuals forms a concrete social community; hence, God elects Abraham, Isaac, and Jacob to create a chosen people. Newbigin believes that election in the Bible is predominantly corporate and, for him, the actual focus is not election of individuals but an election of a people.

According to Newbigin, the essential aspect of election is that God, through this process of election, carries out his mission so that all may be saved.[62] This particularistic strategy is meant to serve universal purposes, that is, the salvation of all.[63] The Bible, however, contains several examples that show that this central missiological aspect of election is often misunderstood:

> [The Bible] teaches that God's people have constantly misunderstood what it means to be God's people. God chooses the Jews—according to the Bible—not for themselves but for the sake of the world. They were chosen to be His witnesses to the world. When they forgot or denied this, and behaved as though they were God's favorites, God punished them, and finally took away their position from them.[64]

According to Newbigin, God's intention with election is this: "He desires to knit together into one holy family the whole race of men broken by sin. Therefore He chooses one man, one race, in order that through them others may be saved. Each one who has been reconciled to God has to be the means by which others are reconciled."[65] God's intent with election is not to choose individuals here and there to recreate at least a small group of what God purposed in the first creation. Election has a broader perspective, that is, that all may be what God originally intended by the creation of the world. God purposes a re-creation, or a second creation,

---

61. Newbigin, "Why Study the Old Testament?," 72.
62. Ibid., 75.
63. Newbigin, *A Faith for This One World?*, 82.
64. Newbigin, "Why Study the Old Testament?," 72.
65. Newbigin, *Sin and Salvation*, 45.

of the whole human race in Christ, so that it may be what was intended by the first creation.[66]

For Newbigin, God's plan for salvation begins with the election of Israel and culminates with the election of Christ. Israel's election is inextricably linked with the election of Christ so that this election, then, as a part of the redemptive process, takes place with reference to Christ, and reaches its fulfillment in his work. The election of Israel points to the election of Christ, and Israel must understand itself in light of Christ, in connection with the unique midpoint. The election of a people, by which God purposes to save the world, is an essential part of "the faith which Jesus accepted from Israel, in which his own deeds and words were rooted and without which they cannot be understood."[67]

The Bible begins with the creation of the world; later, Israel is chosen to be God's people living among other people; and then, with Christ, the biblical perspective on election becomes narrowed to comprise one single person. Previously, a whole people was the bearer of universal salvation, but now a single person becomes the bearer of cosmic salvation, which is made known and accomplished in the life, death and resurrection of Jesus. Yet, salvation remains hidden and entrusted as a secret, a secret to be made known for all nations. What is true about the election of Israel is also true about the election of Christ: election has a universal purpose. Thus, Newbigin believes the "total fact of Christ" is a particular event, which has significance for the whole world and its history.

As the last part in the history of God's election, the church is chosen: "Then at once the story broadens out again. The tribes of men, proleptically present on the day of Pentecost, are gathered in, until at the end we

---

66. In his dissertation, Hunsberger makes a helpful comparison between Karl Barth and Newbigin's understanding of election. Hunsberger shows how Barth primarily uses the term in relation to God's electing action, while Newbigin primarily uses the term in relation to the electedness of human persons. This semantic divergence reflects a difference in the two structures of thoughts. Thus, as Hunsberger summarizes, "For the one, it [election] refers to the origins of the mission of God in the deepest recesses of his 'willing.' For the other, it speaks of the method by which the ultimate purposes of God are being carried forward." See Hunsberger, *Bearing the Witness of the Spirit*, 85. Barth begins with the election of Christ and then incorporates within that perspective the particularity of the chosen community. Newbigin, on the other hand, begins with the election of a people. This is, according to Hunsberger, the reason why Newbigin takes "Abraham as his point of departure, while Barth begins emphatically from the election of Jesus." See Hunsberger, *Bearing the Witness of the Spirit*, 86.

67. Newbigin, *A Faith for This One World?*, 61.

have a vision which includes all the nations and the entire cosmos."[68] In this way, Newbigin believes that the whole of human history is to be understood from one center, Jesus Christ. The church must, as was the case for Israel, understand itself in the light of Christ, in connection with this unique middle point in history.

Based on the Johannine "Great Commission" (John 20:21), Newbigin believes that mission originates from the Father who sends the Son to the world and, just as the Father has sent the Son, the Son sends the church to the world. For Newbigin, the church must continue the mission of Christ, replacing Christ in the world.[69] God revealed himself in Christ and today God reveals himself in the church. Accordingly, the people of God are the new temple where God today dwells, since "[t]he dwelling place of God upon earth did not end with the crucifixion. Out of that defeat, He fashioned a new temple, the Body of Christ."[70] This people, in which God has taken up residence, is appointed to be a sign for the fall and rise of the nations:

> This church, then, the one new family created by God in Christ out of all tribes and nations and peoples, is set by God in the midst of the world as the sign of that to which all creation, and all world history moves. It is the body of Christ, the new man, the second Adam, the new human race, growing up into its full stature and drawing into itself men of every kind. It is here that the world is given the opportunity to see and accept its true destiny; accept or reject it, for both possibilities remain open.[71]

Consequently, election should not be primarily understood as a special privilege, but as a special responsibility. Christians should not be preoccupied with the reason, but with the purpose of their election. Therefore, it is mistaken when Christians "are concerned more to probe backwards from their election into the reasons for it in the secret counsel of God than to press forward from their election to the purpose for it, which is that they should be Christ's ambassadors and witnesses the ends of the earth."[72] Rather, Newbigin's approach is this: "God could have cho-

---

68. Ibid., 80.

69. Newbigin, "The Basis, Purpose, and Manner of Inter-faith Dialogue," 263; Newbigin, *The Household of God*, 50, 82, 103; Newbigin, "Presiding at the Lord's Supper," paragraph one.

70. Newbigin, "Will God Dwell on the Earth?," 100.

71. Newbigin, *Is There Still a Missionary Job Today?*, 16–17.

72. Ibid., 75.

sen others, but he has chosen us. We cannot say why. But we know the wherefore: he has chosen us to be the bearers of his promise of blessing of all mankind."[73] Thus, Hunsberger remarks that Newbigin in this way changes the perspective "from an inner, personal, theological-psychological one into an interpersonal, socio-anthropological one."[74]

With reference to the New Testament, Newbigin asserts that humans are incorporated into Christ when they are chosen. When a person is elected, this person becomes a part of the body of Christ, a distinct social entity which has been sent to the world. Newbigin believes that the life of Christians must be social, as well as synonymous with a life in common love as a witness to the world. Thus, the church can only fulfill its task of reconciling people to God in Christ "insofar as she is herself living in Christ, a reconciled fellowship in Him, bound together in the love of the Father."[75] This also means that the church's ecumenical unity has significance for its witness to the world. God's chosen people consists of "men of all kinds and sorts [who] are reconciled in one body through the cross."[76] If these people must be an instrument to reconcile all people, Newbigin asks, how can those who are unreconciled with each other fulfill this purpose? Our disunities, he remarks, have introduced a false particularity, which is dissimilar to the particularity of being a distinctive people in the world for the sake of the world.[77]

Within the framework of Newbigin's theology, election is not only the very heart of ecclesiology, but ecclesiology also composes the very heart of missiology. We find clear expressions of this especially in his early writings: "[T]he centre of God's plan for salvation is an actual community of men and women called by God for this purpose (. . .) that through them God's love may reach others, and all men be drawn together into one reconciled fellowship."[78] Later, I will show how this church-centered missiology becomes the pivot point of a larger missiological debate in the ecumenical movement of the mid-twentieth century, and how Newbigin attempts to modify his stance.[79]

---

73. Newbigin, *Christian Witness in a Plural Society*, 25.
74. Hunsberger, *Bearing the Witness of the Spirit*, 95.
75. Newbigin, *The Household of God*, 169.
76. Newbigin, *A Faith for This One World?*, 81.
77. Ibid., 82.
78. Newbigin, *Sin and Salvation*, 46.
79. See 2.4 below.

2.3.2 Election and Necessity

Election evokes an important question: Does election not convey some sort of discrimination or arbitrary favoritism? Newbigin questions, "how can it be that among all the tribes of the ancient world, *one* should be God's people? How can it be that the Christian Church, one particular strand of human history, should be the exclusive bearer of God's saving grace for mankind?"[80] He answers himself, asserting that God does not work in this way by chance, but by necessity: "God *must* deal with us according to the principle of election."[81] In addition, he says, "[God's love] *must* be worked out through election."[82] Three matters substantiate this necessity. First, election says something about the nature of salvation:

> What is it that you are really asking for? Are you asking for a relationship with God which is in principle accessible to everyone individually apart from any relationship with his neighbor? That is in fact what the unredeemed ego in each of us really wants. At the most secret and central place of our being, do we not constantly want to be in that position where we do not have to be debtor to any other man? (. . .) His purpose is precisely to break open that shell of egoism in which you are imprisoned since Adam first fell and to give you back the new nature which is content to owe the debt of love to all men. And so God deals with us through one another.[83]

As this demonstrates, God contrives his mission through the election of a concrete and particular people, which says something essential about the nature of salvation, namely that there exists an association between the content and method of salvation. As Newbigin explains, "[t]he means which God employs for our salvation are congruous at every step both with the nature wherewith He endowed us, when He created us and the world of which we are a part, and with the end to which He leads us, which is that all things should be summed up in Christ."[84] When God chooses to act in this particularistic way, it is related to the fact that salvation revolves around love: "[L]ove only exists in actual concrete human

---

80. Newbigin, *A Faith for This One World?*, 78; italics original.
81. Newbigin, *The Household of God*, 110; italics mine.
82. Newbigin, "The Duty and Authority of the Church to Preach the Gospel," 30; italics mine.
83. Newbigin, *A Faith for This One World?*, 79.
84. Newbigin, *The Household of God*, 110.

relationships" and therefore a community is called "in order that through them God's love may reach others, and all men be drawn together into one reconciled fellowship."[85] Thus, Newbigin believes it has to do with an "inner necessity of love's nature," that God's love reaches others through election.[86] As salvation has to do with breaking down isolation and egotism, God chooses a people who, in solidarity with and devotion to others, are supposed to share salvation: "The end is the healing of all things in Christ, and the means therefore involve each of us from the very beginning inescapably in a relationship with our neighbour (. . .). We cannot be saved except through and with one another (. . .). [Salvation] relates us to God only through a relationship with our neighbour."[87]

Second, election says something about the nature of God. According to Newbigin, many believe that it is "self-evident that particular events cannot demonstrate universal truths, that God is present always and everywhere, and that the idea that one particular series of events could be regarded as in any exclusive sense the acts of God, is impossible."[88] Thus, Newbigin asserts that this viewpoint is a rejection of the Christian faith in a personal God. In contrast to this, however, Newbigin states, "if we believe in a personal God, we must believe that it is possible for him to act and therefore to choose the times and places of his actions."[89] These two viewpoints express a significant divide in human thinking. Newbigin does not believe that God is a composite of theoretical, abstract dogmas but a personal being with a will to choose and act. Therefore, it is possible for God to choose a people to play a special role in history.

Third, election suggests human nature is social; therefore, the meaning of human existence is found in the social and historical life of humanity. In this way, Newbigin claims that election reveals important insights into the nature of salvation, God and human life.[90]

---

85. Newbigin, *Sin and Salvation*, 45–46.

86. Newbigin, "The Duty and Authority of the Church to Preach the Gospel," 29–30.

87. Newbigin, *A Faith for This One World?*, 79.

88. Ibid., 78.

89. Ibid.

90. Hunsberger has similar explanation of these three aspects in his *Bearing the Witness of the Spirit*, 102–4.

2.3.3 Election and Ecclesiology

In conclusion, election is an anchoring idea in Newbigin's ecclesiology. Consequently, a situation in which a whole society is baptized,[91] and where Christianity becomes the official religion of a whole society, is unthinkable to Newbigin.[92] Thus, we can begin to answer what makes the church a distinct social entity in the world according to Newbigin.

First, he believes that election must play a crucial role in our understanding of the church: The church is a people created by God in Christ out of all tribes, nations and peoples. Transcending all social and cultural barriers, it is defined by an identity more profound than all other given identities, implying that all other given identities be seen in a new light.[93] This was a major challenge for the early church, where Jews and Gentiles had to eat together, worship the same God, and let their former understanding of their identities be determined by a new and more fundamental identity.

Second, Newbigin believes that election must play a crucial role in our understanding of mission: Ecclesiology and missiology cannot be separated. Through election, God contrives his mission so that all may be saved,[94] and w1hen election is understood missiologically, as in this case, particulari1ty and universality are held together. Thus, Newbigin believes that there exists an inescapable particularity about the church. However, this particularity has a universal scope,[95] and this particular strategy, election, must serve universal purposes: The salvation for all. This must have fundamental consequences for the structure of the church. The church must be turned outward to the world, to which its life, words and deeds must serve and witness. Therefore, Newbigin insists: "The question has to be asked—and is repeatedly asked—whether the traditional forms of the ministry which have been inherited from the 'Christendom' period are fully compatible with the faith that the Church is called to be a missionary community."[96]

In summary, Newbigin asserts that the church is a people of all tribes and nations and peoples, called into existence in the midst of

---

91. Newbigin, *Honest Religion for Secular Man*, 106.
92. Ibid., 102.
93. See 3.4.3 in chapter 3 below.
94. Newbigin, "Why Study the Old Testament?," 75.
95. Newbigin, *A Faith for This One World*, 82.
96. Newbigin, "Developments During 1962," 8.

the world as the sign for all creation. There cannot be any distinction between presence and witness. The church does not have a mission. By being the church, the church *is* mission. Thus, the life and the mission of the church is one and the same. God realizes his intentions through the church in particular and, thus, God's chosen people should reveal his intention for the whole world. According to Newbigin, the world is called to be the church, and, like Israel, the church is meant to be a light in the world, which is living in darkness. Thus, there is a fundamental difference between the church and the world, namely that God works in a special way in the church. God chooses a people to play a special role in history, and in a special way realizes his intentions in this people.[97] This leads us to the next section, where this subject will be developed further in terms of missiology.

2.4 Missiology

The middle of the twentieth century saw a theological integration of church and mission, and a development of a trinitarian understanding of mission in the ecumenical movement. Major portions of Newbigin's early writings are an important part of these developments and to understand his missiological considerations, thus, it is important to know the conversations of the ecumenical movement, which I will therefore consider here. Therefore, contrary to the other sections in this chapter, I will here outline the theological discussion of which Newbigin is a part, in order to help us better understand his theological intentions. I will begin by sketching the larger conversational context to which Newbigin belongs, followed by an exposition of his own position, and, finally, show how this debate relates to his understanding of the distinctive identity of the church.[98]

---

97. As we shall see later, Newbigin is well aware that the church not only *reveals* but also *hides* God's intentions for the whole world because of its sinful corruption. See 2.4.4 below.

98. The following analysis relies heavily on my article "Missional Church: A Historical and Theological Analysis of an Ecclesiological Tradition."

2.4.1 Church and Mission in the Ecumenical Movement

The theological integration of church and mission is an important result of the efforts of the ecumenical movement in the mid-twentieth century with the nineteenth century revivals in Germany and England as an important backdrop. In 1792, the father of the modern mission movement, William Carey, encouraged his contemporary Christians to participate in world mission. This calling appealed to many in Germany and England. However, the official churches were not willing to make a range of catechumenal, diaconal and missional tasks integral to their being. Therefore, various mission organizations were established which, on behalf of the church, sought to respond to the Great Commission. Consequently, a disintegration of church and mission occurred, and "mission" and "church" became two different bodies, with two different tasks. Thus, while the first body was responsible for the proclamation and spread of the gospel in foreign countries, the second body supported this foreign mission, but was primarily responsible for upholding and sustaining the already converted Christians in the so-called Christian West. In this way, the modern missionary movement contributed to the separation of church and mission. The beginning and the middle of the twentieth century, witnessed a theological reintegration of church and mission in the ecumenical movement.[99] This is a very complex process, and I will only present some of the more important aspects here.

In 1910, the first major world mission conference was held in Edinburgh. During the ten days of this conference, the delegates were preoccupied with how the non-Christian part of the world could be reached. Hence, the conference was not, first and foremost, a conference about mission theology, but about mission strategy. The delegates, with few exceptions, represented Western churches, and the theological relationship between church and mission was not focused on, as the missionary activities were regarded as a separate body engaged with operations on the fringe of, or fully outside of, the existing Christian Western body called "the church." In accordance with this, the mission organizations developed their "own independent organizational structure within or alongside of the organized Churches."[100] Hence, the mission organizations and the churches regarded themselves as two separate entities.

---

99. See Andersen, *Towards a Theology of Mission*, 15–33.
100. Ibid., 15.

In 1928, the International Mission Council held its first major conference since its founding in 1921. The conference was held in Jerusalem, with the mission organizations and the churches facing one another, the old schism between church and mission now in question. In contrast to Edinburgh, the conference in Jerusalem had more delegates from non-Western countries, indicative of the direction Christianity was headed. Furthermore, the destruction of the First World War intervened between the conference in Edinburgh and the conference in Jerusalem. These recent historical events resulted in a weakening of faith in the "Christian" West, leading eventually to a abandonment of the conceptual divide between the Christian West and the "pagan" non-West. Furthermore, it essentially resulted in the churches again thinking about themselves as missionary entities in the Western world.[101]

In 1938, a third notable conference was held in Tambaram, about twelve miles south of Madras, India. This conference was the first world mission conference preoccupied with an exposition of the theological relationship between church and mission.[102] The developments observed in Jerusalem continued here, as the European and American delegates were now a minority.

As is evident in many of the reports from group sessions, the understanding of the Christian church played an important role at this conference, and was represented by two main positions. The first position regarded mission as the very nature of the church: Christ passed on his mission to the Apostles, and the church's task is now to continue Christ's mission on earth. Hence, the church is very central to God's salvific work.[103] The other position considered mission as an addendum to the church, and this position differentiated between the nature and the function of the church. No one subscribing to this point of view saw mission as belonging to the *esse* of the church; mission was instead regarded as a task and function on par with other functions.[104] However, it was generally agreed upon that mission is a very important task.[105]

---

101. Ibid., 25–27.

102. Nissen, *Mission og Enhed*, 64.

103. See, for example, International Missionary Council, *Tambaram Madras Series VII*, 35, 41; Nissen, *Mission og Enhed*, 67.

104. Ibid., 69–70.

105. See the report from the group session on "The Church, its Nature and Function," in International Missionary Council, *Tambaram Madras Series VII*; Nissen, *Mission og Enhed*, 68–71.

In general, the delegates of the Tambaram conference expressed an agreement on the close connection between church and mission, and furthermore, the conceptual divide between the Christian West and the pagan non-West was given up, opening up the possibility for an understanding of the church's obligation to be in mission everywhere.[106]

However, even though Tambaram expressed agreement over the close relationship between church and mission, the conference did not lead to an understanding of the deeper theological relation between church and mission, since mission was not placed at the *esse* of the church, but rather, was understood as an addendum.[107] Neither at this conference, nor at a later conference held in Whitby, Canada, in 1947, was a consistent understanding of the relationship between church and mission reached. Thus, appropriately, the following subject was chosen for the 1952 conference in Willingen, Germany: The Missionary Obligation of the Church.[108]

At the conference in Willingen, an intense discussion of the relationship between church and mission took place, especially in the group session which worked with the subject "The Theological Foundation of the Missionary Obligation." However, the report from this group session was not accepted by the conference at large. Two things are worth noting on this point. First, the report expressed a close connection between church and mission. Second, the report emphasized that God is working actively in the world, outside as well as inside the church.[109] In fact, it was emphasized that the work of God *in the church* is the less significant, and that the true task of the church is to show how God is working in the world, for example, in political and social movements. Therefore, the church ought not to consider itself as something separate from the world, but as one part of God's activity in the world. This last point of view was the main reason why the report was not accepted.[110] Thus, a new committee was appointed, with Newbigin as chairman and Paul Lehmann, Russell Chandran and Karl Hartenstein making up the rest of the committee. The new report was named "A Statement on the Missionary Calling of

---

106. Bosch claims that First World War, socialism, fascism, and Marxism weakened the faith in a so-called Christian West. See Bosch, *Transforming Mission*, 370.

107. Nissen, *Mission og Enhed*, 73.

108. Goodall, *Missions Under the Cross*, 10; Goheen, *As the Father Has Sent Me*, 48–49.

109. Nissen, *Mission og Enhed*, 106.

110. Lehmann, "Willingen and Lund," 434–35; Nissen, *Mission og Enhed*, 110.

the Church," and, in contrast to the original report, the word "church" was included in the title: A clear signal of the theology behind it. What is most notable about this new report is that the mission of God was tied exclusively to the church.[111]

The two reports mentioned make it clear that there existed two major missiological positions at the conference in Willingen, the first position having a world-centered approach to the theology of mission, and the second a church-centered approach. Nevertheless, the conference in Willingen must be regarded as an event which contributed to a theological reintegration of church and mission. While the difference between the two reports is the notion of how broadly we ought to understand the scope of the mission of God, both reports expressed that church and mission are closely connected.[112]

It should also be mentioned that at the conference in Willingen a new understanding of mission emerged, asserting that mission does not originate in the church, but in the Triune God. After the conference, this understanding was expressed using the important term *missio Dei*.[113] Over time, the two aforementioned missiological positions at the conference in Willlingen came to represent two different interpretations of the *missio Dei* concept. The first interpretation can be designated with the expression *missio Dei generalis*, and the latter with the expression *missio Dei specialis*.[114] The first expression emphasizes that God first and foremost contrives his mission in the world independently of the church, while the latter emphasiszes that God contrives his mission in and through the church. In the years after Willingen, the church-centered position gained ground, but already at the mission conference in Uppsala, Sweden, in 1968, this position was in decline.[115]

In this presentation of the larger context to which Newbigin belonged, I have briefly outlined how in the early to mid-twentieth century,

---

111. Nissen, *Mission og Enhed*, 113–16.

112. See also Ahonen, "Antedating Missional Church," 573–76. For an analysis of the debate concerning the two reports, see Flett, *The Witness of God*, 152–57.

113. I will later present Newbigin's understanding of this concept. See 2.4.3 below.

114. The expression *missio Dei specialis* was for the first time used by Vicedom in his book *Missio Dei: Einführung in eine Theologie der Mission*, 43 (published in 1960). The expression *missio Dei generalis* was introduced by Berentsen in his article "*Missio Dei*: Nøkkelbegrep til Bestemmelsen av et Hovedproblem i Etterkrigstidens Protestantinske Misjonstenkning," 4 (published in 1983).

115. Engelsviken, "*Missio Dei*," 482–84; Berentsen, "*Missio Dei*," 6.

both a theological reintegration of ecclesiology and missiology and a trinitarian understanding of mission emerged. In the following, I will first explore Newbigin's own position on the relationship between church and mission, followed by an exploration of his appropriation of a trinitarian understanding of mission.[116]

2.4.2 Church and Mission in the Theology of Newbigin

The missiological starting point for Newbigin is the mission commandment in the Gospel of John ("as the Father has sent me, I am sending you"). In continuation of the insights that were gained in the ecumenical movement, Newbigin accentuates the inner-trinitarian sendings, that the Father sends the Son, that the Father and the Son send the Holy Spirit, and that the Father, the Son and the Holy Spirit send the church to the world. For Newbigin, the *missio Dei* is the starting point from which the *missio Christi* and the *missio ecclesiae* derive.[117] The *missio Dei* leads to the sending of Jesus, and with the sending of the Holy Spirit, a *missio continuata* is set in motion. Even though there cannot be a clear identification of the *missio Dei* and the *missio ecclesiae*, Newbigin's understanding of the *missio Dei* shows a close relationship between church and mission. Even so, it is important to note that Newbigin's understanding of the *missio Dei* is first and foremost historical, not ontological, that is, he unfolds his trinitarian approach to mission in relation to redemptive-history as narrated in the biblical story, and does not present theo-ontological reflections on the nature of the Trinity abstracted from history.[118]

Newbigin is a child of the missiology developed from Tambaram to Willingen, and approves of a church-centered missiology. He sees the importance of the theological reintegration of church and mission like this: "The separation of these two things which God has joined together must be judged one of the great calamities of missionary history, and the healing of this division one of the great tasks of our time."[119] For

---

116. See 2.4.2 and 2.4.3 below.

117. It should be noted that Newbigin in fact very rarely uses the *missio Dei* concept. He makes the case without using that particular language very often. A few times he did, however, use the term. Newbigin uses the concept eight times in his article "Recent Thinking on Christian Beliefs," 260–64, and he uses the concept four times in his article "Reply to Konrad Raiser," 51–52.

118. Goheen pointed to this in a correspondence in June 2010.

119. Newbigin, *One Body, One Gospel, One World*, 26.

Newbigin, the church is the most important tool in God's mission, and mission is the essential nature and calling of the church.[120] Nowhere in Newbigin's writings is God's mission separated from the church. As he puts it, "the centre of God's plan for salvation is an actual community of men and women called by God for this purpose (. . .) that through them God's love may reach others, and all men be drawn together into one reconciled fellowship."[121]

At the conference in Accra, Ghana, in 1958, the integration of the International Mission Council and the World Council of Churches was an important topic of discussion. The two international councils themselves expressed an organizational disintegration of church and mission, which had been theologically overcome in the previous decades. Newbigin summarizes the conclusions from the conference in three statements: (1) The Church is Mission: It is not possible to talk about the church without talking about mission and vice versa; (2) The Home Base is Everywhere: The church on every continent is facing a mission task; and (3) Mission in Partnership: One church cannot supercede another church and the global church must work on its common mission task in fellowship.[122]

At the conference in Accra, the theological integration of church and mission was thereby accomplished, resulting in the integration of the International Mission Council and the World Council of Churches at the conference in New Delhi in 1961. In the time between the conference in Willingen and the conference in Accra, Newbigin was involved in the International Mission Council and the World Council of Churches joint committee which aimed to lay out an integration plan.[123] At the conference in Accra, Newbigin was elected as President and later as General Secretary of the International Missionary Council. In 1959, he was elected as General Secretary of the International Mission Council.[124]

---

120. See, for example, ibid., 25–27; Newbigin, "The Bishop and the Ministry of Mission," 242.

121. Newbigin, *Sin and Salvation*, 46.

122. Bosch, *Transforming Mission*, 370; cf. Newbigin, *One Body, One Gospel, One World*, 25–38.

123. Newbigin, *Unfinished Agenda*, 153–54.

124. Newbigin's role in this process has been analyzed by Laing in his dissertation, "The Calling of the Church to Mission and to Unity."

2.4.3 Church and Mission in Light of a Trinitarian Perspective

By the end of the 1950s and into the early 1960s, a shift occurred in Newbigin's missiology. In the late 1950s, Newbigin reached the conclusion that his missiology had been too Christocentric and ecclesiocentric:

> Already at New Delhi I had recognized that the missiology of *One Body, One Gospel, One World* was not adequate. It was too exclusively church-centred in its understanding of mission. Only a fully Trinitarian doctrine would be adequate, setting the work of Christ in the Church in the context of the overruling providence of the Father in all the life of the world and the sovereign freedom of the Spirit who is the Lord and not the auxiliary of the Church.[125]

Therefore, in the beginning of the 1960s, Newbigin began to develop a trinitarian framework for his missionary ecclesiology. In 1963 Newbigin writes: "A true doctrine of missions must make a large place for the work of the Holy Spirit; but it is equally true that a true doctrine of missions will have much to say of God the Father. The opinion may be ventured that recent ecumenical thinking about the mission and unity of the church has been defective at both of these points."[126] Even though, in his early writings, Newbigin used trinitarian formulas in relation to the mission of the church, he still believed that his understanding of mission was "Christocentric in a way that neglected the work of the Father and the Holy Spirit."[127] The ecumenical movement made Newbigin think this through anew, and his first attempt to understand the mission of the church in a trinitarian context can be found in his book *The Relevance of Trinitarian Doctrine for Today's Mission*. Here Newbigin's missiology clearly develops from a Christocentric orientation to a Christocentric focus with a trinitarian breadth, even though he never developed this comprehensively.[128] I now turn to consider how Newbigin came to understand mission explicitly in relation to the Father, the Son and the Holy Spirit.[129]

---

125. Newbigin, *Unfinished Agenda*, 187.
126. Newbigin, *The Relevance of Trinitarian Doctrine for Today's Mission*, 31.
127. Goheen, *As the Father Has Sent Me*, 115.
128. Goheen, "As the Father Has Sent Me, I Am Sending You," 356–57.
129. Goheen has presented an analysis of this, which I find no reason to criticize and which I rely on. See Goheen, *As the Father Has Sent Me*, 115–64.

(a) The Father

As Goheen asserts, there are three matters of importance when we look at Newbigin's understanding of mission in relation to the Father.[130] First, the Father is the creator and upholder of the world. Jesus came not into a foreign world, but into his Father's world.[131] God has not condemned his world but upheld it. In Newbigin's words, God the Father "is ceaselessly at work in all creation and in the hearts and minds of all human beings whether they acknowledge him or not, graciously guiding history toward its true end."[132] Thus, the Father loves and cares for his creation and therefore he sends his Son to the world, a world which he has created but which has "fallen from his true estate and [is] involved in a common sin against the creator."[133]

Second, the Father is the source of mission. Even though Newbigin does not use the term *missio Dei* very often, it is still important to him to emphasize that mission originates in the Triune God.[134] Newbigin affirms the inner-trinitarian sendings, that the Father sends the Son, that the Father and the Son send the Holy Spirit, and that the Father, Son and Holy Spirit send the church to the world, implying that mission begins with God and not the church. As Goheen explains, Newbigin acknowledges that,

> God is at work in history *in some sense* in movements of national liberation, of scientific discovery, of cultural renaissance, and reform in non-Christian religions. But it is essential to press further in what sense God is at work in these movements. Newbigin's dilemma was how to affirm the uniqueness of Christ without denying God's work in the world, to probe the relation between what God has done in Christ and what God is doing in the life of humankind as a whole.[135]

When Newbigin uses the term *missio Dei*, it is tied to Christ, the Holy Spirit and the church. By way of contrast, David J. Bosch uses the term also with respect to God's creational work, stating that "in creation God was already the God of mission, with his Word and Spirit as 'Missionaries'

---

130. Ibid., 134–36.
131. Ibid., 135.
132. Newbigin, *The Gospel in a Pluralist Society*, 135.
133. Newbigin, *A Faith for This One World?*, 61.
134. See n117 above.
135. Goheen, *As the Father Has Sent Me*, 131; italics original.

(cf. Gen 1:2–3)."[136] The term *missio Dei* is here used to express God's work as a whole, as Bosch regards God's redemptive activities as an integral part of his creational and upholding work. In the writings of Newbigin, however, we do not find such a corresponding use of the term *missio Dei*. He never uses the terms *missio Dei* or *mission* in relation to God's creational and upholding work; God's mission is exclusively tied to Israel, Christ and the church.[137] According to Newbigin, God nevertheless works in the world, namely as the upholder and ruler of the world.

Third, the Father is the ruler over the world. To Newbigin, the Father rules over both the world and world history, and it is within world history that the Father composes his mission.[138] He chooses first Israel, later Christ and finally the church. The Father has created all things and is the ruler over all things, he is the ruler of history and directs the course of history according to his will, and he upholds all things. With the Father's ordering of all things, Jesus complies. In Jesus, God's kingdom is revealed, yet, still remains hidden. The church cannot take control over history, but must be an obedient and suffering witness. The whole world is a part of this history. The church must witness that God is the ruler of history and that biblical history comprises the framework of human existence. The end of history is hidden, but the understanding of history is revealed to the Christian community as a secret, which must be made known to all. The Father sends the Son to inaugurate his kingdom on earth.

(b) The Son

Newbigin looks to the Gospel of John as he tries to understand the relationship between the mission of the church and the Son. As the Father has sent the Son, so the Son sends the church to the world. The church takes over the place and mission of the Son. Jesus proclaims that the kingdom of the Father is near and inaugurates the end-time, which has been promised, announcing the arrival and the presence of the kingdom of God in history. Jesus not only proclaims, but also realizes the kingdom of God, inaugurating the kingdom of God in his life, words and deeds. And at the center of the life of Jesus is his accomplishment of salvation by his

---

136. Bosch, *Witness to the World*, 239.

137. Berentsen, "*Missio Dei*," 10.

138. Later I will show how Newbigin critiques any attempt to separate salvation history from world history. See 2.5 below.

death and resurrection. Jesus gathers a community, which partakes in the salvation and the powers of the kingdom. This community is "commissioned to annouce the presence of the kingdom and to perform the works that authenticate its presence."[139] The presence of the kingdom of God is hidden and not made known for everyone. Yet, "in its hiddenness it is revealed to those whom God through his Spirit grants the gift of faith."[140] Newbigin believes that Jesus carried out his mission through the power of the Spirit and that the church in the same way must carry out its mission in the power of the Holy Spirit. The Son forms a people, which he sends into the world, and then sends the Holy Spirit to strengthen this people.[141]

(c) The Holy Spirit

It is important for Newbigin to stress that the Holy Spirit is God's gift to his people in the last days. Therefore, the work of the Holy Spirit must be understood in an eschatological context. Christ established the *eschaton* and sent the Holy Spirit to the church on the day of Pentecost. The Holy Spirit realizes the end-time reign of God in the world. Furthermore, he believes that mission is primarily the work of the Holy Spirit; the church is a result of the Holy Spirit's activities.[142] Newbigin argues that it is the Holy Spirit who leads Philip to the Ethiopian eunuch (Acts 8), who prepares Ananias to meet Paul (Acts 9), who prepares Peter to meet a pagan army officer (Acts 10), who initiates the first mission to the Gentiles (Acts 13), and who guides the apostles on their journeys (Acts 16).[143] The Holy Spirit walks in front of the church, and in this way mission can take place outside the church. This implies that the mission of God not only changes the world, but also the church. The Holy Spirit leads the church and convicts the world.[144] Newbigin refers to Acts 10 as a good example of this as we here see how the Holy Spirit directs the Roman officer Cornelius. Even so, Newbigin believes that mission is always somehow connected to the church. There would not have been a history of conversion if Peter

---

139. Newbigin, *The Open Secret*, 42.

140. Ibid., 53.

141. This is of course a very short outline of Newbigin's understanding of the ministry of Jesus. For a more comprehensive analysis, see Goheen, *As the Father Has Sent Me*, 136–53.

142. Newbigin, *The Open Secret*, 56–58.

143. Ibid., 58–59.

144. Ibid., 59.

had not gone to the house and spoken with Cornelius, proclaiming the gospel.[145] Thus, the Holy Spirit's work "outside the church cannot be separated from the church."[146]

In summary, it is clear that Newbigin believes the church's mission to be fully understable only in a trinitarian context. By the end of the 1950s and in the early 1960s, Newbigin's theology of mission transitions from a Christocentric orientation to a more balanced trinitarian orientation.[147] However, even though Newbigin develops a trinitarian framework for his understanding of the mission of the church, he nevertheless maintains a strong Christological focus as he again and again ties together Christology, ecclesiology, and missiology.

Newbigin, however, has some reservations about the expression "the church as an extention of the incarnation."[148] He believes that the unity of the divine and human in Christ is not analogous to the church, and in addition, if the church were an incarnation of God, it would have no need "to point beyond itself to Christ."[149] Yet, Newbigin emphasizes that the sending of the church is a continuation of the incarnation of the Son, and that the mission of Christ must also be the mission of the church. This double sending is the axis of Newbigin's missiology.

As I have shown in this section, Newbigin believes that an inescapable particularity is an integral part of God's mission in the world. Newbigin's understanding of the mission of God can appropriately be expressed with the term *missio Dei specialis*, as he believes that God carries out his mission through election—first through Israel, then Christ and finally the church. It is a fundamental presupposition in Newbigin's missiology that the church is a distinct social entity, which is meant to embody the mission of God in the world.

2.4.4 Missiology and Ecclesiology

In conclusion, within Newbigin's theological framework, God's mission is embodied in the church as a distinct community. This exploration into

---

145. Ibid., 59–61.
146. Goheen, *As the Father Has Sent Me*, 156.
147. Ibid., 62–64.
148. See Newbigin, *The Reunion of the Church*, 55–83.
149. Ibid., 61, see also 59–61.

missiological thoughts has also shown that a scenario in which a whole society is baptized, and where Christianity becomes the religion of a whole society, is unthinkable for Newbigin. Thus, we can add a new layer to our understanding of the distinctive identity of the church according to Newbigin.

It is a fundamental assumption for Newbigin's missiology that the church is a distinct social entity, meant to embody the mission of God in the world. God's redemptive activities are in a special way tied to the church as a distinct social entity, and, in and through the church, God is recreating in a way that he is not recreating in the world. Thus, the church is purposed to function as an example for the world. Hunsberger refers to several theologians who claim that the church serves as a prototype for what God intends for the world. For example, Charles Van Engen writes, "their being [is] a sort of showcase, a prototype, of what He intends for all mankind (. . .). In their communal, practical everyday life they must really *be* that exhibition model which they are intended to be."[150] Along the same lines, Robert Martin-Achard writes, "the evangelization of the world is not primarily a matter of words and deeds; it is a matter of presence—the presence of the People of God in the midst of mankind and the presence of God in the midst of His People."[151] These statements lie in immediate continuation of Newbigin's thoughts concerning Israel and the church's role in the world, namely, that God chooses Israel and the church to "reveal and effect God's will for all mankind."[152]

Further, Newbigin states that the church is a "foretaste of the restoration of creation to its true harmony in and for God's glory, and of man to his true relation to the created world."[153] The church is an expression of a re-creation, or a second creation, of the human race in Christ so that it must be what he intended by the first creation. God's redemptive powers are at work in the church, and in the church the power of sin is broken. Therefore, the church is the "body of Christ actually present in the world, a place where the light of God really shines and the life of God really pulses."[154]

---

150. Van Engen, *The Growth of the True Church*, 134, 144–45. In the original text "be" is capitalized; the emphasis is added.

151. Martin-Achard, *A Light to the Nations*, 31.

152. Newbigin, "The Duty and Authority of the Church to Preach the Gospel," 29.

153. Newbigin, *The Household of God*, 67.

154. Ibid., 55.

However—and this is an important point to underscore—history teaches us that the church is certainly not always an example to follow, or a role model for the world. Newbigin is well aware of this, stating "the Church, even the New Testament Church, has never been a simple expression of the love of God; it has always been also at the same time a contradiction of the love of God."[155] Hence, Newbigin also states, "[a]t no point, therefore, is it sufficient for the Church to point to its own good deeds. It must always be penitently aware of the fact that even the best of its good deeds cannot mediate for man the ultimate judgment and mercy of God."[156] Ideally, the church reveals God's intentions for the whole world, but because this is not always the case, the church must refer to Christ, in whom God's purpose for the world is most clearly expressed.

2.5 Eschatology

In this section, I will analyze Newbigin's eschatology with the aim of disclosing its significance for the distinctive identity of the church. As Schuster explains, Newbigin summarizes world history in five major themes: Creation, the fall, election, redemption, and consummation.[157] Thus, I will begin with an exploration of these themes.

2.5.1 The Old Age

The Christian faith claims that God is the creator of all things. The Bible is universal history, which begins with the creation of the world. God creates the world through Christ and creates the human in his image. Newbigin believes that the *imago Dei* must largely be understood as a fundamental relation to God.[158] Furthermore, he says, "the nature of man is that he was made in love, by love, for love. Love is the source and end of his being. Therefore man cannot live alone (. . .). When God created man He did not create an individual; He created man-and-woman. For God is not an individual; God is personal but He is not a person. He is a

---

155. Newbigin, *A Faith for This One World?*, 90.

156. Ibid.

157. Schuster, *Christian Mission in Eschatological Perspective*, 66.

158. Newbigin, *A Faith for This One World?*, 61–68; Newbigin, *Sin and Salvation*, 16–18.

Trinity, Father, Son, and Holy Spirit, one God."[159] God created the world with orders and good structures in an original state of *shalom*.

A general belief of the Christian faith is, furthermore, that humankind "is fallen from his true estate and involved in a common sin against the creator."[160] Therefore, God set in motion a rescue plan. What God is doing "in Christ is the culmination of a plan which begins with the choosing of a people," whose intent is the salvation of all.[161] As we have seen, Newbigin believes that the majority of the biblical story can be regarded as a story about election, first of Israel, later of Christ and finally of the church.[162] It is, however, noteworthy that Newbigin does not believe that salvation history can be separated from the natural history of the world.[163] According to him, world history must be understood in accordance with a number of events in the stories that are described in the Bible, and which center around the life, death and resurrection of Jesus: "[Salvation history] is part of world history, that part from which we understand the whole. It is the clue to world history (. . .). The special story with which it [the Bible] is concerned is in no kind of isolation from the rest of the world's history but is bound up with it."[164] Thus, it is important for Newbigin to emphasize that there are not two different histories, a sacral and a profane history, or a salvation history and a secular history. Why is this so? Newbigin clearly emphasizes this in order to protect the church from being drawn into a private sphere, something he does again and again, especially in his later writings.[165]

Eschatology must begin fundamentally with an understanding of the New Testament's account of two ages, which overlap or lie alongside one another.[166] The old age begins with the fall, and ends with the return of Christ. The new age extends from Christ's coming (but does not, however, end with the return of Christ). Newbigin's thought on the old age begins with his foundational belief that God has created good struc-

---

159. Newbigin, *Sin and Salvation*, 17–18.
160. Newbigin, *A Faith for This One World?*, 61.
161. Ibid.
162. See 2.3.1 above.
163. Newbigin, *A Faith for This One World?*, 80.
164. Ibid.

165. Cullmann differentiates between world history and salvation history. He believes that the two histories were separated with the fall and will be united again with the *Parousia*. See Cullmann, *Christus und die Zeit*.

166. Newbigin, *The Household of God*, 153.

tures and worldly orders. Newbigin states that these structures have an outward form as established religious, cultural, and political structures. Their inward reality is what Paul calls "the principalities and powers of this age," which no longer honor God, but oppose his good intentions.[167] As Newbigin puts it,

> [These] structures are necessary for the maintenance of human life as it is. Christ has not destroyed the powers (. . .). Anarchism has a respectable history, but Christians are not anarchists, for Christ has not destroyed the powers. But, on the other hand, it is equally necessary to insist that the authority of the structures is provisional and not final or absolute. Christ has disarmed the powers. Christians, therefore, are revolutionaries. They believe that structures can be and have to be changed, and that no structure, even the most venerable (. . .), has absolute authority. Only Christ has absolute authority, and in Christ we are called to keep all structures, under review and to change them when necessary.[168]

Thus, according to Newbigin, "the world" is a manifestation of the old age and "[i]t is too easy for us to use the biblical word 'world' as a mere abstract noun without really thinking of the concrete reality which the word denotes."[169] So, for example, when Paul speaks in this way about powers and principalities, Newbigin believes he is speaking about fallen structures in the world. Here Newbigin clearly follows Hendrick Berkhof in his understanding of the powers and principalities as worldly structures, and not only as spiritual beings.[170]

2.5.2 The New Age

A new age, however, was promised in the Old Testament; Christ inaugurates this new age and the kingdom of God. In the words of Newbigin,

167. Newbigin, *The Gospel in a Pluralist Society*, 105.
168. Newbigin, *Bible Study on Romans 8*, 8.
169. Newbigin, *The Household of God*, 154.
170. See, for example, Newbigin, *The Gospel in a Pluralist Society*, 103, 105, 111, 131. Berkhof has written two important books about this: *Christ and the Powers* and *Christ the Meaning of History*. Newbigin's understanding of the concept of "powers and principalities" in the New Testament is not commonly accepted among scholars. Also, the paragraph above is the closest we come to a definition of "the world" in the writings of Newbigin. Thus, it is not possible to present a major exposition of what he exactly understands by "the world."

> The central proclamation of the New Testament is that in Christ the new age has already dawned. In the words of the very first proclamation of the gospel, 'The Kingdom of God has come near.' In Christ the powers of the new age are at work. The domain of Heaven has touched that of earth and God's rule is actually being exercised in the world through Jesus. Those who accept Him come within the sphere of operations of the powers of the Kingdom: they may in fact be said to have been translated out of the present age into the new age which is to come. The new age is no longer something in the distant future. It is already present proleptically. Christians have already, as it is said, tasted the powers of the age to come.[171]

In regards to this saying, Schuster rightly states that Newbigin's view of this kingdom is strictly Christocentric.[172] For example, Newbigin argues that the message of the kingdom of God is distorted if it is separated from the name of Jesus.[173] Hence, there can be no separation of the kingdom from the king. On the one hand, Newbigin is emphasizing that the kingdom of God is present here and now in this world: "The new age is no longer something in the distant future. It is already present proleptically. Christians have already, as it is said, tasted the powers of the age to come."[174] On the other hand, Newbigin asserts that the kingdom of God is a future reality: "In the center of the picture is the hope of a new world, a recreated universe in which the travail of history shall find its completion and its rest."[175] Accordingly, these two aspects of the kingdom of God must be held together: "The tensions in the teaching of the New Testament about the kingdom are not, therefore, to be rationalized away. The kingdom is both present and future."[176]

Newbigin believes that the new age is defined by the following threefold affirmation: "Christ has died, once for all disarming the principalities and powers. Christ has risen, and now reigns at the Father's side until his enemies submit. Christ will come again, and the glory of his reign will be manifest to all."[177] He also states: "The presence of Jesus

---

171. Newbigin, "The Kingdom of God and the Idea of Progress," 27.
172. Schuster, *Christian Mission in Eschatological Perspective*, 101.
173. Newbigin, *Mission in Christ's Way*, 9–10.
174. Newbigin, "The Kingdom of God and the Idea of Progress," 27.
175. Ibid., 46.
176. Newbigin, "The Kingdom of God and Our Hopes for the Future," 12.
177. Newbigin, *The Gospel in a Pluralist Society*, 111.

strips the masks of righteousness and piety from the face of the powers. It does so precisely because in him the kingdom of God is veiled, hidden in a humble and powerless man."[178] In addition to this, he says, "the powers of this age, not knowing the Lord of Glory when He came to His own, rejected and condemned Him."[179] Moreover, Newbigin also asserts that the crucifixion of Christ unmasks the nature of the powers and principalities, because this event discloses that they act against the good intentions of God, and in a profound sense, are in rebellion against God. They act "not as his instruments but as his enemies."[180] Finally, Newbigin states that Christ now sits at his Father's right hand, and is made Lord not only over the church but also over the whole world.[181] When Christ returns, this universal lordship will be visible.

2.5.3 The Church as Sign, Instrument and Foretaste

Newbigin believes that the church finds itself in conflict between the old age and the new age, implying that the church must expect suffering. Where the church is faithful to the gospel, and thus creates a presence of the kingdom, "there will be a challenge by word and behavior to the ruling powers. As a result there will be conflict and suffering for the Church."[182] Newbigin also states, "the New Testament makes it plain that Christ's followers must expect suffering as the normal badge of their discipleship, and also as one of the characteristic forms of their witness."[183] On this point, Schuster tells us that Newbigin's belief is that the church "must not give in to the temptation to live according to the paradigm of the present, but to live according to the Spirit. Only thus the church is true to its calling to be an eschatological community, a regenerate humanity."[184] The kingdom of God has broken into the world, and the church is a sign, instrument and foretaste of this kingdom.[185]

---

178. Ibid., 105.

179. Newbigin, *The Household of God*, 154.

180. Newbigin, *Honest Religion for Secular Man*, 139.

181. Newbigin, "Can the Churches give a Common Message to the World?," 516, 518; Newbigin, *The Household of God*, 158–59.

182. Newbigin, *The Gospel in a Pluralist Society*, 136.

183. Newbigin, *Trinitarian Faith and Today's Mission*, 42.

184. Schuster, *Christian Mission in Eschatological Perspective*, 64.

185. Newbigin, *Mission in Christ's Way*, 12.

But why must Christ's victory and the kingdom of God remain hidden? Why is the church only a sign and a foretaste of the kingdom? Newbigin would reply to this by claiming that humans should have the freedom to respond freely to the gospel.[186] Hence, Newbigin states that God mercifully withholds the final revelation. Until the return of Christ, his reign will "be known not by sight but by faith, not in full enjoyment but in foretaste, not in complete manifestation but in signs which point beyond themselves to a reality greater than themselves."[187] Since the victory of Christ remains hidden, the life and mission of the church will never be triumphant. The mission of the church will always remain a mission under the cross.

Furthermore, the kingdom of God will not appear clearly, because the church is still full of the seeds of its own corruption. Therefore, the church does not fully establish God's kingdom. God's kingdom is a given fact, but Christian communities encompass "*at the very* best only signs, pointers to help men and women to turn round so that it becomes possible for them also to believe in the reality of that kingdom, to have a foretaste of its liberating power, to follow the way of the cross and to find in it life—a life that death cannot threaten."[188] It is, however, the belief of the church that Christ has prevailed, and that his victory will one day be known for all. This is the hope of the church even under the most hopeless circumstances.[189] Also, the Holy Spirit has been given to the church as a visible sign testifying that the new age has dawned: "The Spirit is given us in order that we may witness, for He is the primary witness to Christ, (. . .) granting signs of the hidden victory."[190]

Thus, the church must learn from Christ as it discerns how to exist in the world. For example, it must understand its mission in light of the mission of Christ. Newbigin explains,

> We have to remind ourselves again of the significance of the little word 'as.' It is the manner in which the Father sent the Son that determines the manner in which the church is sent by Jesus. Its mission is governed by the manner of his. We are reminded again of the pattern of his mission as it is outlined for us in the four gospels. And lest the full meaning of that word 'as' should

---

186. Newbigin, *The Household of God*, 126.
187. Ibid., 126–27.
188. Newbigin, *Mission in Christ's Way*, 12; italics mine.
189. Newbigin, "The Present Crisis and the Coming Christ," 120–21.
190. Newbigin, *The Household of God*, 157.

> be missed, he shows them his hand and his side. It was the scars of the passion in his risen body that assured the frightened disciples that it was really Jesus who stood among them. It will be those same scars in the corporate life of the church that will authenticate it as indeed the body of Christ, the bearer of his mission, the presence of the kingdom. It will not be enough for the church to place a cross on the top of its buildings or in the centre of its altars or on the robes of its clergy. The marks of the cross will have to be recognizable also in the lives of its members if the church is to be the authentic presence of the kingdom.[191]

Later Newbigin states,

> Jesus stood in their midst and said 'peace be with you', showed them the scars of that atoning passion by which alone peace is made between sinful men and women and their holy Creator; and then sent them out to be the bearers of that peace into the life of the world—but always in conformity with the way by which peace was made, the way of the cross.[192]

To Newbigin, the church must exist in the world as Christ existed in the world. The church must not destroy the powers because of the evil they do, but seek "to subvert them from within and thereby to bring them back under the allegiance of their true Lord."[193] As Christ unmasked the powers, the church must do the same.

Newbigin understands this very concretely and seeks, through an analysis of the history of Western culture, to unmask this culture's most fundamental assumption. Newbigin's ambitious intention is to show that the axioms of Western culture are a result of a "socio-cultural construct" and therefore can be questioned.[194] Newbigin's project is not only ambitious, but also quite radical, for he desires to question assumptions that seem to be so obvious to humans in Western culture that they are held unconsciously. Newbigin exposes these unexamined assumptions by taking a radically different starting point for human thought, that is, for Newbigin, the starting point is not human rationality, but Christ. He believes: "The Christian tradition offers the gospel of Jesus Christ as the

---

191. Newbigin, *Mission in Christ's Way*, 23.
192. Ibid., 30.
193. Newbigin, *Truth to Tell*, 82.
194. Goheen, *As the Father Has Sent Me*, 379.

light of the world while the classical tradition offers autonomous reason disciplined by scientific methods as the light of the world."[195]

Newbigin, however, is not fully consistent in his reflections about the church's relation to society. On the one hand, he believes that the church must serve society, must be willing to suffer and not take control over the world. On the other hand, he states that the church must impact society and its public doctrines. This represents a significant tension in Newbigin's theology, on which he does not seem to present a thoroughly thought-out reflection. In the last section of this chapter, I will discuss this tension in further detail.[196]

2.5.4 Eschatology and Ecclesiology

In conclusion, after having sketched the most important aspects of Newbigin's eschatology, it is possible to add yet another layer to our understanding of the distinctive identity of the church according to Newbigin. The analysis in this section has pointed to a fundamental difference between the church and the world, namely that the kingdom of God, in a special way, is manifested in the church. According to Newbigin, the church is set firmly in an eschatological framework, and, consequently, the identity of the church can only rightly be understood from an eschatological perspective.[197] Therefore, he can say that the church "*is* an eschatological reality."[198]

Newbigin also asserts that God created the world in an original state of *shalom* with orders and good structures. However, these structures no longer honor God, but oppose his good intentions and, therefore, the church exists in a hostile environment. In the midst of this world, however, the kingdom of God has broken in. The church is a space in the world where the powers of the new age are active in a special way. Hence, the church finds itself in a conflict between the old age and the new age. In this situation, it must "not give in to the temptation to live according to the paradigm of the present, but to live according to the Spirit. Only thus the church is true to its calling to be an eschatological community."[199]

---

195. Ibid., 381.
196. See 2.8 below.
197. Newbigin, *The Household of God*, 18–19.
198. Newbigin, "Review of God's Order," 546; italics mine.
199. Schuster, *Christian Mission in Eschatological Perspective*, 64.

Just as Christ submitted himself to the powers and principalities and unmasked them, the church is called on to do the same. However, the church acknowledges only Christ as Lord and, therefore, it will inevitably question the most fundamental assumptions of its surrounding society. By its very existence, by its way of life, and by its understanding of reality, the church will constantly relativize the morality and religiosity of the surrounding society.

2.6 Social Ethics

Newbigin never dealt with social ethics in a systematic way or devoted a major book to the topic. Nevertheless, he deals with ethics throughout his writings. He believes that the disestablishment of Christendom involve a questioning of accepted Christian practices and patterns of behavior: "In a sacral type of society these patterns are regarded as part of the ultimate constitution of things, bound up with the final realities which cannot be questioned. Secularization destroys these certainties and puts men in a position where they have to make conscious decisions about matters which were formerly taken for granted."[200] Hence, in a post-Christendom society, the church must represent a distinct social order. In fact, "the most important contribution which the Church can make to a new social order is to be itself a new social order."[201] Thus, the calling of the church to be a distinct social order within society will be the focus of this section. In the final section of this chapter, I will return to the implications of this for the relationship between church and society.[202]

2.6.1 The Church as a Distinct Social Order

Newbigin states that the Christian community must believe, embody and proclaim the gospel. Hence, the gospel is not announced as a disembodied gospel, but rather, a community which represents the gospel. This community lives by the gospel and invites others to live by it. As Newbigin states: "How is it possible that the gospel should be credible, that people should come to believe that the power which has the last word in human affairs is represented by a man hanging on the cross? I am suggesting that

---

200. Newbigin, *Honest Religion for Secular Man*, 138.
201. Newbigin, *Truth to Tell*, 85.
202. See 2.8 below.

the only answer, the only hermeneutic of the gospel, is a congregation of men and women who believe it and live by it."[203] According to Newbigin, being a distinct social order within society is not one of several optional activities of the church. He says,

> A congregation cannot say: 'This Church is not interested in social service: it is interested in something else.' It is not this kind of question that we are dealing with. We are dealing with a question which concerns the integrity of the Church itself, its fundamental character as a Church (. . .). It is a question of whether the Church in its fundamental character is a servant Church; whether it is possible to have in any valid sense a Christian congregation, or a Christian liturgy, or a Christian ministry in which this concern for the poor is not integrally involved.[204]

Hence, it is clear that Newbigin believes that it is a part of the identity of the church to be a distinct social order within society. He also expresses it in this way: "It is a disastrous misunderstanding to think that we can enjoy salvation through Jesus Christ and at the same time regard action for justice in the world as a sort of optional extra—or even as an inferior substitute for the work of passing on the good news of salvation."[205] Newbigin believes that Christ is the new fact, the new datum, wherefrom Christian ethics spring.[206] The Christian has been given salvation as a totally undeserved gift, and the life of the Christian must be an act of thanksgiving, a continuous response to the living Lord himself.[207] He reflects that God teaches, guides and rebukes his people with his commandments, which leads the church to be involved in the social, political and economic life of the world.[208]

Newbigin's reflections on the social task of the church are closely connected to his eschatology. Schuster claims that Newbigin believes that the church "must not give in to the temptation to live according to the paradigm of the present, but to live according to the Spirit. Only thus the church is true to its calling to be an eschatological community, a

---

203. Newbigin, *The Gospel in a Pluralist Society*, 227.

204. Newbigin, "The Church as a Servant Community," 260.

205. Newbigin, "Jesus, Saviour of the World," 109. Here I quote from Goheen, *As the Father Has Sent Me*, 293.

206. Newbigin, *Christian Freedom in a Modern World*, 83.

207. Newbigin, *Honest Religion for Secular Man*, 141–42.

208. Wainwright, *Lesslie Newbigin*, 241.

regenerate humanity."[209] Christians have been given a new life by God, fit for the new age. The kingdom of God has broken into the world and the church manifests this kingdom in the world.[210] The church is not to be identified with the kingdom, but it is a sign, instrument and foretaste of the kingdom.[211] Therefore, Christians are not to wait passively for the full realization of God's Kingdom, but they must "act as agents of the Kingdom in the various sectors of public life where they work."[212] The church as a distinct social order is inescapably part of the new eschatological reality inaugurated with the coming of Christ:

> The works of mercy, of healing, of liberation—all are part of the breaking in of a new reality. They are parts of it and therefore signs of it (. . .) the deeds of healing and liberation must not be separated from the new reality of which they are a part. They are part of the overflowing of God's grace. Jesus' deeds of love were not part of a contrived programme with some ulterior purpose: they were the overflowing of the love which filled his whole being. Just so, the Church's deeds of love ought to be—not contrived signs but natural and spontaneous signs of the new reality in which we have been made sharers through Christ. Those who have received so much cannot keep it to themselves. It must overflow in love to others.[213]

2.6.2 The Church as a Servant Community

How, then, is the church supposed to act in society? The all-dominant theme in Newbigin's writings is that the church must be a servant community: The church must care for its neighbors,[214] feed the hungry, clothe the naked, give help to the victims of disasters,[215] struggle against injustice and oppression,[216] and participate in creating good, just orders in society. Newbigin remarks, however, that political action is "not the only

---

209. Schuster, *Christian Mission in Eschatological Perspective*, 64.
210. Newbigin, *The Good Shepherd*, 94.
211. Newbigin, *Mission in Christ's Way*, 12; Newbigin, "Does Society Still Need the Parish Church?," 62; Newbigin, "Church, World, Kingdom," 106.
212. Newbigin, "Evangelism in the Context of Secularization," 156.
213. Newbigin, *The Good Shepherd*, 93.
214. Newbigin, *Unfinished Agenda*, 208.
215. Newbigin, "Developments During 1962," 7.
216. Newbigin, *The Good Shepherd*, 94, 107.

means, and probably not the most fundamental means by which society will be changed."[217]

Hence, to Newbigin, the "fundamental form"[218] or "authentic nature"[219] of the church must be the form of a servant. This must be understood Christologically: "It will be a church which is in the world but not of the world. That over-used phrase has been replaced in recent talk by the phrase 'a church for others,' and we can accept that description provided that the preposition 'for' is rightly understood. It has to be understood Christologically. The church is to be 'for' others in the same sense in which Christ was and is 'for' the world."[220] Newbigin observes that when Jesus was done with all his teaching about the kingdom of God, he stooped down and washed his disciples' feet. Here, Newbigin states: "It is when the Church is in that position that our message of the Kingdom will be credible."[221] He points to the early church as an example of how the church must let this servant nature impact its life. Goheen summarizes this well:

> [The early church] was able to take solidarity with and justice for the poor into its very congregational life. He points to the office of the diaconate that was concerned for the care of the poor, widows, underprivileged, and marginalized (. . .). The deacon who was responsible throughout the week for the poor, sick and underprivileged stood up at the time of intercession to share the urgent concerns for prayer. He also brought this concern to the heart of the liturgy when, at the point of the Lord's Supper, he collected gifts for the poor and then was responsible for their distribution.[222]

This point of view leads Newbigin to criticize the church for failing to be a servant in both the past and in the present. First, Newbigin argues that the church often has been so entrenched in the established order that it has not taken the side of the weak, marginalized, and oppressed. It has

---

217. Quoted in Wainwright, *Lesslie Newbigin*, 248.

218. Newbigin, "Bible Studies Given at the National Christian Council Triennial Assembly, Shillong," 131; cf. Goheen, *As the Father Has Sent Me*, 303.

219. Newbigin, "The Church as a Servant Community," 261.

220. Newbigin, *Your Kingdom Come*, 27.

221. Newbigin, *The Good Shepherd*, 95.

222. Goheen, *As the Father Has Sent Me*, 304–5. Newbigin deals with the office of the diaconate in the early church in the article "The Church as a Servant Community," see 258–60.

sought prestige, rather than humble service. It has indulged in the advantages of being a part of the established order, rather than serving the poor. Newbigin claims the church today often "creates the impression of being a society which accepts, and is content to benefit from the established order, and at the same-time to reach out the hand of charity as far as possible to those who are the victims of that order."[223] Therefore, the time has now come when "we must somehow find ways by which the Church as a corporate body, in its ordinary life, its liturgy, its ministry, its congregational fellowship can be recognizably a body which is on the side of the oppressed."[224] Second, Newbigin states that powerful denominational structures, nationwide agencies for evangelism, and social action have led to social responsibility "no longer [being] seen as the direct responsibility of the local congregation except insofar as they are called on to support them financially. But if the local congregation is not perceived in its own neighborhood as the place from which good news overflows in good action, the programs for social and political action launched by the national agencies are apt to lose their integral relation to the good news and come to be seen as part of a moral crusade rather than the gospel."[225]

2.6.3 Social Ethics and Ecclesiology

In conclusion, Newbigin believes that the disestablishment of Christendom involve a questioning of accepted Christian practices and patterns of behavior, suggesting that the social practices of the church now become more and more distinctive. But while he does not present any major analysis of how the church's practices differ from those of the surrounding society, he clearly believes that the church's way of life is distinct.[226] I have, in my exposition of Newbigin's ecclesiology, missiology, and eschatology, tried to briefly show that Christology plays an important role in his theology. This is also to some extent true concerning his ethical considerations. Newbigin believes that Christ is the new fact, the new datum, from which Christian ethics spring.[227] The Christian has been given salvation as a totally undeserved gift, and the life of the Christian

---

223. Newbigin, "The Church as a Servant Community," 263.
224. Ibid., 264.
225. Newbigin, *The Gospel in a Pluralist Society*, 229.
226. See, for example, Newbigin, *Honest Religion for Secular Man*, 143.
227. Newbigin, *Christian Freedom in a Modern World*, 83.

must be an act of thanksgiving and a continuous response to the living Lord himself.[228] Since Christology plays an important role in Newbigin's theology, I cannot, however, keep from wondering why he did not put forward a more expanded Christological ethic. Nevertheless, it is clear that Newbigin believes that it is a part of the identity of the church to be a distinct social order within society. The fundamental motivation for this social order is the life Christ modeled.

2.7 Epistemology

Epistemological analysis occupies a large place in Newbigin's later writings, and his many epistemological analyses have a special aim which must be understood from a missiological perspective. Newbigin is eager to liberate the gospel and the church from the captivity of Western culture. This, he believes, must be obtained "through a resolute assault on the fundamental problem which is epistemology."[229] The theorists Newbigin draws on point out the necessity of a hermeneutic community in the process of acquiring knowledge. This gives Newbigin an opportunity to emphasize the significance of the faith community in the internal teaching and external communication of the gospel. Newbigin uses several sources of inspiration in his attempts to challenge existing epistemological assumptions, including Michael Polanyi and Alasdair MacIntyre, whom he uses to demonstrate that knowledge is tradition-based and socially conditioned. I will now show how the church, according to Newbigin, bears a special understanding of reality, which has Christ as the starting point.[230]

2.7.1 Two Traditions

Newbigin works with two streams of thought, which, he claims, have their respective historical and philosophical roots in Greco-Roman and

---

228. Newbigin, *Honest Religion for Secular Man*, 141–42.
229. Newbigin, *The Gospel in a Pluralist Society*, 25.
230. The analysis in this section relies on my two publications "Lesslie Newbigins postfundamentistiske epistemologi: Om følgerne af opgøret med oplysningstidens epistemologi," 26–37; and *Udfordringer til den vestlige kirke. En studie af Lesslie Newbigins sene forfatterskab.*

Israelite history.²³¹ In antiquity, Newbigin designates the first stream "the classical stream," and in modern time "the rationalistic humanist tradition." The other stream he designates "the Christian tradition." He claims that, throughout history, there has always existed a tension between these two streams. Newbigin does not believe that it is possible to fully identify these two streams throughout all of history. However, he tries to name examples in history in order to demonstrate his point of view. I will give three examples on this.

First, in the classical tradition, truth was regarded as ideas about timeless or eternal truth. This led to the distinction between *theoria* and *praxis*. In the Christian tradition, truth is revealed in history and this truth can be heard or ignored, obeyed or disobeyed. In the Christian tradition, one cannot differentiate between theory and praxis.²³² Therefore, Newbigin argues, these Greek terms are absent in the New Testament because they express a way of understanding things that is foreign to the Bible. In the New Testament, "[t]he operative contrast is not between theory and practice; it is between believing and obeying on the one hand and the refusal of belief and obedience on the other."²³³ So when Jesus says "Follow me," the response is "a single act of faith and obedience; there is no gap between a mental action of believing and a bodily action of following."²³⁴ Followers of the classical tradition could perhaps admire the Jews for "their high moral standards and perhaps for their noble monotheism," but their religion could not play any major role in philosophical investigation.²³⁵ This was also the case when Christianity presented itself as a later development of the Jewish religion. If the Christian tradition was to legitimize itself, it would have to relate to the classical-philosophical world in a genuinely intellectual way. The Christian tradition, thus, faced the following important challenge: "[H]ow could the biblical message be communicated with the world of classical thought without being absorbed into and neutralized by that world of thought?"²³⁶ Newbigin

---

231. See, for example, Newbigin, *The Gospel in a Pluralist Society*, 1–3; Newbigin, *Proper Confidence: Faith, Doubt, and Certainty in Christian Discipleship*, 3.

232. Newbigin, *Proper Confidence*, 14–15.

233. Ibid., 39.

234. Newbigin, *Proper Confidence*, 39. Newbigin follows Dietrich Bonhoeffer who says, "Only the obedient believe, and those who believe are obedient." See Newbigin, *Proper Confidence*, 14–15; cf. Bonhoeffer, *The Cost of Discipleship*, 69.

235. Newbigin, *Proper Confidence*, 3.

236. Ibid., 4.

believes that, in the New Testament, we already see an incipient work of building bridges between these two traditions, to communicate the new and revolutionary message of Christianity in a way that was understandable to the classical world, without the Christian message being neutralized. This is the reason why the author of the Fourth Gospel begins with introducing the word *logos*, a word well-known in the Middle East by both Greeks and Hebrews. However, the term *logos* is defined in a radically new way such that it is identified with Jesus.[237]

Second, to Newbigin, the heart of the Christian message is that God has acted in such a way that this fact must determine all thinking. Also the early church fathers were also challenged by the tension between the Greco-Roman and Israelite tradition. According to Newbigin, this is what we see when Athanasius talks about Christianity as a new *arché*, that is, "a new starting point for all human understanding of the world."[238] Some, such as Tertullian, see no possibility for common dialog between the two traditions. "What has Jerusalem in common with Athens?" he asks, while predicting the answer: "Nothing!" Others, like Origen, an expert of both traditions, seek the greatest possible common ground between the two traditions, Newbigin claims.[239]

Third, an important figure for Newbigin is Augustine, who was a product of the classical world. However, at some point he adopted the biblical story as the starting point of thought, which meant a radical reconstruction of his former way of thinking. Newbigin claims that Augustine, with his famous *credo ut intelligam*, defined a way of knowing which acknowledges how God has revealed himself in Christ.[240] Moving forward in history, Newbigin claims that Aristotle, as a representative for the classical tradition, by a circuitous route, impacted the Christian tradition.[241] For example, Thomas Aquinas, in his work on his *Summa contra gentiles*, tried to unite the old biblical tradition with the new knowledge inspired by Aristotle, among others. Newbigin claims that this has had a lasting impact on Western Christianity. Aquinas believed that theology is superior philosophy, but that philosophy had to be a necessary precursor for theology. Furthermore, Aquinas accepted a distinction between what can

237. Ibid., 4–5.

238. Ibid., 4.

239. Ibid., 5–6; Newbigin never proved his claims concerning Origen and Tertullian.

240. Ibid., 9–12.

241. Ibid., 16–20.

be known by reason alone, and what can be known only by revelation.[242] However, Aquinas believed that when divine revelation contradicts the findings of philosophy, the latter must be rejected. This was not always followed, and resulted in theology becoming so dependent on philosophy that the findings of theology had to be validated by philosophy.[243]

2.7.2 The Rationalistic Humanist Tradition

Newbigin believes that René Descartes, John Locke, Francis Bacon and Isaac Newton became representatives of a new worldview in the seventeenth and eighteenth centuries, which resulted in the collective conversion of Western culture. From the middle of the eighteenth century, analytic rationality became the center of a new European culture. Descartes doubted everything in order to attain indubitable knowledge and, on the basis of what could not be doubted, he sought true and objective knowledge about other matters. This was the starting point of the vision that, according to Newbigin, led to nothing less than a collective conversion of Western culture which, over time, made significant scientific gains.[244] The Enlightenment thinkers believed that they lived in an age of reason. The inner nature of the new culture employed the analytic powers by which humans could obtain total control over nature, at least in principle. The basic intellectual driving force in the culture was to understand everything in terms of basic physical laws. One could not accept anything but proven facts. Newbigin claims that this new vision had eschatological implications. Where one previously had thought that history moved towards an end, when Christ should come again, the great hope now became scientific improvements that could help the human race live in an even better world. What carried the vision forth was, according to Newbigin, a rationalistic humanist tradition.[245]

---

242. Ibid., 17.

243. Ibid., 16–19. In many ways, Newbigin argues like Karl Barth. But whereas Newbigin states that there exists a *radical* discontinuity between the gospel and the world, Barth argues that there exists an *absolute* discontinuity, as Newbigin puts it. Cf. Newbigin, *The Gospel in a Pluralist Society*, 14, 152, 195, 197; Newbigin, *The Finality of Christ*, 36–39; Newbigin, *Christian Witness in a Plural Society*, 10; Newbigin, "The Basis, Purpose and Manner of Inter-Faith Dialogue," 261.

244. Newbigin, *Foolishness to the Greeks*, 23–26.

245. The rationalistic humanist tradition in the Middle Ages is far from sufficiently described by Newbigin. However, if Newbigin is right about his hypothesis, it will

Newbigin criticizes the rationalistic humanist tradition in two ways, the first critique leading to the second. First, Newbigin criticizes autonomous reason, calling it an illusion. In this, Newbigin relies on the Hungarian scientist Michael Polanyi.[246] Polanyi stated in the middle of the twentieth century that science had been blinded. He argued that scientists have taken for granted the possibility of obtaining objective truth. He argued for the absurdity of objective knowledge by pointing out the subjectivity of the process of acquiring knowledge, something insufficiently acknowledged.[247] Therefore, Polanyi developed the expression "personal knowledge" in opposition to "objective knowledge." He stated that reason always operates in a context of authority and tradition.[248] Thus, the assumption that reason is a neutral arbitrator of truth is the result of an uncritical acceptance of the epistemology of the Enlightenment. According to Polanyi, even the most intransigent rationalistic disciplines work within a context of tradition. Newbigin agree with Polanyi on this.

This leads us to the second aspect of Newbigin's critique of the rationalistic humanist tradition. Newbigin criticizes the opposition of faith and revelation on one hand, and critical reason on the other. Newbigin calls this a false dichotomy, one that contends that the Christian tradition does not contain a rational discourse. Rather, Newbigin suggests that we must decide which tradition should be allowed to shape the rational process. Newbigin believes that both the rationalistic humanist and the Christian tradition are socially embedded. In both traditions, humans inspire each other and work together, and in this way carry a tradition forward. According to Newbigin, rationality previously functioned in

---

be very difficult to differentiate strictly between these two traditions, the rationalistic tradition being influenced by Christianity and vice versa. When Newbigin analyzes the rationalistic tradition from the Enlightenment, he seems to rely on certain more acknowledged epistemological points of view. Newbigin's own analysis does not seem to be very nuanced. Yet, Newbigin on the one hand acknowledges that Western society is a highly diverse society, as I will show later. See 2.8 below. This seems to contradict that he only conceives of one single rationalistic humanist tradition. Also, his writing style is essayistic and one often wishes for references in his argumentation.

246. The three most important books by Polanyi are *Science, Faith, and Society* (1946), *Personal Knowledge: Toward a Post-Critical Philosophy* (1958), and *The Tacit Dimension* (1966). For an analysis of how Newbigin was influenced by Polanyi, see especially chapter 2 in the dissertation of Weston, "Mission and Cultural Change." For an exposition of Newbigin's epistemology, see Sherman, *Revitalizing Theological Epistemology*, 203–49.

247. See, for example, Polanyi, *Personal Knowledge*, 71.

248. Ibid., 203–4.

a context of revelation, in a tradition that had its roots in the work of Augustine. At the time of the breakthrough of the Enlightenment, this context was replaced by a context in which reason functioned dependent upon its own autonomy. As we shall see later, Newbigin not only uses Polanyi's conclusions to present an epistemological critique, but also applies these conclusions to ecclesiology.[249]

Newbigin views the dominance of the rationalistic humanist tradition as problematic. Consequently, only those people who have a modern, Western scientific education can be a part of the dialogue. Not without irony, he quips that any others might be charming and valuable for the tourist industry, but they will never be regarded as constructive partners in the conversation, only candidates for modernization.[250] Therefore, Newbigin asks, "How, in this situation, does one preach the gospel as truth, truth which is not to be domesticated within the assumptions of modern thought but which challenges these assumptions and calls for their revision?"[251] He asserts that there are elements in the Christian faith that ought not be wiped out by the modern, Western paradigm, and he thus seeks to restore these elements.[252] This leads us to look closer at the Christian tradition itself.

---

249. See 2.7.3 and 2.7.5 below. When Polanyi was once confronted with the possibility of drawing theological consequences from his research results, he was skeptical. In the beginning of the 1970s *The Polanyi Society* was established, an international academic network with an associated journal, and representatives from this network and George R. Hunsberger have had discussions of Newbigin's understanding of Polanyi's writings and whether it is legitimate to draw theological consequences from Polanyi's epistemological insights. I will not enter these discussions here. See the Polanyi Society's journal, *Tradition and Discovery* (2000–2002).

250. Newbigin, *Foolishness to the Greeks*, 22.

251. Newbigin, *The Gospel in a Pluralist Society*, 5.

252. Polanyi's scientific critique seems to have pointed out important weaknesses in former ways of thinking about science. Today Polanyi and Newbigin's critique of the epistemology of modern science seems antiquated. Much postmodern philosophy dissociates itself from Cartesian epistemology. Many contemporary philosophers of science would say that interpretation is conditioned by the scientific system's plausibility structure, which to a great extent creates, and is created by, culture and social environment. This is described in Thomas Kuhn's book *The Structure of Scientific Revolutions*. So, one could say that modern, Western culture has returned to Augustine's *credo ut intelligam*, which is now acknowledged as the assumption for all knowledge. Newbigin's critique is legitimate as a critique of modernity, but is antiquated in relation to postmodern culture.

2.7.3 The Christian Tradition

For the interest of the basic survey of this book, it is especially important to note Newbigin's reflections on the Christian discourse of rationality. To Newbigin the heart of the Christian message is that God has acted in history to reveal himself. This means that Christianity offers a whole new *arché*, a new starting point for the understanding of the world. As Newbigin states, "the Christian tradition of rationality takes as its starting point not any alleged self-evident truths. Its starting point is the event in which God made himself known to men and women in particular circumstances—to Abraham and Moses, to the long succession of prophets, and to the first apostles and witnesses who saw and heard and touched the incarnate Word of God himself, Jesus of Nazareth."[253]

Newbigin observes, with regret, that reason and revelation in the history of philosophy have often been contrasted in the debate about sources and criteria for knowledge:

> When reason is set against revelation, the terms of the debate have been radically confused. What is happening is not that reason is set against something which is unreasonable, but that another tradition of rational argument is being set against a tradition of rational argument which takes as its starting point a moment or moments of divine self-revelation and which will therefore naturally continue to say, not 'We discovered,' but 'God spoke and acted.' From another tradition of rational discourse it is of course possible to say that 'God' does not exist and that the language of revelation has to be translated into the language of discovery. 'God spoke to Moses' will perhaps be translated as 'Moses had a religious experience.' The lines are then laid down for a dialogue between two traditions of rationality, not between reason and revelation.[254]

There exists a long Anglican tradition that regards Scripture, tradition and reason as three sources and criteria for the faith of the church. Newbigin believes that this triad is a more adequate solution than the Catholic "Scripture and tradition," as reason is emphasized more clearly.[255] To Newbigin, the process of knowing implies revelation, tradition and reason. When revelation and reason are contrasted, the premises of the

---

253. Newbigin, *The Gospel in a Pluralist Society*, 63.
254. Ibid., 62.
255. Ibid., 52–65.

debate have been confused. When revelation and reason are regarded as opposed, separate, or competing criteria, the nature of reason is misunderstood.[256] As is clear from the quotation above, Newbigin believes that revelation and reason must be understood in connection with each other. In the Christian tradition, from the revelation in Christ a tradition for the proper use of reason derives. Hence, Newbigin does not want to get rid of reason; he wants to reform reason, suggesting that reason must be guided by Christian revelation and tradition. It is notable that Newbigin does not pay much attention to "experience" here.

Polanyi's effort to reform epistemology is especially directed against objectivism, that is, the illusion that we can know objectively. Polanyi insisted that the process of knowing always implies subjective participation in, and conscious acknowledgement of, the tradition from which one is thinking. Newbigin shares Polanyi's epistemological critique. In the Christian tradition, reason does not operate in a vacuum. Here, rationality is also embedded in social conditioning, namely the faith community. Newbigin believes that Christians live in a community that is a part of an unbroken tradition going back to the biblical actors, who have indwelled the story which the Bible tells us.

In his book *Proper Confidence*, Newbigin refers to the titles of two philosophical works which illustrate his understanding of the relationship between reason and religion. First, he refers to an English translation of the work, *Religion within the Limits of Reason*, by Immanuel Kant. However, Newbigin claims that his position is better illustrated by Nicholas Wolterstorff's book *Reason within the Limits of Religion*.[257] In connection with this, Newbigin emphasizes that human reasoning is embodied in tradition and culture, and that religion throughout history has shown how powerful it is in shaping culture.

In addition to this, Newbigin states that even though Christians have these sources available, the Holy Spirit must still live in Christians to guide them. This is a gift not only to Christians, but also to others. Just as the Holy Spirit guides Christians, Christians must guide the culture

---

256. Ibid., 57.

257. Newbigin, *Proper Confidence*, 93–94. Newbigin refers to the titles as being respectively *Religion within the Limits of Reason* and *Reason within the Limits of Religion*. No books with such titles exist. Newbigin has apparently changed the titles of the books to make his point clearer. The actual titles are *Religion within the Limits of Reason Alone* (English translation of *Die Religion innerhalb der Grenzen der blossen Vernunft* from 1794) and *Reason within the Bounds of Religion* (published in 1984).

around them by calling into question fundamental assumptions about the world. When Christians express their understanding of reality, it is important that they are both open about the presuppositions for their truth claims, and that their thinking is publicly available so that others can examine it.[258]

In other words, Newbigin claims that the church has its own specific understanding of reality. He employs the language of sociology to express this: "[I]t is essential to recognize that all human thinking takes place within a 'plausibility structure' which determines what beliefs are reasonable and what are not."[259] Newbigin believes that "the gospel gives rise to a new plausibility structure, a radically different vision of things from those that shape all human cultures apart from the gospel."[260] In connection with this, Newbigin believes that it is impossible for the biblical story to be accommodated to modern, Western culture's plausibility structure. The story about a man that dies and is resurrected cannot be accepted within any plausibility structure, except within the one where this is the cornerstone. In all other plausibility structures, this story will become a stumbling block.[261] Therefore, Christians ought not to explain the gospel

---

258. Newbigin, *The Gospel in a Pluralist Society*, 126.

259. Ibid., 228. A plausibility structure can be defined as the patterns for the convictions and practices that are commonly acknowledged in a given culture. Berger and Luckmann's book, *The Social Construction of Reality*, show that society cannot be regarded only as an objective reality, but must also be regarded as a human product. Berger and Luckmann identify three fundamental social processes, which dialectically create a social reality. The following builds on Furseth and Repstad, *Innføring i religionssociologi*, 74–78: The first process is called "externalization." Here, society is understood as a human product, given that we as human beings express ourselves continuingly in activities and create products around us (75). This leads to the other process called "objectifying." Here, society is understood as an objective reality. When a human product obtains facticity outside of the human, these human products obtain a more independent objective character (75). Finally, the third process is called "internalization." Here, the human being is understood as a social product. Through socialization, the objective world becomes a subjective world. The world becomes a meaningful reality. The objective world is recommenced in the consciousness so that the structure of this world becomes determinative for the subjective structure in the consciousness. Furthermore, Berger and Luckmann state that every world demands a social basis for its continuing existence. This social basis is its plausibility structure. A plausibility structure is a cultural framework, which we internalize in our personality, and which forms our understanding of human existence. Through interaction with others, human reality is confirmed as reality and the structure of reality is made plausible. See also Andersen and Kaspersen, *Klassisk og moderne samfundsteori*, 203–6.

260. Newbigin, *The Gospel in a Pluralist Society*, 9.

261. Newbigin, *Proper Confidence*, 93.

on the premises of Western culture, but must refer to the gospel as a new starting point for the understanding of human existence, as an alternative foundation for a new plausibility structure. It is not the task of the church to make the gospel acceptable to modern thought, but to refer to it as a new starting point for understanding reality.[262] Christians should not explain the gospel in the terms of modern culture, but should explain their culture in the terms of the gospel.[263]

Because of this, Newbigin argues that the gospel is a source of a plausibility structure that is foreign to Western culture, and he acknowledges that Christian truth may often be affirmed in conflict with the wider society.[264] However, there is a missional dimension to this tension or dialogue between the Christian plausibility structure and that of Western culture. Newbigin considers how the gospel can be presented to the modern West: "The reigning plausibility structure can only be effectively challenged by people who are fully integrated inhabitants of another."[265] The gospel is not announced as a disembodied gospel, but represented by a community which lives by it, and which invites others to live by it: "How is it possible that the gospel should be credible, that people should come to believe that the power which has the last word in human affairs, is represented by a man hanging on the cross? I am suggesting that the only answer, the only hermeneutic of the gospel, is a congregation of men and women who believe it and live by it."[266]

Newbigin points out several characteristics of the community which effectively function as a hermeneutic of the gospel. Such a community worships God, is centered in the biblical story through teaching, the sacraments and apostolic life, and calls humans to live out this history in the midst of a society determined by another story. He suggests, "A Christian congregation is a community in which, through the constant remembering and rehearsing of the true story of human nature and destiny, an attitude of healthy skepticism can be sustained, a skepticism which enables one to take part in the life of society without being bemused

---

262. Newbigin, "Gospel and Culture," 7.
263. Newbigin, *Foolishness to the Greeks*, 41.
264. Newbigin, "On the Gospel as Public Truth," paragraph three.
265. Newbigin, *The Gospel in a Pluralist Society*, 228.
266. Ibid., 227.

and deluded by its own beliefs about itself."²⁶⁷ Such a community is also characterized by hope.²⁶⁸

Even though the reigning plausibility structure can only be effectively challenged by people who are fully integrated inhabitants of another plausibility structure, this must not lead to Christians living in a ghetto. Christians must learn to live bi-culturally, must learn to live within both the Christian plausibility structure and that of Western culture. Newbigin refers to his own life as an example of this. As a Christian, he lives in the Christian tradition, uses the Christian language as his own language, and uses the Christian story as a clue to understanding his own story, and as a member of British society, he shares his life with others who live in another tradition.²⁶⁹

2.7.4 The Rationalistic Humanist and the Christian Tradition

I find Newbigin to be reductionist in his epistemological reflections. For example, he presupposes that it is possible to talk about *one* rationalistic humanist tradition and *one* Christian tradition. Thus, he has a tendency to generalize and to ignore the diversity of these so-called traditions. We shall now see which axiomatic presuppositions Newbigin believes the rationalistic humanist tradition and the Christian tradition build on. He asks: On what authority do the Christian and rationalistic humanist traditions rely? His answer is that neither tradition relies on something outside itself, and that the fundamental axiom of both traditions must be acquired by faith. It is not possible to argue that people should choose Christ as the starting point for the understanding of the world. To look for a starting point apart from the gospel is a contradiction of the gospel itself.²⁷⁰ Both traditions rely on the assumptions that the universe is accessible to rational understanding. Like the scientist, the Christian must dwell within a tradition: One must acquire its central concepts through which one must understand the world; one must internalize them and dwell in them; one must trust the Christian tradition and have confidence in others as authorized interpreters of it, reaching the point where

---

267. Ibid., 229.
268. Newbigin has a longer description of these characteristics. See ibid., 227–33.
269. Ibid., 65.
270. Newbigin, *Proper Confidence*, 94.

he or she can say: "Yes, I believe in this."[271] Thus, this knowing is not a matter only of the mind, but also of the heart and will. It is discipleship.

Newbigin points out three differences between the rationalistic humanist tradition and the Christian tradition.[272] First, the scientific tradition begins with "I have discovered" in contrast to the Christian tradition, which begins with "God has spoken."[273] Newbigin tries to explain the difference using Martin Buber's distinction between "I-Thou-knowledge" and "I-It-knowledge."[274] Whereas "I-It knowledge" presupposes that the knowing subject is in control and praises autonomous reason, "I-Thou knowledge" relies on inter-personal trust and communication.[275]

Second, the scientific tradition seeks to attain a limited knowledge within the rule-boundedness of nature, while the Christian tradition seeks to expose a more profound knowledge with its rationality. Newbigin writes about the Christian tradition:

> Unlike the scientific tradition (...) this tradition is not confined to a limited set of questions about the rational structure of the cosmos. Specifically, unlike science, it concerns questions about the ultimate meaning and purpose of things and of human life—questions which modern science eliminates as a matter of methodology. The models, concepts, and paradigms through which the Christian tradition seeks to understand the world embrace these larger questions. They have the same presupposition about the rationality of the cosmos as the natural sciences do, but it is a more comprehensive rationality based on the faith that the

---

271. Newbigin, *The Gospel in a Pluralist Society*, 49–51. Newbigin's understanding of the starting point of the Christian tradition is very similar to Barth's. Newbigin often refers to Karl Barth and seems to appreciate his writings. From Newbigin's autobiography, we know that Newbigin before his return in 1974 was looking forward to reading Barth's 14-volume systematic theology. The autobiography gives insight into Barth's impact on Newbigin. See *Unfinished Agenda*, 30–31, 115–20, 131–39. At first Newbigin found Barth's understanding of the atonement unclear but later Newbigin comments, "I had not yet learned to appreciate either Barth or his theology as I was to do later." See Newbigin, *Unfinished Agenda*, 30–31, 115. On how Barth influenced Newbigin, see also Le Roy Stults, *Grasping Truth and Reality*, 49–50, 274–75.

272. Goheen lists two major differences between the rationalistic humanist tradition and the Christian tradition, which correspond to the first two differences, which I mention. See Goheen, *As the Father Has Sent Me*, 385–87.

273. Newbigin, *The Gospel in a Pluralist Society*, 60.

274. Buber, *Ich und Du*; Newbigin, *The Gospel in a Pluralist Society*, 60–61.

275. Goheen, *As the Father Has Sent Me*, 387.

author and sustainer of the cosmos has personally revealed his purpose.[276]

Newbigin claims that it is possible for the Christian tradition to incorporate origin and nature, while it is not possible for the scientific tradition to do so. Thus, he asserts that the Christian tradition contains a more broad rationality, which is more adequate than the rationality of the rationalistic humanist tradition.

Third, the rationalistic humanist epistemology is not embedded in history, as "[w]e are not, in this view, part of a story, a drama of creation, fall, redemption, and consummation."[277] In contrast to this, the Christian tradition claims that we as human beings are fundamentally embedded in universal history. In this history, Christ is the center and the clue to the understanding of human existence.[278]

2.7.5 Epistemology and Ecclesiology

In conclusion, this analysis allows us to add yet another layer to our understanding of the distinctive identity of the church, according to Newbigin: The church is a social embodiment of a tradition, with a special understanding of reality, which takes Christ as a starting point. Newbigin expresses a close connection between revelation, the Christian community and rationality. First, the Christian church is obligated to operate within the bounds of the divine revelation. Thus, Newbigin believes that Christ must be the starting point for the church's understanding of reality.[279] Second, the church has an obligation to its own tradition and must, therefore, understand reality in accordance with this tradition. However, the limits of this tradition are difficult to discern, and "[t]radition, therefore, is not a source of authority separate from Scripture."[280] Third, reasoning is socially conditioned. The church must be a hermeneutic community that maintains and communicates an understanding of the gospel and thereby the world. The church will very often if not always represent an understanding of the world that is different from the one present in society. The church takes Christ as its starting point, while this

276. Newbigin, *The Gospel in a Pluralist Society*, 49.
277. Ibid., 2.
278. For an exposition of Newbigin's theology of history, see n282 below.
279. Newbigin, *Truth and Authority in Modernity*, 38.
280. Ibid., 49.

is not the case for society. Christology plays an important role for Newbigin's epistemology, with Christ functioning as an *episteme*, as a distinctive source for the church's understanding of the world.

2.8 Conclusion

2.8.1 The Distinctive Identity of the Church

Newbigin's writings represent an important theological critique of Christendom, whereby all significant perspectives of Newbigin's critique of Christendom can in one way or another be related to missiology, and thus, one may say that missiology frames his critique of Christendom.[281] Those who critique Christendom have different emphases. For some, it is decisive to re-envision the distinctive identity of the church, while for others it is decisive to re-envisage the missional identity of the church. Newbigin's main concern is the latter rather than the former. We have, however, seen that Newbigin, in his critique of Christendom, also argues that the church will more often than not be a distinct social entity within the society in which it lives, which is a common thread in his writings developed in various ways. At times, Newbigin contrasts the distinctive identity of the church with the Christendom settlement, but often this is not the case. Against the fusion of church and society, which is designated as *corpus Christianum*, Newbigin argues that the church, *corpus Christi*, will often times be different from society and must by her very nature be engaged in mission.

In each of the past five sections, I have shed light on what Newbigin believes the church is fundamentally meant to be, what the distinctive identity of the church is. It turns out that, to Newbigin, there is an inescapable distinctiveness tied to ecclesiology, missiology, eschatology, social ethics, and epistemology, which is further rooted to the church. It is important for me to say that the analysis I have presented does not exhaustively capture the distinctiveness of the identity of the church. I do not believe that it is possible to present such an analysis. It is also important for me to add that this analysis also does not exhaustively capture the distinctiveness or the identity of the church in the writings of Newbigin. That would be a very wide-scale task indeed. For example, an exposition of Newbigin's ecclesiology would normally involve a clearer

---

281. See 2.2 above.

focus on the sacraments and how the church should organize itself. I have only focused on the most fundamental aspect of Newbigin's ecclesiology, namely election. Also, I have only identified and focused on five important themes which inform the distinctive identity of the church in Newbigin's theology. Other themes could have been chosen.[282]

I have at the end of each the five major sections in this chapter briefly pointed out that Christology plays a central role for Newbigin's theology, creating a fundamental duality between Christ and all he brings into the world on the one hand, and the fallen world on the other.[283] I will now briefly point to certain central aspects of Newbigin's thinking which show how Christology plays a central role in his understanding of the church as a distinct people (ecclesiology), which expresses God's mission in the world (missiology), manifests the kingdom of God in the world (eschatology), embodies a distinct social order (social ethics) and which is a social embodiment of a tradition for a special understanding of reality (epistemology). At the same time, I will clarify how almost all of Newbigin's theological reflections are in the end grounded in the church, and how Newbigin understands the distinctive identity of the church.[284] I will here sum up the findings of this chapter.

282. I could also have included Newbigin's theology of history, where he argues that Christ is the center of world history, and that Christ should be the clue to our understanding of world history. Thus, the church, according to Newbigin, will always represent a different understanding of history than the society of which it is a part. Newbigin claims that world history comprises a coherent whole, which has a special meaning. Newbigin does not claim that the Christian faith offers a theoretical interpretation by which we can understand every detail of the course and development of world history; rather, it interprets the framework of human existence. He states that the Christian faith is an interpretation of world history. Christology also plays an important role for his understanding of history. God created the world in Christ, Christ's life on earth—the total fact of Christ, as Newbigin likes to say—is the midpoint of history and Christ shall bring history to an end. Hence, Christ is the alpha and omega of history. When Christians proclaim the gospel, they simultaneously make the bold contention "that God really has a purpose for the world and for all men, and that we have the secret of that purpose, and that all men should join with us in obeying and fulfilling that purpose." See Newbigin, "Why Study the Old Testament?," 75. This leads Newbigin to an even bolder contention, namely, that the church holds the secret of and the clue to the meaning of history. According to Newbigin the understanding of history, which the church bears, will always be unique, because Christians interpret history with Christ as a starting point. The world does, however, not acknowledge this as a starting point for the understanding of history.

283. See 2.3.3, 2.4.4, 2.5.4, 2.6.3, and 2.7.5 above.

284. Hunsberger ends his dissertation on Newbigin's theology of cultural plurality by constructing a triangular mission model, where the corners are made up of

The church as a distinct people: God chooses a people who must function as a prototype, to show what he intends for the whole world, and who shall reveal and effect God's will for all mankind. This chosen people *is* a people called out of all tribes, nations, and peoples. The church is a chosen people sent to the world and determined by an identity, which is more fundamental than all other given identities.[285] This chosen people is a provisional incorporation in Christ. Here, people become a part of the body of Christ, a distinct social entity in the world.

The church as mission: In the writings of Newbigin, Christology, ecclesiology, and missiology are closely interwoven. The church takes over the place and mission of Christ in the world. First, the Son is incarnated into the world, and then the church is, in continuation of this incarnation, sent into the world. The life of Christ is a pattern for the life of the church in the world; the church must continue his life in the world and is meant to embody the mission of God in the world. The very existence of the church and its witness to the world cannot be separated.[286]

The church as an eschatological reality: The church exists in a world that does not acknowledge Christ as Lord and which is in rebellion against God. In the midst of this world, Christ inaugurates, proclaims and manifests the kingdom of God, and the church is a provisional foretaste and sign of this kingdom. The very existence of the church expresses the breakthrough of the kingdom of God in the world. For Newbigin, Pneumatology is in many ways a part of eschatology. Hence, the Spirit is given to the church as a sign of the new age that has been inaugurated. It is the task of the church to unmask and demonstrate for the world that the world is in rebellion against God.[287]

The church as a distinct way of living: The most important contribution which the church can make is to be itself a new social order. Christ

---

gospel, culture, and church. See Hunsberger, *Bearing the Witness of the Spirit*, 235–79. In connection with this, Bevans states that Newbigin's countercultural theology is tied to these three central concepts. Bevans states that Newbigin believes that modern, Western culture is deeply secularized, that the church must function as a contrast community, and that the gospel deeply contradicts every culture. See Bevans, *Models of Contextual Theology*, 120–25. Neither Hunsberger nor Bevans make clear to what extent Christology functions as a theological resource for Newbigin or how Newbigin's understanding of the distinctiveness of the church has a clear christological focus.

285. See 2.3 above.
286. See 2.4 above.
287. See 2.5 above.

is the new fact, the new datum, wherefrom Christian ethics spring. The church *is* a different kind of social order in society.[288]

The church as a social embodiment of a tradition for a distinct way of viewing the world: The church interprets reality often times quite differently than the world, and is a socially embodied tradition for a special way of interpreting reality. In this tradition, Christ functions as an *episteme*, as a distinctive resource for the church's understanding of reality.[289]

I regard Newbigin's main conclusions concerning the distinctive identity of the church quite positively. However, one often wishes that he had explained many of his ideas in further detail. Newbigin's theology has been described as *ad hoc* theology, but his writings nevertheless maintain, to a large extent, coherence.[290] Also, he certainly could have developed a stronger theology of creation, which would have changed many theological emphases. For example, in his epistemological reflections he seems to emphasize the Christological starting point so much that the First Article of the great creedal tradition of the church, the creation of the world, almost seems to disappear into thin air. Instead, he could have developed a stronger notion of humans living in a common, mutual world, and when Christ is then proclaimed, this is done in this shared, mutual world, acknowledging the created world as a common frame of reference. Thus, at times his understanding of the Christian rationality discourse and the church seem very narrow.

Also, since Christology plays such an important role in his writings, I ponder why he did not put forward a Christological ethic. Several times, Newbigin touches on ethical matters, but he never develops this in detail.[291]

Below, I will draw on this analysis, and present three central aspects of Newbigin's understanding of the distinctive identity of the church, with special reference to its role in a post-Christendom society. It is here that I am more critical of Newbigin.

---

288. See 2.6 above.

289. See 2.7 above.

290. Hunsberger, *Bearing the Witness of the Spirit*, 42.

291. In the next chapter, we shall see how John Howard Yoder presents such a christological ethic.

2.8.2 The Role of the Church in a Post-Christendom Society

The Church as Minority in a Post-Christendom Society

Newbigin believes that Christians must understand themselves as a minority, implying that the church must be an alternative community, in contrast to society. This has both a historical and a theological background. First, Newbigin believes that in the last three centuries the church has left the Christendom era behind and "has moved into a new situation. A new ideology has replaced the Christian vision as the *cultus publicus* of Western Christendom. It is the vision which dawned in that remarkable experience which those who shared it called 'the enlightenment.'"[292] Given that the time of Christendom is over, the churches in Western culture must come to terms with new cultural premises. The church must take into account that Christians now make up a minority in a secular society.[293] Second, due to theological reasons Newbigin believes that Christians will often be a minority in any given society. He does not believe that the church should try to reestablish the old Christendom. The church cannot accept a role as the protected chaplaincy[294] and the spiritual arm of society.[295] Newbigin says that the church in Western culture has "in general failed to realize how radical the contradiction between the Christian vision and the assumptions that we breathe in from every part of our shared existence is."[296]

The church is made up of different people called out from society. The church must therefore never fuse into a unity with society. When the church realizes its distinctive stance, it is driven to share the gospel with others, Newbigin believes.[297] This must have fundamental consequences for the structures of the church. The church must be turned outwards to the world, to which it must serve and witness. Therefore, according to Newbigin: "The question has to be asked—and is repeatedly asked—whether the traditional forms of the ministry which have been inherited from the 'Christendom' period are fully compatible with the faith that the

---

292. Newbigin, *Your Kingdom Come*, 28–29.
293. See 2.2 above.
294. Newbigin, "Christ, Kingdom, and Church," 4.
295. Newbigin, *Your Kingdom Come*, 28.
296. Newbigin, "Evangelism in the City," 4.
297. See 2.3 above.

Church is called to be a missionary community."[298] For Newbigin, this implies that the church must develop new, flexible structures necessary for embodied witness in various areas of a diverse Western society.

The Church in a Diverse Post-Christendom Society

Newbigin acknowledges that Western society is a highly diverse society. This means that the church must be present in various segments of society. Goheen remarks, however, "a basic inconsistency remains in Newbigin's understanding of the structure of the missionary church. Two different and inconsistent images lie side by side: the church formed in the undifferentiated villages of India, and the new flexible structures necessary for the differentiated society of the West. The image of the church of the undifferentiated Indian village was etched on his mind."[299] To my mind, there can be no doubt that Newbigin primarily stresses that the church must develop new flexible structures necessary for the diversity of Western societies, so that the church may become present in various segments of these societies.

According to Newbigin, the church has two fundamental tasks in relation to its surrounding society. On the one hand, the church is obligated to adjust to its cultural context, while, on the other hand, it is obligated to guard itself against conforming to this cultural context. Newbigin expresses the tension in this difficult balancing act with the concept of "challenging relevance."[300] He says that when the gospel only challenges and does not become a part of the culture, it leads to irrelevance; and when the gospel becomes conformed to culture without challenging it, this leads to syncretism.[301] The church must guard itself against both ir-

298. Newbigin, "Developments During 1962," 8; see also 2.3 above.

299. Goheen, *As the Father Has Sent Me*, 273.

300. See, for example, Newbigin, "Christ and the Cultures," 12; Newbigin, "Mission in the 1980s," 154–55. In the article "Christ and the Cultures" Newbigin explains the background of this expression. Newbigin states that Alfred G. Hogg, who in the beginning of the twentieth century was in dialogue with several Hindus, inspired him. Newbigin refers to Hogg's book *Karma and Redemption* (1909), where Hogg—according to Newbigin—writes about his efforts to be both relevant and challenging. Hogg, however, never writes anything about this in *Karma and Redemption* (1909). Newbigin should have referred to Hogg's book *The Christian Message to the Hindu* (1945), where Hogg reflects upon this. Goheen has also noticed this. See Goheen, *As the Father Has Sent me*, 358.

301. Newbigin, *Foolishness to the Greeks*, 7; see also Newbigin, "The Cultural

relevance and syncretism. The latter has become a reality for the church in Western culture, according to Newbigin, and he therefore tends to stress the antithetical side of the gospel and the church.[302] Often it is said that the gospel must be contextualized into different cultures. What is interesting in relation to this is that Newbigin, in his considerations concerning contextualization, often focuses on the church. Reasonably, one could say that we, in the theology of Newbigin, find incipient resources for a development of an ecclesiological contextualization theory.

Concerning how the church must become present in various segments of society, Newbigin also highlights the scattered laity, who must bear witness in different sectors of society. Newbigin says,

> I do not believe that the role of the Church in a secular society is primarily exercised in the corporate action of the churches as organized bodies in the political or cultural fields (. . .). On the contrary, I believe that it is through the action of Christian lay people, playing their roles as citizens, workers, managers, legislators, etc., not wearing the label 'Christian' but deeply involved in the secular world in the faith that God is at work there in a way which is *not* that of the 'Christendom' pattern.[303]

In this way, Newbigin believes that individual members of the church are called to serve within various areas of the dominant culture.[304] As Newbigin explains,

> I am thinking of groups of men and women in say a particular profession, or a particular sector of commerce or industry or in one of the sectors of education or politics, who can wrestle on the basis of direct personal involvement with the claims of

---

Captivity of Western Christianity as a Challenge to a Missionary Church," 67–68.

302. Newbigin, *The Good Shepherd*, 67; see also Newbigin, "Christ and the Cultures," 5.

303. Newbigin, "Baptism, the Church and Koinonia," 127; italics original.

304. On this Goheen explains: "Newbigin's stress on the callings of individual believers in the world is not unique. He developed his position in the context of the ecumenical tradition's growing emphasis on the laity. J. H. Oldham and the Oxford World Conference on Church, Community, and State in 1937, the establishment of lay academies throughout Europe after 1945, the founding of the Ecumenical Institute at Bossey in 1946 led by Suzanne de Dietrich and Hendrick Kraemer, the establishment of WCC Department on the Laity in 1955 led by secretary Hans-Reudi Weber and important books by Kraemer (1958) and Yves Congar (1957) on the laity and the church; all are highlights in this growing concern for the laity that shaped Newbigin." See Goheen, *As the Father Has Sent Me*, 305.

Christian obedience in particular situations, who can share experiences of the grace of God in this wrestling, who can pray and worship together out of the midst of these shared experiences. I believe that, in our kind of society, such groups will have to be the basic units of the church if it is to be a sign to the world of the reign of God in Jesus.[305]

In connection with this, we find in the writings of Newbigin an emphasis on the church as a corporate body, and on the individual members of the church who must be deeply involved in the secular world in order to shape various areas of society. This leads us to the third and final aspect of the church's role in a post-Christendom society, which I have chosen to highlight here.

The Church Shaping Various Areas of a Post-Christendom Society

Because the church is a distinctive community which embodies a special understanding of history and reality, it must hold a prophetic and critical stance in a post-Christendom society. This implies that the church will inevitably to some degree relativize the morality and religiosity of its surrounding society.

Newbigin asserts that this was the case for the early church. At that time, the religious societies were, for example, described with the Greek words *thiasos* and *heranos*, but the early church deliberately chose the name *ecclesia* to describe its identity. In other words, the early church did not see itself as a private religious society, but as a public assembly.[306] As Newbigin suggests, "it saw itself as a movement launched into the public life of the world, challenging the *cultus publicus* of the Empire, claiming the allegiance of all without exception."[307] Hence, it is the task of the church "to unmask and expose these idolatrous assumptions that give shape to the political and economic order."[308]

As we have seen earlier, Newbigin believes that the story of the Bible cannot fit into the plausibility structure of modern, Western culture. In connection with this, Newbigin states: "The reigning plausibility structure can only be effectively challenged by people who are fully integrated

---

305. Newbigin, *Priorities For a New Decade*, 6.
306. Newbigin, *Your Kingdom Come*, 27.
307. Ibid., 28; see also 2.2 above.
308. Goheen, *As the Father Has Sent Me*, 403.

inhabitants of another."³⁰⁹ The Christian community must believe, embody and proclaim the gospel. The gospel, therefore, is not announced as a disembodied gospel, but as a community which lives by the gospel, and which invites others to live by it. At the same time, the church must challenge the premises on which modern, Western culture relies. The church must call the Western world to repentance. Goheen rightly says that Newbigin spells out both a critical and a constructive task for the church in society.³¹⁰ In this, I agree entirely with Newbigin.

The question is whether Newbigin goes further than this. Should the church not only challenge but also impact and intentionally shape society? To this, his answer is "yes." Newbigin believes that the idea of a neutral secular society is a myth.³¹¹ The choice is not a choice between a religious or a neutral public space, but a choice between Christ and idolatry. Therefore, a privatization of the gospel and a retreat from the public space will lead to idolatry. Newbigin claims that where Christ is not present in society, an idol takes his place.³¹² Therefore, the church must occupy public space and shape society from its Christian standpoint. For example, in a discussion of education he says:

> How is this world of assumptions formed? Obviously through all the means of education and communication existing in society. Who controls those means? The question of power is inescapable. Whatever their pretensions, schools teach children to believe something and not something else. There is no 'secular' neutrality. Christians cannot evade the responsibility which a democratic society gives to every citizen to seek access to the levers of power.³¹³

Yet another and even better example is this: "[T]he church today cannot without guilt absolve itself from the responsibility, where it sees the possibility, of seeking to shape the public life of nations and the global ordering of industry and commerce in light of the Christian faith."³¹⁴ The Constantinian church claimed this responsibility and Newbigin understands this in positive terms. Hence, the church is obligated to shape

---

309. Newbigin, *The Gospel in a Pluralist Society*, 228.
310. Goheen, *As the Father Has Sent Me*, 402.
311. Newbigin, *The Gospel in a Pluralist Society*, 211–21.
312. Newbigin, *Foolishness to the Greeks*, 115, 124.
313. Newbigin, *The Gospel in a Pluralist Society*, 224.
314. Newbigin, *Foolishness to the Greeks*, 129.

various areas of society, such as art, science, politics and economy. But the church does not, Newbigin admits, have authority over these spheres, as was believed in the age of Christendom. Still, the church must intentionally shape these areas of society. In other words, Newbigin believes that the church should enforce Christian values in society. Newbigin's "particularistic" ecclesiology, however, implies that the church cannot expect that society will be fully Christianized because Christians often will compose a minority in society. Nonetheless, he advocates that the church should Christianize society.

This leads to the question of whether Newbigin's thinking leads to imperialism in the public space, and ultimately to coercion. Newbigin obviously tries to guard himself against such a critique. He argues that the gospel and the story, which the church is called to proclaim in the public space, must be interpreted in light of the cross. Sometimes the gospel has been made an argument for imperialism, but according to Newbigin, at the very heart of the gospel lays a denial of imperialism.[315] He draws attention to this as an important point of orientation for the action of the church in the public space,[316] but he never evades the fact that he wants the church to impact and shape society. It is here that I believe Newbigin goes too far. He fails to acknowledge that the church is not called to Christianize society, but to make people disciples of Christ (Matt 28:20). There is a difference here. The church should unmask society and show that it does not acknowledge Christ as Lord and does not want to follow him. It is not the task of the church to Christianize society, but to call people to repentance.[317] Yet, society may pick up practices from the church, the church in this way being an important and legitimate inspiration for society.

Newbigin actually goes further than this. In the the mid-1990s, Newbigin promoted a notion of a Christian society. He advocated this in lectures at King's College in London in 1995 and at a colloquium in Leeds in 1996. As he explains: "Since a Christian society, as I am trying to imagine it, would be a society where those in authority both affirm explicitly their allegiance to the Christian faith as their guiding light in all the decisions they have to make, and affirm the right of others to hold and express different beliefs, such a society would have to be one in which

315. Newbigin, *The Gospel in a Pluralist Society*, 155, 159.

316. Goheen has a fuller description of this. See Goheen, *As the Father Has Sent Me*, 401–3.

317. I will qualify these arguments in chapter 4.

opportunities for discussing the business of the public square would have to be maximized."[318] Furthermore, he says,

> They have to take the responsibility of government, knowing well the dangers which this involves. And, if my argument is right, when they have this responsibility, they will have to use the powers entrusted to them in accordance with the understanding of the purpose of human life which we have in Christ. They will therefore seek a kind of government which is not neutral but Christian, knowing that those who hold other beliefs will protest, and ensuring that they have the freedom to protest (...). Their vision would be not that of a neutral, secular society, nor that of a theocratic society of the type sought by Islam, but of a Christian society, a society whose public life is shaped by the Christian beliefs about human person and human society.[319]

Newbigin believes that because the Christian church ensures a preservation of freedom for dissent and disobedience, it is capable of providing a framework for a pluralistic society. In this way the church can reflect that God is not only Lord of the church but also of the world.[320] Thus, the church can be a "faithful and confident witness to God's rightful rule over the world."[321]

I disagree with Newbigin on this. What he is suggesting is to my mind foreign to the New Testament and early Christianity. In this situation, Christians were a persecuted minority in society. But even though the situation Newbigin is imagining is unthinkable for the New Testament and early Christianity, could it not be envisioned today? I do not think so. Let me present two short reflections on this. First, to my mind, the New Testament unfolds its thinking about the life of the church from within a context where a Christian society would be unthinkable. If the church exists in a Christian society, how is it then supposed to think about the suffering and persecution that the New Testament displays as a central mark of the church? Second, his proposal concerning a Christian society seems to contradict his own thinking about the powers and principalities as fallen structures in this world that act against the good intentions of God, and which, in a profound sense, are in rebellion against God.[322]

318. Newbigin, "Can a Modern Society Be Christian?," 107.
319. Ibid., 105.
320. Newbigin, *Truth to Tell*, 34.
321. Newbigin, "Can a Modern Society Be Christian?," 108.
322. See 2.5.1 above.

It appears, however, that Newbigin eventually came to the conclusion that it was a mistake to speak about a Christian society and, in his last years, completely avoided using the phrase.[323] Newbigin mentions two reasons for this. First, the phrase led people to think about an attempt to reestablish the old Christendom, which was never his intention.[324] Second, Newbigin says, "I have come to see that all attempts to envisage a Christian society in the sense of one which has achieved a stable state amid the conflicting claims of different religions and ideologies are illusory. I do not think that the Bible authorises us to expect any such thing within history. I think we have to recognise that until the second coming of Christ we live in a world where the truth can only be affirmed in conflict. What we must pray for is that we may learn to engage in this conflict exclusively with the weapons of the spirit."[325]

In this chapter, I have given an introduction to Newbigin's life and work, presented his evaluation of the rise of Western Christendom, and suggested that Newbigin's ecclesiology, missiology, eschatology, social ethics, and eschatology all shed light on the distinctive identity of the church and its role in a post-Christendom society. I now turn to the writings of John Howard Yoder.

---

323. Newbigin, "On the Gospel as Public Truth," paragraph three.
324. Newbigin, *Foolishness to the Greeks*, 102.
325. Newbigin, "On the Gospel as Public Truth," paragraph three.

PART III

John Howard Yoder

3
Following the Way of Christ in the World

JOHN HOWARD YODER PRESENTED "a fairly complete, systematic account of Christian theology," even though he disclaimed being a systematic theologian.[1] His ecclesiology is woven into this larger systematic theological framework. In this chapter, I will try to sketch the most important aspects of his understanding of the distinctive identity of the church with special reference to its role in a post-Christendom society. In particular, I have chosen to analyze three major themes of his theology—ecclesiology, social ethics, and eschatology—with the aim to show how each of them sheds light on the distinctive identity of the church. Since the interconnectedness of Yoder's thoughts makes it difficult to separate out his theology, the three themes will be necessarily interrelated.[2]

3.1 Introduction

John Howard Yoder was born December 29, 1927, in Smithville, Ohio. Yoder was raised in Oak Grove Mennonite Church, in northern Ohio, where his grandfathers had successively provided leadership for over one hundred years.[3] After high school, Yoder applied for admission at two universities, and though he secured acceptance and scholarships at both institutions, his parents wanted him to start at Goshen College, the Mennonite institution where they both had studied.[4] Out of respect for his parents, he enrolled at Goshen College, and in two years he completed

---

1. Murphy, "John Howard Yoder's Systematic Defense of Christian Pacifism," 42; see also Stoltzfus, "Nonviolent Jesus, Violent God?," 38–40.

2. A part of this chapter has been published in Danish in my article "Kirkens mulighed for at genvinde sig selv."

3. Nation, *John Howard Yoder*, 3.

4. Ibid., 13–14.

a bachelor's degree in Biblical Studies.[5] After graduating, he returned to Ohio, where he worked at a greenhouse in Barberton. The following summer he participated in a peace team, which visited Mennonite congregations around the United States and promoted peace making.[6] Then Harold Bender, dean of Goshen Biblical Seminary, created a European assignment for Yoder, wishing for him to study theology at a European university.[7]

Twenty-one years old, Yoder arrived in France to begin a Mennonite Central Committee assignment on April 1, 1949.[8] Three years later, he married Anne Marie Guth, a French Mennonite, with whom he had seven children. While Yoder worked in Europe, he also studied at the University of Basel, where he studied with Walther Baumgartner in Old Testament, Oscar Cullmann in New Testament, Karl Jaspers in Philosophy, and Karl Barth in Dogmatics, among others.[9] Upon returning to Ohio in 1957, Yoder again worked at a greenhouse until 1958, when he began teaching at Goshen Biblical Seminary in Indiana. In 1962, he successfully defended his doctoral dissertation, which analyzes the disputations between Reformed Christians and Anabaptists in early sixteenth-century Switzerland. In his dissertation, Yoder examined these disputations between the Swiss Anabaptists and the Swiss Reformers with the goal of clarifying the theological and ethical commitments of the Anabaptists.[10]

From 1959 to 1965, Yoder worked as an administrative assistant for overseas missions at the Mennonite Board of Missions. He also served the World Council of Churches as "an adjunct staff member of the Commission of World Missions and Evangelism, and as a consultation speaker for the Commission on Justice, Peace and the Integrity of Creation."[11] From 1960 to 1965, he was a part-time instructor at Mennonite Biblical

---

5. Ibid., 14.

6. Ibid., 16.

7. Zimmerman, *Practicing the Politics of Jesus*, 33, 101.

8. Nation, *John Howard Yoder*, 16, 77; Zimmerman, *Practicing the Politics of Jesus*, 33.

9. Nation, *John Howard Yoder*, 18; Zimmerman, *Practicing the Politics of Jesus*, 101–2, 105.

10. Yoder defended his dissertation at the University of Basel and it was publish under the title, *Täufertum und Reformation in der Schweiz: I. Die Gespräche zwischen Täufern und Reformatoren 1523–1538*.

11. Nation, *John Howard Yoder*, 22.

Seminary in Elkhart, Indiana, later becoming a full-time Professor of Theology at Goshen Biblical Seminary in Goshen, Indiana (1965–68) and later still, at Associated Mennonite Biblical Seminary in Elkhart, Indiana (1968–1977). From 1965 to 1973, he was also the Associate Director of the Institute of Mennonite Studies. From 1970 to 1973, he was president of Goshen Biblical Seminary, was ordained in 1973 at Oak Grove Mennonite Church in Smithville, Ohio, and from 1975 to 1976 served at the Tantur Ecumenical Institute in Jerusalem. Finally, from 1977 to 1984, he was a part-time Professor of Theology at Goshen Biblical Seminary, and from 1977 to 1997, he finished out the later years of his illustrious career as a Professor of Theology at the University of Notre Dame.[12]

During these years, Yoder wrote hundreds of articles and more than twenty books.[13] His book, *The Politics of Jesus*, has sold over 100,000 copies and has been translated into more than ten languages. Yoder spoke German, French, and English fluently, and he lectured in more than twenty countries.[14] It has often been emphasized that Karl Barth influenced Yoder, and in many ways this is true. Like Barth, Yoder centered his theology in Christology and rejected any attempt to derive moral standards and knowledge about the divine will from the natural law.[15] Yoder, however, never became a protégé of Barth. He was too critical of the theology of Barth, (for example, in regard to Barth's view of war) and they, furthermore, never had a good relationship.[16] Thus, sometimes the influence of Barth seems overestimated. It may be at least as important to emphasize Oscar Cullmann's influence on Yoder, Yoder adhering to Cullmann's view of the state, his pacifism, and his understanding of the concept of "powers and principalities" in the New Testament. It is also worth noting that the majority of Yoder's courses at Basel University were in Biblical Studies—nine courses from Cullmann.[17]

12. Ibid., 21–24.

13. See Nation, *A Comprehensive Bibliography of the Writings of John Howard Yoder*. Several books, compiled by unpublished and published material by Yoder, have been published posthumously. This bibliography does not include these books.

14. Nation, *John Howard Yoder*, 25–26.

15. On Yoder's rejection of the natural law as a source of divine revelation, see, for example, Yoder, *The Christian Witness to the State*, 33–35, 79–83.

16. On Yoder's critique of Barth's view of war, see Yoder, *Karl Barth and the Problem of War and Other Essays on Barth*.

17. For example, Shin overlooks the influence of Cullmann. Shin expands intensively on the influence Barth had on Yoder. He mentions, however, nothing about the influence of Cullmann. See "Two Models of Social Transformation," 26–28. Carter

Yoder deliberately identified himself with the Anabaptist vision, even though Protestantism, Evangelicalism, and Catholicism influenced him and his theology.[18] He did not, however, regard his theology as Mennonite theology, but as catholic in the broadest sense.[19] More than any other Mennonite theologian, Yoder brought the Anabaptist theological tradition, with its emphasis on discipleship and nonresistance, into dialogue with mainstream Christian ethics in North America.[20] Yoder had ecumenical awareness, and he contributed to the Mennonite church's opening up to the ecumenical world to a greater extent. He admitted the need to learn from others, and at the same time, he believed that the Anabaptist tradition represented important insights that could benefit all Christians.[21] John Howard Yoder died December 30, 1997, the day after his seventieth birthday.

3.2 Constantinianism

3.2.1 Constantinianism and the Theological Project of Yoder

Yoder believes that Constantine's conversion is a symbol for a new era in the history of Christianity. He presents a strong critique of Constantinianism, which he believes expresses a heresy that continues to impact the church in the Western world to a great extent. He states that major changes in the relationship between the church and its surrounding society began before 200 AD and rapidly took shape with Constantine.[22] However, Yoder is not primarily interested in historical details concerning how sincere Constantine's conversion was, what he believed or the date of

---

also emphasizes the influence Barth had on Yoder, while the influence of Cullmann seems less emphasized. See Carter, *The Politics of the Cross*, 61–90. For an overview of which courses Yoder took at Basel University, see Zimmerman, *Practicing the Politics of Jesus*, 105.

18. Carter, *The Politics of the Cross*, xx–xxi, 32.

19. Yoder, "Introduction," 8; Rasmusson, "Revolutionary Subordination," 40.

20. As I referred to in chapter 1, Webber and Clapp say, "Almost singlehandedly, Yoder has caused the theological world to take seriously the Anabaptist ecclesiology and social ethics." See *People of the Truth*, 133.

21. For an exposition of Yoder's thoughts on ecumenism, see Nation, *John Howard Yoder*, 77–108. See also *Radical Ecumenicity*.

22. Yoder, "The Otherness of the Church," 57; Yoder, "The Pacifism of Pre-Constantinian Christianity," 49–54; Yoder, "The Constantinian Sources of Western Social Ethics," 135.

the punctual downfall of the church.²³ LeMasters rightly points out that Yoder uses Constantinianism as a provocative metaphor without proving his contentions historically.²⁴ LeMasters claims, nevertheless, that several of Yoder's assertions can be documented by historical studies.²⁵ At times, however, Yoder has a tendency to oversimplify in his references to the pre-Constantinian Christians as a major homogeneous group, a point which will be exemplified later.²⁶ As mentioned, Yoder does not refer to many historical studies of the events associated with Constantine's conversion. Instead, he is preoccupied with the larger overriding conditions with an interest in the *theological* significance and consequences of this shift.²⁷

Yoder uses both the expressions "Christendom" and "Constantinianism." They do not, however, function synonymously. The term "Christendom" marks the so-called Christian Europe of the Middle Ages, and is in this way a geographical and historical term.²⁸ The term "Constantinianism" expresses, first and foremost, a heresy with profoundly theological implications. Hence, Christendom is a consequence of Constantinianism. Both Christendom and Constantinianism are heretical, according to Yoder. He often, however, also refers to Constantinianism, in historical

---

23. Yoder, "The Constantinian Sources of Western Social Ethics," 135. However, Yoder deals with these matters a few times. See, for example, Yoder, "The Meaning of the Constantinian Shift," 57–59. The conversion of Constantine has received much attention by historians and theologians across the centuries. For example, it has been debated how sincere Constantine's conversion was, and to what extent he used the church to foster his political agendas, etc. LeMasters refers to several books which discuss these topics. See LeMasters, *The Import of Eschatology*, 102–7.

24. LeMasters, *The Import of Eschatology*, 91, 101–2, 128.

25. LeMasters says, "Yoder's account of Constantine's use of Christianity as an ideology to foster his political agenda is not without support from historical studies (. . .). Through exacting historical analysis on Constantine of the sort which Yoder does not seem to have undertaken." LeMasters refers to Alistar Kee, who "portrays the emperor and his reign in a fashion that is clearly congenial to Yoder's account." See ibid., 106.

26. For example, LeMasters suggests that the statement that Christians who lived before Constantine in general were pacifists is challenged by the findings of Helgeland, Daly and Burns in *Christians and the Military*, 87–93. Cf. LeMasters, *The Import of Eschatology*, 92.

27. Recent years, Yoder's use of the expressions as "Christendom" and "Constantinianism" has been debated in several books. For example, see Leihart, *Defending Constantine*; and Roth, *Constantine Revisited*. Here, I have chosen not to enter this debate but to present my own understanding of this aspect of Yoder's writing.

28. See, for example, Yoder, *Preface to Theology*, 233.

terms, as the fundamental reorientation in the relationship of church and world, which Constantine became a symbol of.[29]

Yoder challenges Constantinianism throughout major parts of his writings, and when various aspects of Yoder's theology have been analyzed previously, many have noted that his critique of Constantinianism plays an important role in his theology. This may be an overstatement, but Constantinianism almost seems to comprise the essential background of his theological project as a whole.[30] For example, as Yoder suggests, "the fourth-century shift continues to explain much if not most of the distance between biblical Christianity and ourselves, which is a distance not simply of time and organic development, but of disavowal and apostasy."[31] Moreover, Chris K. Huebner asserts that Constantinianism is perhaps the most recurring theme in Yoder's theology.[32] Thus, he deals with the problem of Constantinianism throughout his whole work.[33] Doing this, Yoder does not refer to Constantinianism to actualize his theological project, but it is probably more accurate to say that the struggle against Constantinianism is a driving motivation for him. This is not to say, however, that his fundamental driving force is entirely negative. He indeed developed a constructive theology, proposing ways for the church to live more faithfully in the world.

Since Yoder quite often challenges Constantinianism, and since his theological project to a great extent can be considered as an expression of

---

29. Yoder, "The Constantinian Sources of Western Social Ethics," 135; Yoder, "The Meaning of the Constantinian Shift," 63; Yoder, "The Otherness of the Church," 57. "The world" in the Bible can mean "the earth," "the universe," "nature" or "creation." In the creation narratives, "the world" is regarded as "good" and Paul can say that through the world we are able to discover God's "eternal power and divine nature" (Rom 1:20). "The world" in the New Testament most frequently connotes a refusal to worship God or to acknowledge Jesus as Lord. See, for example, John 7:7, 14:17, 15:19, 16:33, 18:36; Rom 12:2; 1 Cor 1:20; Eph 2:2; 2 Tim 4:10; Jas 4:4; cf. Stone, *Evangelism after Christendom*, 192–93. Yoder follows this dual understanding of "the world," but most often he uses the term not to signify the creation or the universe but the fallen structures of the world that no longer is conformed to the creative intent. Yoder defines "the world" in this sense as "*structured unbelief.*" See Yoder, "The Otherness of the Church," 62; italics original. See also 3.5.3 below.

30. In his fine introduction to Yoder's theology, Carter does not really make it clear how crucial the critique of Constantinianism is for the theological project of Yoder as a whole. See Carter, *The Politics of the Cross*, 201.

31. Yoder, "The Constantinian Sources of Western Social Ethics," 144.

32. Huebner, *A Precarious Peace*, 57.

33. Kerr, *Christ, History and Apocalyptic*, 170.

Following the Way of Christ in the World

a strong critique of Constantinianism, it is natural to begin here as I seek to understand his theological intentions and his understanding of the distinctive identity of the church.

3.2.2 Consequences of Constantinianism

For Yoder, Constantinianism is "a metaphor for a shift in the relationship between church and world that has had, and continues to have," ramifications which profoundly corrupt the Christian church and Christian theology.[34] Yoder unfolds the consequences of Constantinianism in many ways and most of these are, in one way or another, related to ecclesiology, social ethics, and eschatology. Thus, I will here give a brief introduction to the most important aspects of the ecclesiological, ethical and eschatological consequences of Constantinianism, later expanding on these themes.

Yoder asserts that the Constantinian shift had severe consequences for ecclesiology, believing that the most pertinent fact about this shift was that "two visible realities, church and world, were fused."[35] Before Constantine, the church was a minority. After Constantine, the church was everybody. Christianity now became the official religion of the society, all citizens were baptized and considered Christians—"except a few Jews, who did not count"[36]—and the entire social order was now declared Christian, which meant that there was no longer a contrasting other realm to call "the world." This, ultimately, led to the church severely compromising its identity as a distinct community of faith.[37] As I will demonstrate later, a separationist stance with respect to the state is, for Yoder, not merely a possible implication of obedience to Christ in some settings, but an intrinsic part of Christian obedience in every context.[38]

The Constantinian shift also had severe consequences for Christian ethics. Before Constantine, the church represented a way of living, which differed significantly from the society in which it lived. After Constantine, the church was filled with people for whom repentance and faith were absent. This meant that the ethical requirements set by the church

---

34. LeMasters, *The Import of Eschatology*, 101.
35. Yoder, "The Otherness of the Church," 57.
36. Yoder, "The Meaning of the Constantinian Shift," 62.
37. Yoder, "The Otherness of the Church," 57; LeMasters, *The Import of Eschatology*, 93.
38. See, for example, 3.3.1 and 3.3.7 below.

had been "adapted to the achievement level of respectable unbelief."[39] This change of Christian ethics also had consequences for the distinctiveness of the church. As Christian ethics were applied to the whole society, a distinction between church and society could no longer be maintained. Furthermore, Yoder believes that the pre-Constantinian Christians were pacifists, "rejecting the violence of army and empire not only because they had no share of power, but because they considered it morally wrong."[40] This exemplifies Yoder's description of the pre-Constantinian Christians as a homogeneous group. Nonetheless, he argues that Christians, as a consequence of Constantinianism, stopped being pacifists. The rise of Constantinianism also led to a change in the understanding of the church's ethical responsibility. Before Constantine, the church did not try to *control* the world, but *witnessed* to the world. After Constantine, managing the world became part of the church's self-understanding.

Yoder believes that the Constantinian shift also led to a major revision of eschatology: "Before Constantine, one knew as a fact of everyday experience that there was a believing Christian community," but Christians had to trust, despite their experience, that God was governing history.[41] After Constantine, one had to believe that there existed an invisible community of believers within the nominally Christian mass, "but one knew for a fact that God was in control of history" through the dominion of the Empire.[42] This understanding presupposes that "the *state* was unequivocally in the realm of redemption" and a manifestation of God's reign.[43] In this way, the church now came to express that the state was an incarnation of the ultimate values of God's work in the world. As I will show later, Yoder believes this to be false.[44]

---

39. Yoder, "The Otherness of the Church," 57.

40. Yoder, "The Constantinian Sources of Western Social Ethics," 135.

41. Ibid., 137.

42. Ibid.

43. Yoder, "The Otherness of the Church," 59; italics mine.

44. See 3.5.3 below. Yoder believes that Constantinianism also had epistemological consequences. With the rise of Western Christendom, secular philosophy and biblical wisdom merged, and common sense and natural law became important sources for moral knowledge. See Yoder, "The Meaning of the Constantinian Shift," 63–74. Hence, these epistemological consequences are also related to Christian ethics. I will turn to the epistemological aspects of the Constantinian shift later on. See 3.6.1 below.

3.2.3 Constantinianism and Modern Western History

Yoder is not only preoccupied with Constantinianism in the fourth century, but in fact also reads "Constantinianism back into the Old Testament, so that rulers such as Solomon and David, or any attempt to use secular power to do God's work can be seen as prequels, as it were, to Constantine."[45] I will deal with this later.[46] Here, I will instead explore Yoder's belief that Constantinianism still impacts the church in modern times. Even though many contend that the Constantinian era is phasing out, and some even state that we left the age of Constantine behind long ago, Yoder believes that Constantinianism throughout history has occurred in new disguises, and still impacts the church of today. In the article "The Constantinian Sources of Western Social Ethics," he gives a number of examples of this, presented in chronological order.

First, Yoder identifies a form of Constantinianism which exits even when society cannot any longer be considered as a Christian empire. Yoder believes that the Reformation and the Renaissance led to the rise of nationalism, with the state replacing the old Christendom as the definition of cultural identity and historical meaning. With this change, it became more important to belong to a specific country than to the unity of Christendom. According to Yoder, the social arrangement of Constantinianism remained, but on a national scale. Under this arrangement, "[o]ne could now have wars, even holy wars, against other Christian nations."[47] With this development, "[t]he basic Constantinian vision remained, only on a much smaller, provincial scale."[48] This is what Yoder calls neo-Constantinianism.[49]

Second, Yoder believes that a new form of Constantinianism emerged at the time of the Enlightenment. Religious liberty and disestablishment led to an institutional separation of church and state, yet, the state retained the moral blessing of the church through the church's moral identification with the state.[50] As Yoder suggests, even when separation of church and state is seen as theologically desirable, "a society where this separation is achieved is not a pagan society but a nation structured ac-

---

45. Doerksen, *Beyond Suspicion*, 147.
46. See 3.3.1 below.
47. Yoder, "The Constantinian Sources of Western Social Ethics," 141.
48. Ibid., 142.
49. Ibid., 141–42.
50. LeMasters, *The Import of Eschatology*, 97.

cording to the will of God."[51] The moral identification of the church with the nation remained despite institutional separation. Thus, according to Yoder, with the Enlightenment, the social arrangement of Constantinianism had been changed deeply and formally, but remained informally powerful. This is what Yoder calls "neo-neo-Constantinianism."[52]

A third form of Constantinianism is evident within nations with an officially anti-Christian stance, such as some Marxist states, because Christians within these nations remain patriotic. Even when they are persecuted, they claim that their beliefs do not make them disloyal to the nation. Further, the Christians often "espouse the political views of their government in ecumenical meetings."[53] In some cases, the churches are disestablished, but in other cases the churches are still financially supported by a Marxist regime. This continuing moral identification, despite mutual ideological disavowal, is what Yoder calls "neo-neo-neo-Constantinianism."[54]

Fourth, yet another possible permutation of Constantinianism is identifying "God's cause and Christians' loyalty with a regime which is *future* rather than present: with a 'revolution' or 'liberation' which, being morally imperative, is sure to come."[55] In this case, Constantinianism is manifested in a more acquirable system of power "yet to come, with which Christians should proleptically identify."[56] This is what Yoder calls "neo-neo-neo-neo-Constantinianism."[57]

Each of these permutations of Constantinianism highlights a common "basic structural error," which Yoder identifies as "the identification of a civil authority as the bearer of God's cause."[58] As he explains,

> Each view along this progression is clear in rejecting the former one as having been wrong, and in blaming the blindness of earlier generations of churchmen for having accepted such identification with an unworthy political cause. This sense of rightness over against the others blinds each generation to the

51. Yoder, "The Constantinian Sources of Western Social Ethics," 142.
52. Ibid.
53. LeMasters, *The Import of Eschatology*, 97.
54. Yoder, "The Constantinian Sources of Western Social Ethics," 142–43.
55. Ibid., 143; italics original.
56. Ibid.
57. Ibid.
58. Ibid.; see also Yoder, "Christ, the Hope of the World," 147–53; LeMasters, *The Import of Eschatology*, 98.

fact that the basic structural error, the identification of a civil authority as bearer of God's cause, has not been overcome but only transposed into a new key.[59]

In his critique of Constantinianism, Yoder unfolds an ecclesiology, social ethics, and eschatology, while at the same time outlining important aspects of the church's distinctive identity. On the one hand, Craig A. Carter states that Yoder primarily considers Constantinianism to be an eschatological heresy.[60] On the other hand, Bryan Stone thinks that Yoder primarily regards Constantinianism as an ethical heresy.[61] Below, I will unify the three aforementioned theological themes.

3.3 Ecclesiology

3.3.1 The Diasporic Existence of the People of God

One cannot truly understand Yoder's ecclesiology without also considering the church's Jewish background. In the article "It Did not Have to Be," Yoder states that in the first century, there did not exist a single, normative Judaism. He argues that within Jewish society, there existed several competing Judaisms.[62]

This leads Yoder to assert: "Neither Jesus, nor Paul, nor the apostolic communities rejected normative Judaism."[63] This is of course true since, according to Yoder, no such thing existed. But the point is far more fundamental, as he points out: "What Jesus himself proposed to his listeners was nothing other than what he claimed as the normative vision for a restored and clarified Judaism, namely the proper interpretation of the Jewish Scriptures and tradition for this present, in light of the New Age

---

59. Yoder, "The Constantinian Sources of Western Social Ethics," 143.

60. Carter, *The Politics of the Cross*, 155. He leaves surprisingly little space to ethics in his survey of Yoder's critique of Constantinianism; see 155–78.

61. Stone, *Evangelism after Christendom*, 120. Stone does, however, acknowledge that Yoder also considers Constantinianism to be an eschatological heresy; see 124. Yoder says, "The most important error of the Christendom vision (. . .) is its illegitimate takeover of the world; its ascription of a Christian loyalty or duty to those who have made no confession, and thereby, its denying to the non-confessing creation the freedom of unbelief that the nonresistance of God in creation gave to a rebellious humanity." See Yoder, "Why Ecclesiology Is Social Ethics: Gospel Ethics Versus the Wider Wisdom," 109.

62. Yoder, "It Did Not Have to Be," 47–48.

63. Ibid., 49; in the original text this sentence is in italics.

which he heralded."⁶⁴ Jesus' work took place within the Judaisms of his time and Paul extended "a messianic Judaism to the Gentile nations as his way of practicing Judaism (. . .) and the Gospel of John did not seek to condemn 'the Jews' in general, but only a certain part of what he took to be the Jewish 'establishment.'"⁶⁵

This, moreover, leads him to suggest that the Jews did not in fact reject Christianity. Believers in Jesus went to the synagogues, and the Temple at Jerusalem was open to them until its destruction.⁶⁶ Therefore, at the time of Jesus, one could be both a Jew and a follower of Jesus.⁶⁷

In response to Yoder's article "It Did not Have to Be," Professor of Judaic Studies, Peter Ochs, confirms: "Many Jewish movements rejected the claims of many other Jewish movements, but without rejecting the membership of the other claimants in the people of Israel."⁶⁸ In another article, Yoder adds, "instead of thinking of 'Christians' and 'Jews' in the early centuries as separate bodies existing over against each other, we must think of two initially largely overlapping circles. The circle 'Church' and the circle 'Jewry' overlapped for generations."⁶⁹ In this way, Yoder established an understanding of how Christianity grew out of Judaism.⁷⁰

Following this, he attempts to investigate how Judaism shaped early Christianity. According to Yoder, one of the defining marks of the Judaism that shaped early Christianity is the notion of *diaspora*.⁷¹ This did not only define the Judaism at the time of Jesus, but, as he argues, the normal state for the Jewish people is existence in diaspora. Therefore, he tries to trace this theme throughout the entire Old Testament.

In Genesis 9–10, we see how the dispersion began and how God commanded it. In rebellion against God, humankind, however, sought to live in one place.⁷² Even so, God responded graciously and restored

---

64. Ibid.

65. Peter Ochs, referring to Yoder, "Commentary," 67; cf. Yoder, "It Did Not Have to Be," 50–51.

66. Yoder, "It Did Not Have to Be," 51.

67. Ibid.

68. Ochs, "Commentary," 67.

69. Yoder, "Jesus the Jewish Pacifist," 69. This also leads him to the final conclusion of the article, namely that the Jewish-Christian schism did not have to be.

70. I have only given an account of the most important conclusions in the article, *It Did not Have to Be*. Yoder of course discusses this in much more detail.

71. See, for example, Yoder, "Jesus the Jewish Pacifist," 77.

72. Cf. Doerksen, *Beyond Suspicion*, 44.

the centripetal motion. Hence, in Genesis 11, we read how humankind is spread out over the whole earth and how it was God who scattered it for its own good. As Yoder notes: "This scattering is still seen as benevolence in the missionary preaching of Paul" (cf. Acts 14:16–17; 17:26–27).[73] In this way, he argues that diversity—diverse identities, languages and cultures—is an original divine intent.[74] Later on in Genesis, we read about Abraham, who becomes the father of the Israelite people. Yoder remarks that when Abraham was called to leave Chaldea, God told him that through him all the nations of the world would be blessed, and in response "Abraham promised his God that he would lead a different kind of life: a life different from the cultured and the religious peoples, whether urban or nomadic, among whom he was to make his pilgrim way."[75] This leads Yoder to claim: "The whole point of Hebrew identity since Abraham is a call to be doing something else amidst the world's power arenas. It is only by doing something different that Jewry in fact has survived; it is only in order to be something morally different that Jewry is called to survive."[76] Moreover, he believes that not only Abraham but also Moses and the prophets acknowledged the minority status of God's chosen people.[77] In both the Old and New Testaments, the people of God exist in a hostile milieu. According to Yoder, "Assyria in the age of Isaiah, Babylon in that of Jeremiah, Nineveh in that of Jonah, and then Rome in that of the New Testament Apocalypse are in one sense all the same thing: the great world city, oppressive, drunk on power, worshipping idols, claiming to be the centre of the world, persecuting the saints, and doomed to destruction."[78]

Yoder clearly narrates the story of Israel from a diasporic or exilic point of view and, therefore, he also privileges the antiroyal tradition in the Hebrew Scriptures.[79] Doerksen comments that,

> Yoder is at pains to point out that Israel had no king from Moses through Gideon, largely because a covenant relationship with

---

73. Yoder, "'See How They Go with Their Face to the Sun,'" 63.

74. Yoder, "'See How They Go with Their Face to the Sun,'" 64; see also Yoder, "Meaning After Babble," 132.

75. Yoder, "The Original Revolution," 27; cf. Num 23:9.

76. Yoder, "Jesus the Jewish Pacifist," 85.

77. Yoder, "Let the Church Be the Church," 116.

78. Yoder, "'See How They Go with Their Face to the Sun,'" 77.

79. Doerksen, *Beyond Suspicion*, 40.

God seemed to imply that no king but God was needed. Yoder reads Israel's longing for a king simply as a desire for conformity to pagan nations, and suggest that kingship is only then accepted under the conditions of charismatic leadership (Northern kingdom), or a dynastic succession (Southern kingdom).[80]

In his unfolding of the antiroyal strand of the Hebrew Scriptures, Yoder often refers to the recognition of Yahweh as a warrior and the king of Israel. This is the most important reason for rejecting that Israel should adopt the institution of kingship and, moreover, he reminds us that even when Israel got a king, he stood under the words of Yahweh.[81] In Yoder's words,

> In pagan empires, justice was the word of the king. In the Hebrew experience, that was not so. Justice could not be above the pagan emperor since it was he who edicted it, and the priests celebrated his empowerment to do so. For Jews, justice was knowable otherwise: by the oral Torah, by prophets, later by Scriptures. None of them were dependent upon the king. When there was an Israelite king, he stood under, not over the words of JHWH, and it was because Israelite kings did not obey those words that the two Israelite kingdoms did not last.[82]

Yoder's reading of the Hebrew Scriptures, with this emphasis on exile, has come under significant criticism. Gerald Schlabach asserts that Yoder's reading of the Hebrew Scriptures ignores the basic problem of the "Deuteronomistic temptation," that is, "the problem of how to receive and celebrate the blessing, the *shalom*, the good, or 'the land' that God desires to give, yet to do so without defensively and violently hoarding God's blessing."[83] And following Alain Epp Weaver and also Michael Cartwright, Doerksen states that, "in Yoder's zeal to draw appropriate implications from his emphasis on the exilic strand of the Hebrew Scripture, he hardly mentions issues of returning to the land. This exclusion has a distorting effect on the Old Testament message, as well as a Christian reading of the issue."[84] Furthermore, in order to save his argument, he avoids major discussions of the books of Ezra and Nehemiah.[85]

80. Ibid., 41.
81. See, for example, Yoder, "Jesus the Jewish Pacifist," 71–74; see also Yoder, *The Politics of Jesus*, 76–88.
82. Yoder, "Jesus the Jewish Pacifist," 73.
83. Schlabach, "Deuteronomic or Constantinian," 451.
84. Doerksen, *Beyond Suspicion*, 49; cf. Weaver, "On Exile," 142–65.
85. Doerksen, *Beyond Suspicion*, 50.

Still, Yoder's understanding of Israel exiled in Babylon is central to his argument. In Babylon, the Jewish people now had to live outside of Judaea and without the Temple, the kingship was given up, and Babylon became "the place where they should settle down, buy land and plant crops, make money and marry off their children."[86] This is what Yoder calls "the Jeremiah shift" or "the Jeremiah turn." This shift is of great important to Yoder, as he believes that two ancient turning points represented by Jeremiah and Constantine must be considered as "the two most important landmarks outside the New Testament itself for clarifying what is at stake in the Christian faith."[87] Even though Israel at the time of Jeremiah was exiled, Yoder, as we have seen, clearly understands exile as the normal way of existence for God's chosen people.

Yoder denotes three important, creative innovations in Israel's coping with their Babylonian exile. Hence, three culturally-unique traits were developed, which in time came to "define 'Judaism' and thereby Christianity in return:"[88]

- The phenomenon of the synagogue; a decentralized, self-sustaining, non-sacerdotal community life form capable of operating on its own wherever there are ten households.

- The phenomenon of the Torah; a text around the reading and exposition of which the community is defined. This text is at once narrative and legal.

- The phenomenon of the rabbinate; a non-sacerdotal, non-hierarchical, non-violent leadership elite whose power is not civil but intellectual, validated by their identification with the Torah.[89]

Since the Temple in Jerusalem could not be replaced by another Temple in Babylon, Israel began to gather in "a house of prayer, a synagogue, a gathering of believers around the scrolls of Scripture. Thereby a community was created which needed neither priest nor Temple."[90]

In addition, as Yoder points out, the oldest version of the Talmud was compiled in Babylon and it did for Jews what "the canon of apostolic

86. Yoder, "Jesus the Jewish Pacifist," 77.
87. Yoder, "Introduction," 8.
88. Yoder, "On Not Being in Charge," 171.
89. Ibid. Yoder later admits that he should have added *kashrut* (Jewish dietary laws) and circumcision; see Yoder, "'See How They Go with Their Face to the Sun,'" 67.
90. Yoder, "Jesus the Jewish Pacifist," 78.

writings is supposed to do for Christians. It can provide a fulcrum, or a fixed star, outside the Hellenistic-Roman system, morally and philosophically, although within it politically and geographically, whereby to evaluate both acceptable compromises and unacceptable betrayals."[91] The Hebrew Scriptural canon was also selected in Babylon and these scriptures also helped to shed light on the diasporic existence of Israel.[92] Thus, the Jews discovered in the diaspora that,

> There was within their tradition more of what it takes to survive than they had been aware of while they had been focusing their hopes on an imminent return to Jerusalem. There was, for instance, the set of hero stories stretching from Joseph through Ester to Daniel and his three friends. These Israelites in pagan courts had all stood up victoriously for the one true God, disobeying non-violently, amidst a hostile pagan culture.[93]

Thus, Yoder argues that the normal existence for the church is existence in diaspora and exile. This notion of exile preconfigured the Christian understanding of the church's existence in the world.[94]

Yoder also notes another important aspect of the exilic situation in Babylon, namely, that the Jewish people were called to seek the peace and welfare of the places where God has sent them (cf. Jer 29:4–7). Not only in Babylon, but also in a broader perspective, Israel was called to exist for the nations. Like Israel, the church is scattered for mission and called to exist for the world. As Weaver states: "The continuity of this exilic vision with Yoder's ecclesiology should be clear: the church is the community called to go out into the world, into diaspora (Matthew 25), a community that refuses to wield violent force, pointing instead to God's sovereignty."[95]

---

91. Ibid., 80.

92. Yoder, "'See How They Go with Their Face to the Sun,'" 56–57. In addition, Yoder argues that Babylon became the cultural center of Judaism from Jeremiah up until the Middle Ages: "The people who re-colonized the 'Land of Israel,' repeatedly, from the age of Jeremiah to that of Jochanan ben Zakkai, and again still later, were supported financially and educationally from Babylon, and in lesser ways from the rest of the diaspora. Our palestinocentric reading of the story is a mistake, though a very understandable one. It was imposed not only on Christians but also on many Jews because of the way the first-century events became legend." See ibid., 57.

93. Yoder, "Jesus the Jewish Pacifist," 78.

94. I will clarify this in my exposition of Yoder's understanding of the expression "powers and principalities" in the New Testament. See 3.5 below.

95. Weaver, "On Exile," 146.

More than anything else, Rabbinic Judaism shaped early Christianity. Yoder argues that the notion of diaspora was a defining mark of Rabbinic Judaism, a movement which emerged earlier than Christianity. As Yoder states that we can say that "Rabbinic Judaism" begins around 200 with the redaction of *Mishna*, around 135 with the defeat of Bar Kochba, or around 70 with the loss of the Temple, or perhaps still earlier, with the foundation of the school of Hillel "depending on the variables we consider important, but the life which the rabbis define has been going since 586 BCE."[96] The defining texts of Rabbinic Judaism were the massive collection called the *Mishna*, which was codified by Judah the Great and is dated around year 200.[97] These texts were of a faith that knew "how to affirm the life of a biblical people away from home, deep in exile, and deeply wounded by loss and dislocation (. . .) the texture of a life lived apart: apart from other traditions, other communities, as well as apart from dimensions of human life that threaten rather than serve as a vehicle for a life lived in imitation of God."[98]

Yoder's exilic argument should obviously be seen in connection with his critique of Constantinianism. Michael G. Cartwright explains that "Yoder's argument is directed at overthrowing the assumptions of Constantinian Christianity as they have shaped *virtually all* forms of religious practice in western civilization since the second century CE."[99] After Constantine, all citizens were baptized, the church included everybody, and Christianity became the official religion of the society. As a result, there was no longer anything to call "the world," which led to a severe compromising of the integrity of the church as a distinct community of faith.[100]

Against this, Yoder argues that the church is God's distinct people. The church submits itself to God, and this religious affiliation cannot be suspended by any other affiliation in the world. Hence, Yoder states: "No political nation, no geographical homeland to which one belongs by birth, can take precedence over the heavenly citizenship of a Christian in one's new birth."[101] Thus, the church has a citizenship not of this

---

96. Yoder, "Jesus the Jewish Pacifist," 77.
97. Ibid., 76.
98. Ochs, "Editors' Introduction," 2.
99. Cartwright, "Editors' Introduction," 22; italics original.
100. Yoder, "The Otherness of the Church," 57.
101. Yoder, *He Came Preaching Peace*, 23.

world.[102] The Christian community must form and nurture a common life determined by Christ, gathering to discern what it means to follow him.[103] As Yoder extrapolates,

> Now the usual name of this new society which Jesus created is 'church.' But when we use the word 'church' in our day we mean by it a gathering for worship, or the group of persons who gather for worship, or who might so gather, and who otherwise have little to do with each other. Sometimes it even means the building they meet in, or the organization which provides an officiant at the meeting, or even the national agency which manages the pension fund for the officiants' widows. But the word which Jesus used in the Aramaic language, like the equivalent word which the New Testament writers used in the Greek language, does not mean a gathering for worship nor an administration; it means a public gathering to deal with community business. Our modern terms *assembly, parliament, town meeting*, are the best equivalents. The church is not just a certain number of persons nor a specific gathering of persons assembled for a particular religious rite. The church is God's people gathered as a unit, as a people, gathered to do business in His name, to find what it means here and now to put into practice this different quality of life which is God's promise to them and to the world and their promise to God and service to the world.[104]

3.3.2 Believers' Church

Yoder claims that there exist three basic types of ecclesiologies: the theocratic vision, the spiritualist reaction, and the believers' church. The first type of ecclesiology envisions a "renewal of the church that hopes to reform society at large with one blow."[105] From this perspective, both the merging and the separation of church and state are considered as "the common Christian takeover of all society for the greater glory of God, which is common to both polities."[106] Thus, power in society is

---

102. Yoder, "The Peace Testimony and Conscientious Objection," 58.

103. Along the same lines, Volf states that, "a person cannot be fully initiated into the Christian faith without being socialized into a Christian church," in *After Our Likeness*, 173.

104. Yoder, "The Original Revolution," 30–31; italics original.

105. Yoder, "A People in the World," 71.

106. Ibid.

best exercised by Christians, but "[t]he preacher or prophet must not seek to govern the State or the economy—that would be to relapse into clericalism—but it shall be governed by men who in their Christian calling do what God demands as the preacher has interpreted it to them."[107] Yoder points to John Calvin as a representative of this type of ecclesiology.

The second type of ecclesiology is a reaction against the theocratic type of ecclesiology. This type of ecclesiology remains, however, within the framework of the theocratic vision to which it reacts, simply moving the focus from society to the spiritual.[108] Yoder points to Philipp Jakob Spener as a representative of this type of ecclesiology.

The third type of ecclesiology, the believers' church, "stands not merely between the other two but over against both of them."[109] It is not really a synthesis of the two preceding ecclesiological models, but in fact a genuinely third option. With spiritualism, it criticizes "the formalism of official theocratic churchdom."[110] However, it instead seeks to renew the church according to Scripture's vision and the expressive character of the disciples' fellowship. Like the theocratic vision, it criticizes the "individualism and elite self-consciousness" of spiritualism.[111] Stemming from this, it does not seek to establish a Christian society, but a covenanted fellowship by those who follow Christ.[112] The church is for believers and for those who accept Christ as Lord and want to follow him. As we shall now see, this community embodies a number of distinctive practices.

3.3.3 Five Practices of the Early Church

Yoder points to five practices of the early Christians which he believes outline the contours of the life of the early church, although not claiming that this is a comprehensive list.[113] Still, these five practices were very

107. Ibid., 72.
108. Ibid.
109. Ibid.
110. Ibid.
111. Ibid.

112. This analysis follows ibid., 68–73. Carter has a similar description of Yoder's ecclesiological typology in *The Politics of the Cross*, 184–86.

113. Yoder, "The New Humanity as Pulpit and Paradigm," 43. A presentation of these five practices is found in the books *Body Politics* (1992), *The Royal Priesthood* (1994) and *For the Nations* (1997). Rowell also mentions this and presents a comparative overview of how Yoder changes "the titles of the practices and the order in which

central for the early church and, furthermore, Yoder believes that each of them must be recaptured today.

Yoder calls the first practice "binding and loosing" (cf. Matt 18:15–18). Jesus instructed his disciples on what to do when a sister or brother sins. The first step is to try to resolve the matter in private, one to one. If this does not bring resolution, the second step is to take along one or two others, to serve as witnesses. If this does not bring resolution, then, thirdly, the matter is taken to the gathered church. If this does not bring resolution, then the offender is to be excommunicated. If the problem is solved, the community is restored. Thus, what the disciples bind, will be bound in heaven, and what the disciples loose, will be loosed in heaven. Yoder believes that the activity of the disciples is at the same time the activity of God. He makes several observations about this practice. First, this practice can be exercised by all Christians, and not only by the clergy. Second, "[t]he intention is restorative, not punitive."[114] Third, no distinction between minor and major offenses is made. Fourth, the intention is not to protect the reputation of the church, but "to serve the offender's own well-being by restoring her or him to the community."[115] This practice belongs to the church as "a voluntary community whose members have committed themselves to its standards and to its practice."[116] Therefore, if this limitation is not respected, and if it is used outside of this context, it becomes an instrument of oppression instead of liberation.[117] Yoder believes that this practice has been lost in many congregations today.[118]

The second practice he calls "breaking bread together" (cf. 1 Cor 11:20–22). Yoder states that what we today call "Communion," "Eucharist" or "Lord's Supper" was an actual meal in the early church. The Lord's Supper was an act of "economic sharing among the members of the messianic community."[119] Yoder believes that the early churches were living together almost as a family, and therefore it was normal for the early Christians to share goods with each other. Thus, the Lord's Supper expressed community, concern, and responsibility for one another, not

---

he lists them." See Rowell, "Ecclesiology of John Howard Yoder," 25. I follow the order and titles from *Body Politics*.

114. Yoder, *Body Politics*, 3.
115. Ibid.
116. Ibid., 5.
117. Carter, *The Politics of the Cross*, 196.
118. Yoder, *Body Politics*, 1–13.
119. Ibid., 21.

symbolically but concretely. Yoder asserts that this social and economic dimension of the Lord's Supper is also lost for most of today's churches.[120]

The third practice is "baptism" (cf. Gal 3:27–28). Baptism initiates persons into a new people, which profoundly transcends all social and cultural barriers. He says that "[t]he distinguishing mark of this people is that all prior given or chosen identity definitions are transcended."[121] Belonging to Christ relativizes all other belonging, and therefore, Jews and Gentiles could be members of the same community in the early church, eating and worshipping together. In this way, the church is open to all, regardless of race, religion, economic status, or political viewpoint.[122]

Yoder calls the fourth practice "the fullness of Christ" (cf. Eph 4:11–13). He refers to Paul, who speaks about the church as a body, and explains how this metaphor expresses that the church is a social group, and, moreover, that every member of this social group carries a "manifestation of the Spirit for the common good" (1 Cor 12:7). Yoder criticizes churches of today that are being run by pastors treating the members as spectators. Therefore, the church must recover the multiplicity of gifts in the church and the value of every member.[123]

Yoder calls the fifth practice "the rule of Paul" (cf. 1 Cor 14) and it is a consequence of the preceding practices. Thus, if the church acknowledges that all its members have gifts, then these gifts must be shared. Therefore, Paul instructed his congregations to have open meetings where all had the opportunity to share. This fifth practice is a kind of social practice of the church.[124]

These practices tell us something about Yoder's view of the life of the church as they all speak to the processes of the congregation when it is gathered, and all express something about the social significance of the church.[125] Baptism is an expression for interethnic reconciliation. Eucharist can be described as economic sharing. Binding and loosing can be described as conflict resolution. The fullness of Christ can be described as the ability of all members of the community. The rule of Paul is an

120. Ibid., 14–27.
121. Ibid., 28.
122. Ibid., 28–46.
123. Ibid., 47–60. This is further developed in *The Fullness of Christ*. Here, Yoder also states that the rise of Christendom led to an abandonment of the multiplicity of gifts and ministry in the church. See 19–20, 37.
124. Yoder, *Body Politics*, 61–70.
125. This in often stressed in Rowell, "The Ecclesiology of John Howard Yoder."

expression for a social order of sharing at the church meetings."[126] Thus, Yoder summarizes: "There you have before you the fivefold pattern. In each case, the shape of grace is described and prescribed *and practiced* in the early church as a social process pattern, *enabled* and *mandated* as part of the good news of redemption."[127]

3.3.4 The Visibility of the Church

To Yoder, the church is a distinct social entity, which will always visibly in one way or another differ from the society in which it lives. Therefore, it is possible to characterize and identify the church in the world. With the Constantinian shift, the church lost its identity as a Christian community visible over against the world, and he believes "[t]his shift called forth a new doctrinal refinement, namely the doctrine of the invisibility of the true church" (*ecclesia invisibilis*).[128] Yoder claims that both Augustine and Luther emphasized the church's invisibility, owing to their historical contexts. For them, "one had to believe without seeing that there was a community of believers within the larger nominally Christian mass."[129] Yoder asserts that the doctrine of the invisibility of the true church arose "in order to permit the affirmation that on some level somewhere the difference between belief and unbelief," and church and world, still existed.[130] According to Yoder, with the Christendom arrangement, "this distinction had become invisible, like faith itself."[131] In regard to this, LeMasters, however, criticizes Yoder for not concretely clarifying what we are supposed to believe regarding the visibility of church, and how the church is to determine what this visibility requires in various historical situations.[132] This may be true, but Yoder does point out that the church is identified, for example, by baptism, discipline, morality, and martyrdom, and therefore is visible.[133]

126. Ibid., 29.
127. Yoder, "The New Humanity as Pulpit and Paradigm," 46; italics original.
128. Yoder, "The Constantinian Sources of Western Social Ethics," 136.
129. Ibid., 137. For example, Augustine believed that the true church would be 5 percent of the visible church. See Yoder, "The Constantinian Sources of Western Social Ethics," 136; see also Yoder, "The Meaning of the Constantinian Shift," 62.
130. Yoder, "The Otherness of the Church," 57.
131. Ibid.
132. LeMasters, *The Import of Eschatology*, 114.
133. Yoder, "The Otherness of the Church," 56.

3.3.5 The Marks of the Church

Throughout history, shorter and longer lists of marks of the church have been developed. One source tells us that the church is "one, holy, catholic, and apostolic," and another that the church is to be found "where the sacraments are properly administered and the Word of God is properly preached."[134] On this point, Yoder responds more to the first understanding of the church than the last. First, he points out that, more recently, a new way of understanding the church has emerged, one which does not understand the church "by definition" or "as such," but in "relation to what is *not* the church, namely 'the world.'"[135] Yoder says that this "definition demands for the church an existence, a structure, a sociology of her own, independent of the other structures of society."[136] He further states that the Reformers did not fully realize this because they were a part of Medieval Christendom. Second, Yoder criticizes the before-mentioned two-point marks of the church for neglecting the congregation in its strong focus on the pastor:

> The place you would go to ascertain whether the word of God is properly preached in a given church is the preacher or conceivably the doctrinal statement by which the ecclesiastical body is governed. The place you go to see whether the sacraments are being properly administered is again the officiant. The concentration of your attention might be upon his or her way of proceeding or it might focus upon his and her understanding of the meaning of the sacrament. But in either case it does not focus upon the congregation (. . .). How many persons are present, in what attitude they are listening, what they understand, how they respond to what they have heard, to what they commit themselves, how they relate to one another, and with what orientation they return to the week's activities is not part of the touchstone definition of the church.[137]

Yoder refers, therefore, to other suggestions on the marks of the church, which can help rectify this situation. First, he refers to Willem A. Visser 't Hooft, who identifies three fundamental functions of the church, namely

---

134. Yoder, "Let the Church Be the Church," 108.
135. Ibid.; italics mine; Yoder, "A People in the World," 78.
136. Yoder, "Let the Church Be the Church," 108.
137. Yoder, "A People in the World," 76. Yoder presents a similar critique in his book *The Fullness of Christ*, 66.

witness (*martyria*), service (*diakonia*), and communion (*koinonia*).¹³⁸ Second, he refers to Stephen Neill, who suggests three marks that should be added to the traditional Reformation marks, namely *suffering, missionary vitality* and the *mobility* of the pilgrim.¹³⁹ Third, Yoder refers to Menno Simons, who adds four marks, which he designates as *holy living, brotherly love, unreserved testimony* and *suffering*.¹⁴⁰ Yoder presents several critical remarks especially to Hooft and Neill, but, even so, he approves that these additional marks to a greater extent focus on the congregation and on mission.

Building on Simons, Yoder develops four additional marks, which to some degree overlap each other. The first mark of the church regards "the moral nonconformity of Christians" as "an indispensable dimension of their visibility."¹⁴¹ If Christians follow Christ, this will inevitably be a strong witness to society. The second mark of the church is about "church discipline." This Is an expression of love, because the congregation does not allow sisters and brothers to live in sin but seeks a restored community. The third mark of the church is about the church's obligation to present and represent the gospel for the world. The fourth mark of the church is about suffering as an integral part of the life of the church.¹⁴²

These four marks of the church only appear in the article "A People in the World" and do not play an important role in the theology of Yoder. I have chosen to focus on Yoder's additional marks of the church because they show how the church can be identified as a visible social entity in the world, and, furthermore, they show how he believes that the church being the church inevitably will witness to society.

3.3.6 The Church Is the Mission

In an unpublished paper presented to a conference of missionary leaders in Lake Forest, Illinois, in August 1961, Yoder outlines his understanding

---

138. Yoder, "A People in the World," 77; Hooft, *The Pressure of Our Common Calling*.

139. Yoder, "A People in the World," 77; Neill, *The Unfinished Task*.

140. Yoder, "A People in the World," 77–78; Simons, "Reply to Gellius Faber." Menno Simons was a sixteenth century Anabaptist leader.

141. Yoder, "A People in the World," 81.

142. Ibid., 79–89.

of the Great Commission.[143] He asserts that Jesus has risen from the dead, that all power has been given to him, and now he reigns until all his enemies are brought into subjection (cf. 1 Cor 15:20–28). This is, according to Yoder, the context of mission. Therefore, the proclamation of the risen Christ is not propaganda but doxology. *Its motivation is not primordially that men need it but that it is true.*"[144] Still, the church should make disciples of all the nations, that is, all the nations who were to be blessed in Abraham. Hence, there is a continuity of redemptive purpose between the two Testaments. The church must make disciples of all nations, to the "end of the world" (geographically, cf. Acts 1:8), and to "the end of time" (historically, cf. Matt 28:20). Hence, Yoder believes that the nature of the church is essentially missionary.[145] The church is scattered for mission, and thus is called to go out into the world, into the diaspora (cf. Matt 28:18–20).[146] Like the Jewish people, the church is called to seek the peace and welfare of the places where God has sent it (cf. Jer 29:4–7). The witness of the church to society is inextricably linked to the very existence of the church. The very existence of the church and its way of life will inevitably witness to society. Therefore, witnessing to the world is not only an obligation for trained and supported missionaries, but for the whole congregation.[147]

Yoder believes that the church constitutes a new kind of social reality. Thus, when a person accepts Jesus as Lord, this person is drawn into this new distinct sociality in the world. Hence, salvation is fundamentally social and communal. The church is meant to embody God's *shalom* in the world and, in this way, be a foretaste of the peaceable kingdom, which shall one day be fulfilled.[148] The church must, thus, serve as a prototype or paradigmatic example for the world. For example, Yoder states, "my metaphor of 'pulpit' or 'pedestal' expresses the functional necessity of just being there with a particular identity."[149] Hence, it is the distinctiveness of

---

143. Yoder, "Outline Commentary," 1.

144. Ibid., 2; italics mine.

145. Yoder, *The Ecumenical Movement and the Faithful Church*, 27; see also Yoder, "Why Ecclesiology Is Social Ethics," 115.

146. Weaver, "On Exile," 146.

147. For example, Yoder argues that the Great Commission "does not say that the church should send missionaries. It says that all Christians, as they move about, are to be engaged in the task of making disciples." See Yoder, "Outline Commentary," 4.

148. See 3.4.6 below.

149. Yoder, "The New Humanity as Pulpit and Paradigm," 42.

the church that is "the major missionary message and service for larger society."[150] Moreover,

> The political novelty that God brings into the world is a community of those who serve instead of ruling, who suffer instead of inflicting suffering, whose fellowship crosses social lines instead of reinforcing them. This new Christian community in which the walls are broken down not by human idealism or by democratic legalism but by the work of Christ is not only a vehicle of the gospel or only a fruit of the gospel; it is the good news. It is not merely the agent of mission or the constituency of a mission agency. *This is the mission.*[151]

The church's witness to society is, furthermore, linked to the public character of the church. The church will inevitably be visible and public and, as such, the church functions as a pulpit and a public offer to the watching world.[152] The church is a redemptive structure that manifests a distinct social order in a fallen world, and therefore a counter-structure in the world. The Church is "the primary social structure through which the gospel works to change other structures."[153]

It is notable that Yoder never really emphasized how the church lost sight of mission in the European Christendom in the medieval era. Although this has been mentioned by many missiologists, Yoder does not pay much attention to it.[154] Yet, Yoder says: "Alone of all the churches of the Reformation, they [the Anabaptists] insisted that the church is essentially missionary, and that she must be separated from the world, even if that world be Christianized."[155] This, however, never became a central part of his critique of Christendom and, moreover, he never developed a well-thought-out missiology in the traditional sense.[156]

---

150. Yoder, "The Theology of the Church's Mission," 32.
151. Yoder, "A People in the World," 91; italics mine.
152. Yoder, "The Paradigmatic Public Role of God's People," 27.
153. Yoder, *The Politics of Jesus*, 154.
154. Guder, for example, refers to Wilbert Shenk, who has said, "Christendom is Christianity without mission." See Guder, "Walking Worthily," 252. Mennonite theologian Kreider states that the Christendom shift "altered the focus of the church from mission to maintenance." See "Beyond Bosch," 66.
155. Yoder, *The Ecumenical Movement and the Faithful Church*, 34.
156. However, in an unpublished and personal letter to Theron Slabaugh December 10, 1973, Yoder writes, "The Anabaptists arose in the midst of the Christendom situation. They said that that situation was wrong and should not exist, and reacted as if it were not in existence. They therefore assumed that the total population of Europe,

Following the Way of Christ in the World

3.3.7 Ecclesiology

In conclusion, with Constantine, all citizens were baptized and considered Christians, and the entire social order declared Christian.[157] This led to a severe compromising of the integrity of the church as a distinct community of faith. In various ways, the exposition above has shown how the understanding of the church, being a distinct social entity, is an integrative part of Yoder's ecclesiology. As we have seen, Yoder clearly narrates the story of Israel from a diasporic and even exilic point of view.[158] Thus, he argues that the normal existence for the church is existence in diaspora and exile, and that the notion of exile preconfigured the Christian understanding of the church's existence in the world. Accordingly, the community that Jesus formed was distinct from, and non-accommodating towards, the Roman empire. For Yoder, the church being distinct from its surrounding society is an intrinsic part of Christian obedience for all Christians in every context. Distinctiveness is what identifies the gospel accordingly, and preaching the gospel "is proclaiming precisely the plus, the otherness, the more-ness, the non-conformity of the church as the visibility of a city on a hill. It is the savor of the salt"[159] and, thus, the church must be restored "to that posture in the world which is in accord with her message."[160] He believes that God's chosen people are called to be "a distinct community with its own deviant set of values and its coherent way of incarnating them. Today it might be called an underground movement, or a political party, or an infiltration team, or a cell movement. The sociologist would call it an intentional community."[161] God has called a community into existence who must serve instead of rule, suffer instead of inflicting suffering, and cross social lines instead of reinforcing them.[162] There cannot be any distinction between presence and witness. The church does not have a mission, but by being the church the church *is* mission.[163]

---

which had been baptized as Christian, was actually a mission field." See Yoder, "Hoekendijk and Evangelism."

157. Yoder, "The Meaning of the Constantinian Shift," 62.
158. See 3.3.1 above.
159. Yoder, "What Do Ye More than They," 73.
160. Yoder, "Let the Church Be the Church," 115.
161. Yoder, "The Original Revolution," 28.
162. Yoder, "A People in the World," 91.
163. Yoder has, as we have seen, a strong emphasis of the distinctiveness of the

3.4 Social Ethics

3.4.1 The Disassociation of Ethics from Jesus

Yoder exercises a dismissive critique of Constantinianism. If the church is to liberate itself from its Constantinian captivity, it must acquire a new starting point. He believes that Christ must again become a starting point for the understanding of the church's existence in the world. There exist, however, several obstacles that disassociate Christ from social ethics.[164]

In his book, *The Politics of Jesus*, Yoder lists, in short form, several ways mainstream Christian ethics have attempted to separate the immediate connection between the work and words of Jesus, and what it would mean to follow Christ today. In the first edition of the book (1972), Yoder lists six reasons for this dichotomy, and in the second edition of the book (1994), he adds five more.[165]

First, "some theologians have thought of Jesus' ethic as an 'interim ethic,' one that was meant to apply to the very short time period before

---

church. But as is so often said, the church must not only be *not of this world* but must also be *in this world*. Yoder would certainly agree and he also, to some extent, developed an understanding of this. He could, however, profitably have substantiated his understanding of the contextuality of the church. God became flesh and blood. Jesus spoke the language of his fellow humans. He was present in the public space of the villages and towns. He asked his disciples to do the same. Yoder asserts that the cross is normative for Christians, and one could add to this that the incarnation must be normative as well. Unfortunately, his theological tradition did not help him to emphasize the contextuality of the church.

164. Yoder believes that Christian ethics are not knowable apart from Jesus, are not distinguishable from Jesus, and should not differ from his ethical instructions. Yoder clearly bases his social ethics in Christology, rejecting "that the order of nature is itself a vehicle of revelation, parallel or complementary or preliminary to revelation in Christ and Scripture. Yet historical study shows that it has been possible to understand under *order of nature* just about anything a philosopher wanted; stoicism or Epicureanism, creative evolution or political restorationism, Puritan democracy or Aryan dictatorship. We shall do well to avoid thinking of the order of nature as a source of any revelation. Yet at the same time we must recognize that there exists also in the unredeemed world an order, a relation to Him who ordains, and who is none other than our Redeemer." See Yoder, *The Christian Witness to the State*, 33; italics original. Yoder has no intentions of rejecting "the foundation of human society within the creative intention of God," but the order of creation cannot explain, for example, why and how the sword can be necessary as "the calculated measuring out of evil." See ibid., 34. Later, I will return to his understanding of this order in the unredeemed world. See 3.5.3 below. Unfortunately, Yoder never presented a major, systematic treatment of his rejection of "general revelation."

165. Below, I only refer to the second edition of *The Politics of Jesus* (1994).

the passing away of this world."¹⁶⁶ When social ethics must deal with problems of duration, Jesus can be of no help. Second, some have pointed out that Jesus was a rural figure whose ethic can only be applied to a small village. Jesus spoke about "sparrows and the lilies to fishermen and peasants, lepers and outcasts."¹⁶⁷ There is in the ethic of Jesus "no intention to speak substantially to the problems of complex organizations, of institutions and offices."¹⁶⁸ Third, some say that "Jesus and his early followers lived in a world over which they had no control,"¹⁶⁹ therefore, the ethics of Jesus cannot be applied to "the very different situation which prevailed after Constantine."¹⁷⁰ Today, Christians "must accept responsibilities that were inconceivable in Jesus' situation."¹⁷¹ Fourth, the message of Jesus is ahistorical, dealing with spiritual, not social matters. What Jesus proclaimed "was not social change, but a new self-understanding."¹⁷² Fifth, Jesus was a radical monotheist who pointed people away from finite values and "proclaimed the sovereignty of the only One worthy of being worshiped (. . .). The will of God cannot be identified with any one ethical answer, or any given human value, since these are all finite."¹⁷³ Sixth, some argue that Jesus came to give his life for the sins of the world. The kind of life Jesus led is, therefore, irrelevant.

Seventh, in the second edition of the book, *The Politics of Jesus*, Yoder adds that a historical skepticism contends that we cannot know whether "the text says anything clear enough to guide us in the moral life, assuming that we would want to follow Jesus."¹⁷⁴ Eighth, there are some who question whether the texts represent any sort of consistency. Ninth, some argue for wisdom, in favor of moral insights less tied to time and place. Tenth, there is the argument that "[o]ne should not make Jesus too important for ethics," since God would call for a different, perhaps more institutionally conservative, social ethic.¹⁷⁵ Eleventh, some argue

---

166. Carter, *The Politics of the Cross*, 142; see also Yoder, "If Christ Is Truly Lord," 63.

167. Yoder, *The Politics of Jesus*, 6.

168. Ibid.

169. Ibid.

170. Carter, *The Politics of the Cross*, 142.

171. Yoder, *The Politics of Jesus*, 6.

172. Ibid., 6.

173. Ibid., 7.

174. Ibid., 15.

175. Ibid., 17.

that Jesus did not come to teach a way of life. He came as savior, "and for us to need a Savior presupposes that we do not live according to his stated ideals."[176] Therefore, the purpose of the law is entirely negative. Yoder believes that all these arguments bypass the authority of Jesus. We shall now see how Yoder demonstrates how Jesus again must become a guiding norm for Christian social ethics.[177]

3.4.2 Christology and Social Ethics

When one examines how Yoder uses Christology as a resource for Christian ethics, it quickly becomes clear that Christology for Yoder is not an abstract dogma alienated from history. In the theology of Yoder, Christology is first and foremost connected to the historical Jesus.[178] This is not entirely clear when examining Yoder's eschatology but, on the contrary, it is very clear when we look at his ethical considerations. LeMasters regards Yoder's down-to-earth approach to Christology as a strength: "Yoder's approach is advantageous because it seeks to hold Christological construction accountable to New Testament portrayals of Jesus Christ; and, hence, tends to resist the temptation to interpret Jesus 'in our own image.'"[179] Paul Ramsey has, however, criticized Yoder's Christology for being Jesucentric, without sufficient awareness of variable Christological themes.[180] I do not, however, believe that Ramsay does justice to Yoder. When it comes to social ethics, the historical Jesus plays a central role for Yoder.[181] The historical Jesus is so central for Yoder's social ethics because he models the true way of living in the world: Jesus models an example which Christians are called to follow. However, Yoder's voluminous book, *Preface to Theology*, clearly shows how he also dealt extensively

---

176. Ibid., 18.

177. This paragraph is founded on ibid., 1–20. Carter has a similar presentation of this in his book *The Politics of the Cross*, 140–44.

178. Therefore, Yoder appreciates critical efforts that can portray the life of Jesus with historical accuracy. See LeMasters, *The Import of Eschatology*, 63–64. Doerksen characterizes his Christology as Jesuology. See Doerksen, *Beyond Suspicion*, 69–70, 72, 83–84, 91–93, 126–27. Yoder also states that Christology in fact should be Jesuology. See Yoder, "Discerning the Kingdom of," 369.

179. LeMasters, *The Import of Eschatology*, 64.

180. Ramsey, *Speak up for Just War or Pacifism*, 111–13.

181. In the book *The Politics of Jesus*, he draws especially on the Gospel of Luke to describe the life and ministry of Jesus.

with Christology in many other ways. Here Yoder deals with Christology in the Gospels, in the writings of Paul and the author of Hebrews and John, and with the Christology of the Apostles' Creed, and the Councils of Nicea and Chalcedon. He also deals with such central concepts in the New Testament as Son of Man, Servant, Teacher, Prophet, Jesus, Messiah, Christ, Son of God, Lord, and at the end of the book he presents a major systematic treatment of three important Christological themes, Christ as King, Priest and Prophet. Still, we may say that his Christology is indeed Jesucentric, but that is not to say that he did not take variable Christological themes into account.[182] And as I will show later, Christ as exalted by the Father's right hand, the cosmic Christ, plays a central role in Yoder's eschatology.[183] His main concern is to oppose a certain type of Christology which is made abstract or metaphysical.[184]

All of this is to say that for Yoder, Christology must pay attention to the earthly life of Jesus, who participated in localizable history and brought about a new social order for the people of God. Here, we find important sources for a Christian social ethic. Yoder believes that Jesus' life is relevant for Christian social ethics, and that discipleship is a call to all Christians. Following Jesus is the basic task of the moral life, and thus, Yoder views the story of Jesus as a paradigmatic example for how Christians are to exist in the world. Yoder insists that his understanding "is founded in Scripture and catholic tradition, and is pertinent today as a call for all Christian believers."[185]

3.4.3 The Politics of Jesus

Referring to Yoder's book *The Politics of Jesus*, Arne Rasmusson states that "Yoder took issue with the common idea that Jesus and his message are socially and politically irrelevant. One of several lines of arguments for this irrelevancy is that because Jesus did not provide any social ethic the early church had to borrow such ethics from other sources."[186] He continues

---

182. Admittedly, Yoder's book *Preface to Theology* was published after Ramsey wrote his dissertation.

183. See 3.5 below.

184. Yoder, "The Prophetical Task of Pastoral Ministry," 75; Yoder, "'But We Do See Jesus'", 57–58; Shin, "Two Models of Social Transformation," 34–35.

185. Yoder, "Introduction," 8; Cf. LeMasters, *The Import of Eschatology*, 8.

186. Rasmusson, "Revolutionary Subordination," 37.

to say, "Yoder does not deny that the church, in the case as often in other contexts, uses many different sources, but he denies that this demonstrates Jesus' social irrelevance."[187] In positive terms, Yoder believes that Jesus' life is an important source for Christian social ethics. He argues that the gospel Jesus proclaimed was expressed in terms borrowed from politics, and involved definite consequences for the social order.[188]

The essence of the life of Jesus is that he embodied and sustained obedience to God. Consequently, Christians should embody and sustain obedience in accordance with his example. As Yoder asserts, "the sinlessness of Christ is not (as for Anselm) a purely legal formality or, as some understand the OT sacrifices, a matter merely of ritual cleanness; His sinlessness is rather the whole point of His life and His obedience-offering. His sinlessness, His obedience, is what He offered God, and that sinlessness, utter faithfulness to love, cost His life in a world of sinners."[189] Moreover, he adds that, "the work of Christ is, at its center, obedience (Phil. 2 et al). Christ was exactly what God meant man to be; man in free communion with God, obeying God and loving mankind, even his enemies with God's love."[190]

Thus, Jesus did not first and foremost come with new information. The cross, for example, was not a new revelation: The Old Testament foresaw the path the Servant of Yahweh would have to follow; "[n]or was the resurrection essentially new; God's victory over evil had been affirmed, by definition one might say, from the beginning;"[191] the selection of a faithful remnant was also no new idea.[192] What Jesus revealed in his life and words was the original and ultimate intention for humankind expressed at creation.[193] Yoder refers to the Gospel of John to give reason for this. When it is said in the prologue, "there was nothing of what came to be that did not come to be through him," he believes that John is repeating the Genesis report. What is revealed with Christ is therefore precisely the same that underlies creation. Hence, Yoder states, "God has not revealed himself otherwise. He has not revealed a different purpose or character

---

187. Ibid.

188. Yoder, "If Christ Is Truly Lord," 55. For example, he states that the term "kingdom" is a political term.

189. Quoted in LeMasters, *The Import of Eschatology*, 59-60.

190. Ibid., 59.

191. Yoder, "If Christ Is Truly Lord," 57.

192. Ibid., 57–58.

193. Carter, *The Politics of the Cross*, 162.

through creation than what we now encounter through Jesus."[194] The new that Jesus brought forth was that he *embodied* obedience to God and *incarnated* God's way in the world.[195]

For Yoder, there exists a fundamental ethical connection between Christ and the church. Christ determines the life which the church is meant to embody in the world, and Yoder believes, thus, that Christ instructed his disciples in a special way of living life. Yoder gives many concrete examples of this:

> He gave them a new way to deal with offenders—by forgiving them. He gave them a new way to deal with violence—by suffering. He gave them a new way to deal with money—by sharing it. He gave them a new way to deal with problems of leadership—by drawing upon the gift of every member, even the most humble. He gave them a new way to deal with a corrupt society—by building a new order, not smashing the old. He gave them a new pattern of relationships between man and woman, between parent and child, between master and slave, in which was made concrete a radical new vision of what it means to be a human person.[196]

Yet, Christians should not resemble Jesus in every way. For example, Yoder states that Jesus did not oblige his disciples to live celibately or to dress like he did.[197] Still, Christians must follow the instructions Jesus gave. This will lead to an alternative way of living. Yoder believes that the church is "a visible body comprised of believers who join voluntarily to pursue together discipleship in a manner distinct from the ways of the larger society."[198] However, one may ask: How does the hospitality of the church stand out from the hospitality expressed by its surrounding society? Or, how does Christian generosity stand out from the generosity expressed in society? To this, Yoder says that the church is not always different or in every way different. Often, others will act in the same way

---

194. Yoder, *He Came Preaching Peace*, 82.

195. Yoder, "Jesus' Life-Style Sermon and Prayer," 89.

196. Yoder, "The Original Revolution," 29.

197. Yoder, "The Contemporary Evangelical Revival and the Peace Churches," 103.

198. LeMasters, *The Import of Eschatology*, 73. It seems obvious that Yoder has a point when he says that Christians must live a different way of life. Jesus travelled around to villages and preached that people should convert and let their lives have new meaning. See Matt 11:21–23; 22:1–8; Luke 13:3–5; cf. Højlund, *Men han gav afkald*, 200, 204.

because it is normal, humane or democratic.[199] Thus, he says: "It might be that what is different about being Christian in some cases is not what we do or whether we do it, but only why we do it, how hard we try, or how long we stick with it without success."[200]

Still, Yoder's argument implies that the Christian community in its totality constitutes a common ethical commitment different from the wider society. Hence, the motivation for hospitality is different for Christians than for the rest of society. As Christ laid down his life for the world, so Christians must lay down their lives for the world. In this way, the church embodies a mode of ethical reasoning which is fundamentally different from that of the surrounding society.

Yoder believes that one of the important distinctive practices of the Christian community by which it is often set apart from society is its pacifism. I will turn to this later.[201] First, however, we need to look at what Yoder calls "revolutionary subordination," and then we shall see how Yoder believes that suffering is an intrinsic part of the life of disciples of Jesus.

3.4.4 Revolutionary Subordination

In the Epistles, we find a number of texts that can be designated as the *Haustafeln* or the so-called household codes (Col. 3:18–4:1; Eph. 5:21–6:9; 1 Pet. 2:13–3:7). These texts express that children should obey their parents, wives should be subject to their husbands, husbands should love their wives, servants should be submissive to their masters, etc. Yoder notices that we find very similar thoughts and expressions in different literary contexts in the New Testament. This leads him to state that there must have been some kind of pattern in the moral teaching of the early churches.[202] Thus, Yoder believes that these texts express a common ethical instruction "that calls for a willing subordination to one's fellow person."[203] He states that this subordination means "acceptance of an *order*, as it exists, but with the new meaning given to it by the fact

---

199. Yoder, "The Believers' Church and the Arms Race," 156.
200. Ibid.
201. See 3.4.6 below.
202. Yoder, *The Politics of Jesus*, 163–64.
203. Shin, "Two Models of Social Transformation," 68.

that one's acceptance of it is willing and meaningfully motivated."[204] This subordination is mutual and reciprocal, and thus, both the person in the subordinate position and person in the superordinate position must be submissive to each other. Children, women, and slaves must subordinate, while parents, husbands and masters must conform to patterns of servanthood. Furthermore, Christians are to subordinate themselves to the local authorities (cf. 1 Pet 2:13–3:7). Hence, subordination not only has reference to the congregation but also to the order of this world. Therefore, Paul says to the Christians in Rome that they must subordinate themselves to the authorities (cf. Rom 13:1–7). In this relationship, Christians can, however, not expect mutual subordination. Yet, Christians must accept the obligation of subordination.

Yoder denies that Peter and Paul simply borrowed the tradition of subordination unaltered from Hellenistic or Jewish sources. Furthermore, he believes it is unlikely that one of them should have borrowed it from the other. He argues that the tradition is rooted in the teaching and practice of Jesus himself.[205] Hence, Yoder recognizes this pattern of moral teaching in the early churches, in the ministry of Jesus as he subordinated himself to the local authorities. Even when Jesus was confronted with death on the cross, he did not deviate from exercising revolutionary subordination. Following his example of accepting subordination, Christians should "not do this because the new world or the new regime under which we live is not a simple alternative to present experience but rather a renewed way of living within the present (1 Cor. 7:20; John 17:15–16)."[206] Thus, the old order is not violently replaced by the new. Because Christ has freed Christians, they live according to the new order and therefore they can freely accept subordinating themselves to the structures of the present, which are passing away (cf. 1 Cor 7:31).[207] Yoder designates this as revolutionary subordination because he believes that it has a revolutionary impact on personal relationships and worldly structures. This willing, reciprocal subordination is an ecclesial way of life, which will have a "missionary impact" on the structures of the world.[208]

---

204. Yoder, *The Politics of Jesus*, 172; italics original.
205. Ibid., 168–79, 185–86.
206. Ibid., 185.
207. Ibid., 186.
208. Ibid., 185.

Rasmusson regards Yoder's chapter on revolutionary subordination as the most controversial chapter in the book, *The Politics of Jesus*. He believes "that most Christian political, social and moral thought assumes explicitly or implicitly a perspective from above, from sovereignty, from a position of control," and says later that "Yoder's language of revolutionary subordination does not assume this situation of power and control, and that is part of what makes it provocative."[209] According to Yoder, it is foreign to the authors of the New Testament to suggest that Christians should obtain power, or strive to become a part of the ruling elite, in order to set things right and create justice. The authors of the New Testament are concerned with what to do in a situation without power.[210]

3.4.5 Suffering Like Jesus

Jesus said that those who would follow him must deny themselves and take up their cross. What, then, does it mean for Christians to "bear a cross"? For Yoder, as Earl Zimmerman remarks, discipleship is about "being fully present in the world in the same way that Jesus was. Such presence means being willing to experience the same kind of persecution and suffering that Jesus experienced."[211] This is a central aspect of his portrait of the life of a disciple. Yoder states that Jesus suffered death on the cross because he was faithful to God in a world that is in rebellion against God. In the same way, Christians must be faithful to God in a rebellious world. This implies that as Christ suffered, Christians must be willing to suffer and must sometimes even be willing to suffer death. Jesus foresaw this and warned his disciples. Thus, Yoder says: "The cross of the Christian is no different. It is the price of one's obedience to God's love toward all people in a world ruled by hate. Such unflinching love for friend and foe alike will mean hostility and suffering for us, as it did for him."[212]

Yoder believes that Christ, in many ways, informed his disciples about what kind of life they were supposed to live. Even so, Yoder several times says that the cross, more than anything else, is what Christians must imitate. Robert M. Parham criticizes this, as he believes that Yoder's

---

209. Rasmusson, "Revolutionary Subordination," 38, 40.
210. Ibid., 40.
211. Zimmerman, *Practicing the Politics of Jesus*, 142.
212. Yoder, *He Came Preaching Peace*, 19.

thoughts lack consistency.[213] On the one hand, Yoder believes that Christ embodied God's way of life in the world and introduced his disciples to various aspects of this way of life. On the other hand, Yoder states that the cross *alone* shows the way for Christ's followers. While Parham rightly points out this inconsistency in the theology of Yoder, I do agree with Yoder that for both Paul and Jesus, suffering is an important mark of the life of the church in the world.[214] In my mind, this also points out the failure of Christendom. If all are baptized, if the whole society is declared Christian, what kind of suffering must the church then experience? The suffering that Paul and Jesus are imagining is, clearly, not just suffering bound to human life in general. The suffering they talk about is clearly bound to life as *disciples*.

3.4.6 Jesus Was a Pacifist

When Christians experience suffering and persecution, they ought not to answer back with violence. Yoder argues unequivocally that Jesus was a pacifist and that Christians should also be pacifists. Thus, the church should be *a space for peace* in the world.[215] Before turning to this, however, I first turn to a basic problem for Christians who are committed to pacifism out of loyalty to Jesus Christ. That is, as Yoder suggests, the holy wars in the Old Testament.[216]

Reading the Old Testament, we see that violence seems not only to be tolerated, but even fostered and glorified. We read of the holy warfare of the age of Moses, Joshua and the judges; of "[t]he civil legislation of the Pentateuch, with its provision for the death penalty;" and of the imprecatory Psalms; and the prophetic visions, which rejoice at the prospect of the destruction of the enemies of Israel.[217] Hence, Christian pacifists are obliged to explain why wars in the Old Testament seem to be tolerated. In

---

213. Parham, "Ethical Analysis of the Christian Social Strategies," 197.

214. Paul believes that there exists an irresolvable unity between Christians and Christ. Christians are one with and have been united with Christ (Rom 6:5). Christians share their destiny with Christ. Christians share the suffering of Christ (Rom 8:17; 2 Cor 1:5; Phil 3:10). Paul even says that Christians must fill up what is still lacking in regard to the suffering of Christ (Col 1:24).

215. Cf. the title of Hauerwas and Sherwindt's article "The Kingdom of God: An Ecclesial Space for Peace."

216. Yoder, "If Abraham Is Our Father," 85.

217. Ibid., 85–86.

the book, *The Original Revolution*, Yoder lists five major models to explain this apparent contradiction between the Old and New Testaments.

The first explanation states that Jesus announced, "the beginning of a new era or dispensation which purely and simply sets aside what went before."[218] Thus, the Jews had learned much from their forefathers, but now Jesus brought them a new message (cf. Matt 5–7). In this way, Jesus instituted a new dispensation in history. Yoder, however, cannot subscribe to this interpretation. He believes that Jesus in the Sermon on the Mount does not bypass the Old Testament, as the texts Jesus bypasses are not citations from, but rather misinterpretations of the Old Testament. Hence, Jesus is not setting aside what was before. He came to *fulfill* the Israelite faith and Jewish hope.

The second explanation makes a comparison between war and divorce. It states that neither divorce nor war was allowed or intended from the beginning, but because of the hard hearts of men it is now allowed (cf. Matt 19:3–12). As Yoder says: "Now that Jesus has restored the wholeness of the knowledge of God's creative purposes, or the possibility of obeying Him, the concession to men's hard hearts or closed minds is withdrawn."[219] In opposition to this, Yoder objects that wars in the Old Testament were not allowed by God as divorce was, by concession, but were in fact ordered by God, since "[d]ivorce is never commanded in the Old Testament; it is only grudgingly permitted, and that in a context whose main intent is to restrain it and to protect the dignity of woman. Thus even this legislation in its very words supports the theme of 'concession.' This *cannot* be said about a holy war."[220] Therefore, Yoder believes that this argumentation is alien to the message of the Bible.

The third model explains the apparently contradictory views on war in the Old and New Testament as an expression of a pedagogical concession. It states: "Perhaps insight into the destructiveness of violence and the redemptiveness of love is a very refined kind of cultural understanding accessible only to cultures with a certain degree of advancement. It would have been too much to ask for the rough and illiterate tribesmen of the age of Moses and Joshua."[221] This can be compared with "the difference between a parent's commanding a child not to touch matches

---

218. Ibid., 86.
219. Ibid., 89.
220. Ibid., 90; italics original.
221. Ibid., 90–91.

or electric plugs at the age of two and his instructing the child to use matches or an electric plug a few years later."²²² Yoder is hesitant with this explanation because, in this way, one looks down on "the ancient Israelites with a sense of moral superiority," which he believes can hardly be justified.²²³

The fourth explanation emphasizes the fundamentally different contexts in which the Old and New Testament were written. The Old Testament is dealing with commands and permissions to the civil order of the Hebrew people. In this context, commands and permission to use violence to defend the civil order against enemies from outside were given. But the New Testament prescribes no standard for civil order. Thus, nonviolence is the only imperative for the Christian individual and the church. Yoder acknowledges that this explanation has many advantages, but criticizes it, nevertheless, for bypassing the problem rather than solving it. Still, his own explanation, as we shall now see, lies in continuation of this model.

The fifth model is Yoder's own constructive proposal. He suggests that it is important to uncover the concrete historical and anthropological meaning of the holy wars in the Old Testament. He exemplifies this with the story about Abraham, who is told to kill his own son (cf. Gen 22:1–19). Yoder, however, claims that the story has been "systematically misinterpreted in Western ethical thought."²²⁴ The crucial question for Abraham is not how God can make such a repulsive request as killing his son, but how God can ask him to sacrifice his *only* son, when he had promised him great posterity. Yoder argues that, in Abraham's culture, it was not immoral or culturally repulsive to sacrifice one's firstborn son. On the contrary, it was quite normal.²²⁵ The sacrifice of the firstborn son was, however, as insane as it may sound, a sacrifice to God. In the same way, Yoder suggests that Israel's holy wars can be understood as a sacrificial act.

As an example of this, Yoder mentions that "before being attacked, a Canaanite city would be" devoted to Yahweh and, through a ceremony, the whole city would be made a sacrifice to Yahweh.²²⁶ The holy wars

---

222. Ibid., 91.
223. Ibid.
224. Ibid., 94.
225. For further explanation, see ibid., 95.
226. Ibid., 98.

were not a result of strategic planning or preparedness, but they were *ad hoc* charismatic events. Often, the Old Testament emphasizes the pathetic way Israel was involved in war: "Sometimes, especially as in the parade around Jericho and the wars of Gideon, special symbolic measures are taken to dramatize the nonrational, nonprofessional, miraculous character of the entire sacramental battle."[227] When Israel was victorious, it was not because the enemy was hated, but because "Yahweh gave the enemy into their hands."[228] In the chapter, "God Will Fight for Us" of *The Politics of Jesus*, Yoder lists several examples of how God gave Israel victory and how their salvation came from Yahweh.[229] When the enemy was put to death by Israel, the enemy became a ritual human sacrifice. The holy wars were a sign of how they should build their identity not on trusting their own readiness, but on trusting in Yahweh as their king and provider.[230] Because Yahweh was their king and provider, it was unnecessary to have an earthly king like the neighboring nations.[231] The Lord himself brought about the victory. Therefore, when Israel got a king, the holy wars came to an end.

When Jesus began his ministry, the perception of God's chosen people was restructured. This is important for Yoder's argument:

> The identification of the people of Israel with the state of Israel was progressively loosened by all of the events and prophecies of the Old Testament. It was loosened in a positive way by the development of an increasing vision for the concern of Yahweh for *all* people (. . .); it was loosened as well in a negative direction by the development of a concept of the faithful remnant, no longer assuming that Israel as a geographical and ethnic body would be usable for Jahweh's purposes. These two changes in turn altered the relevance of the prohibition of killing.[232]

The new people that Jesus inaugurated should, as Israel was instructed, trust Yahweh as the one who gives victory. The new people should not rely on their own strength or power, but trust Yahweh as their deliberator.[233]

227. Ibid., 99.
228. Ibid.
229. Yoder, *The Politics of Jesus*, 76–92.
230. Yoder, "If Abraham Is Our Father," 99.
231. See also 3.3.1 above.
232. Yoder, "If Abraham Is Our Father," 101; italics original.
233. Yoder, *The Politics of Jesus*, 83–84. One could add that when Jesus rides into Jerusalem on a donkey, it can supposedly show how he trusted Yahweh and not his

On the background of this, I now turn to show how Yoder argues that Jesus was a Jewish pacifist.

As we have seen, Yoder emphasizes that early Christianity and Judaism overlapped for generations.[234] According to the Sermon on the Mount, Jesus did not come to abolish the law or the prophets, but his call was for a greater righteousness than that of other teachers. The intent of the Torah is thus broadened or intensified, not negated. This leads Yoder to state that "Jesus did not reject anything Jewish in calling for love of the enemy."[235] He says: "There must then be, in the mind of Jesus of Matthew, an original intent which we can discern as having been within the Torah itself, which points toward the renunciation of violence and the love of the enemy."[236] Hence, Yoder argues that we find rich sources of what we today would call pacifism in Talmudic Judaism. As he explains,

> Not only did Judaism as defined since Jeremiah forsake their visions of kingship and sovereignty for the historical present under his prophetic guidance, they also forsook violence. The rabbinic corpus is by its nature complex and contradictory. Some passages reject violence completely, even in self-defense; others retain the memory of a judicial system qualified to punish people and of limited wars, since such wars were recorded in ancient histories. But the guidance given by the rabbis for the moral life of the ongoing Jewish community calls for a fundamentally non-violent style of life, even under persecution, on grounds not of strategy or weakness but because that is now seen to be the will of God.[237]

In this way, Yoder is not first and foremost interested in whether what Jesus meant is credible to modern westerners, but whether the proclamation of

---

own power. As God gave victory to the small and weak people of Israel in the Old Testament, God gave victory to a weak Jesus in the New Testament. Yoder, however, denies that Jesus' alternative social strategy is a strategy of weakness. It is a strategy of strength. Hence, following Christ is a way of participating in the *victory* of redemption. See Yoder, "A Theological Critique of Violence," 39–41. Moreover, Yoder believes that this fifth explanation to a greater extent than the fourth model affirms the unity between the Old Testament and the New Testament, which he believes is important for the genuinely historical nature of biblical faith.

234. See 3.3.1 above.
235. Yoder, "Jesus the Jewish Pacifist," 70.
236. Ibid.
237. Yoder, "From the Wars of Joshua to Jewish Pacifism," 81–82.

Jesus was intrinsically credible to his *listeners*.[238] Here, Yoder argues that Jesus did not reject anything Jewish in his renunciation of violence and the love of the enemy.[239]

Yoder believes that throughout the ministry of Jesus, "from the temptation in the desert to the last minute in Gethsemane, political means were offered Him from all sides as short cuts to the accomplishment of His purposes, and He refused to use them."[240] In support of this, Cullmann claims that at least five of Jesus' disciples were Zealots and states that Jesus continually had to come "to terms with the challenge of the Zealot question throughout his ministry."[241] Stemming from this, Yoder concludes,

> This Zealot option represented a real possibility, in fact, a real temptation for Jesus. It was this possibility to which He was particularly drawn in His debate with the tempter in the desert at His baptism, and again at His last trial in Gethsemane. More of His disciples came from the Zealot group than from any other part of Palestinian society, and their expectations were clearly along this line.[242]

---

238. Ibid., 78.

239. Through the centuries, Jewish pacifism has been strengthened. Yoder sums up five ways of explaining this stance: (1) Blood is sacred. Blood is life and belongs to God. (2) The Messiah has not yet come. If anyone could have a right to restore the patterns of divine vengeance, which alone could justify the shedding of blood, it would be the Messiah. (3) Jewish thought is marked by a concern for properly learning the lessons of the Zealot experience. (4) The wisdom with which God presides over the affairs of the *goyim* (the Gentile peoples) is not revealed to Jews in any simple way. As Jews we do know that God does rule over the whole universe, and therefore over all the nations. But the *way* this rule over the nations is exercised is not the same as the way he rules over us through the revealed Torah. (5) Suffering has a place in the divine economy. Why the faithful must suffer is a mystery not yet clear in the Jewish understanding of history. See ibid., 82–83; see also Yoder, "The Nonviolence of Rabbinic Judaism," 141–42. I have here quoted the headings of five paragraphs in Yoder's summary of Jewish pacifism and added an explanation of *goyim* in a parenthesis. In the article, *Jesus the Jewish Pacifist*, Yoder also mentions these five explanations, but here he adds two further reasons, namely, that "the rabbis consistently downplay the wars of the age of Moses, Joshua and the Judges" and "the survival of Israel is promised by God." See Yoder, "Jesus the Jewish Pacifist," 83–84.

240. Yoder, "If Christ Is Truly Lord," 55.

241. Zimmerman, *Practicing the Politics of Jesus*, 123; see also n244 below. For more on how Cullmann influenced Yoder, see 3.1 above.

242. Yoder, "If Christ Is Truly Lord," 22.

Therefore, when Jesus refrained from violent revolution, it was not because it changed too much, but rather that it changed too little. An order created by the sword was, at the heart, not the sort of new community that Jesus had in mind.[243] Jesus could have used violence to bring his kingdom forth by force. But he did not.[244]

In the book, *He Came Preaching Peace*, Yoder argues that following Christ implies that Christians will suffer as Christ suffered. He points out that the authors of the New Testament saw Jesus' suffering on the cross not only as a *sacrifice*, but also as an *example* for Christians:

> Following the example of Jesus himself, the first Christians and the writers of the New Testament were quick to see in the book of the prophet Isaiah a description of the innocent sufferings of Christ. They read there: 'He was counted among evildoers / For our welfare he was chastised / Mistreated, he bore it humbly, without complaint, / silent as a sheep led to the slaughter, / silent as a ewe before the shearers / They did away with him unjustly / though he was guilty of no violence / and had not spoken one false word' (Isa. 53:4-9) (. . .). Yet when we find these same words echoing in the New Testament, it is not only because they are fitting or beautiful words to describe Christ and his sacrifice on behalf of sinful humanity; it is because they constitute a call to the Christian to do likewise. There we read: 'If you have done right and suffer for it / your endurance is worthwhile in the sight of God; / To this you were called, / because Christ suffered on your behalf, / and left you an *example*; / it is for you to follow in

---

243. Ibid., 23-24.

244. Violent revolution was not the only option for Jesus. Yoder believes that Jesus had several options for reacting to the surrounding society. The first option Yoder calls "realism." The Sadducees represent this. The Sadducees were intelligent leaders, who, to a certain degree, had resigned to the rule of the Romans. They tried to make the best of the situation within the realistic opportunities that existed. The second option Yoder calls "violent revolution." The Zealots represented this option. I have already referred to this option. The third option was to escape to the desert. This opportunity was represented by the Qumran society. They withdrew from the tension and conflicts of society and escaped to the desert where they could be pure and perfectly faithful. The fourth option Yoder calls "proper religion." The Pharisees represented this option. They tried to keep themselves clean in the city by keeping rules of segregation. They tried to separate religious concerns from the concerns of the society, and in this way they avoided interfering with the realities of power, politics, and economics. Jesus rejected all these options. Instead, he created a new people, which offered a new way of life by imitating his way of life. This new social order is "the original revolution." See Yoder, "The Original Revolution," 18-33.

his steps, / He committed no sin, / he was guilty of no falsehood; when he suffered he uttered no threats' (1 Peter 2:20–22).[245]

Thus, Christians must be willing to experience the same kind of persecution and suffering that Jesus experienced.[246] But even more, Christians should, as Christ did, refrain from answering violence with violence.[247] Christians must defeat evil by resisting the temptation to meet evil on its own terms: This is "God's method of overcoming evil with good."[248] Jesus foresaw clearly the costly suffering this would mean for himself and his followers.[249] But, as Yoder points out, this is precisely the way Paul believes we see what love is. As Christ laid down his life for the world, Christians should lay down their lives for the world. This leads to a critique of Constantinianism:

> [I]f *kenosis* is the shape of God's own self-sending, then any strategy of Lordship, like that of the kings of this world, is not only a strategic mistake likely to backfire but a denial of gospel substance (. . .). What the churches accepted in the Constantinian shift is what Jesus had rejected, seizing godlikeness, moving *in hoc signo* from Golgatha to the battlefield. If this diagnosis is correct, then the cure is not to update the fourth-century mistake by adding another 'neo-' but repent of the whole 'where it's at' style and to begin again with *kenosis*.[250]

Furthermore, Yoder claims that the pre-Constantinian Christians were pacifists, "rejecting the violence of army and empire not only because they had no share of power, but because they considered it morally wrong."[251] For example, Yoder refers to Tertullian, Origen and Cyprian who were all pacifists.[252] After Constantine, Christians regretfully "con-

---

245. Yoder, *He Came Preaching Peace*, 17; italics mine.

246. For an exposition of this, see 3.4.5 above.

247. Yoder's understanding is similar to that of Cullmann, even though Cullmann believes, based on Luke 22:35-38, that Christians may use the sword in self-defense.

248. Yoder, *He Came Preaching Peace*, 19; Yoder, "If Christ Is Truly Lord," 63.

249. Yoder, *He Came Preaching Peace*, 19.

250. Yoder, "The Constantinian Sources of Western Social Ethics," 145; italics original.

251. Ibid., 135. I have already shown how Yoder often is too categorical when he refers to the pre-Constantinian Christians. See 3.2.1 above.

252. Yoder, "The Pacifism of Pre-Constantinian Christianity," 49. Here Yoder also discusses the role of idolatry in the pacifism in Christian thought in the first two centuries; see 43-49. Yoder, however, never presented any major detailed study of the

sidered imperial violence not only to be morally tolerable but a positive good and a Christian duty."[253]

As we have seen, Yoder argues that the church should be a space for peace in the world. This distinguishes the Christian way of life from the world's way of life. The world will always be characterized by violence and war. Arguing for this, Yoder refers to Jesus, who says that there will be wars until the day that he returns (cf. Matt 24:3–14). God, however, limits the evil in the world:

> It would be perfectly natural if human violence and selfishness destroyed human society. Humans are so constituted, and their sinfulness stands in such stark conflict with the ground of their own existence that humanity could very quickly destroy itself. And yet, what one would expect to happen to sinful humanity does not happen, for God has mandated that the state uphold a measure or order (. . .). However, humanity has fallen away from God, God permits human evil to keep itself under control by using evil against itself.[254]

Argumentation for nonresistant pacifism obtains much space in Yoder's writings. He repudiates all the classical objections against Christian pacifism, and states that "[a]ny attempt to draw from Scripture an approval of war in principle, on the basis of what John the Baptist said to soldiers, what Jesus said before Gethsemane, what Samuel said to Saul, or of Jesus' use of a whip when He cleansed the temple, is condemned to failure."[255] While I have not been able to cover Yoder's position in full, I have attempted to sketch the major lines of his argument. Yoder also showed much interest in the dialogue between the just war tradition and the pacifist tradition,[256] but this I have chosen to leave out of consideration. As Rasmusson rightly points out, "Yoder was a pacifist, but he represents a specific type of pacifism, which he once called the 'pacifism of the messianic community.' He does not think there is one single position

---

pacifism of the early church. For this I refer to Daube, *Civil Disobedience in Antiquity*; Harnack, *Militia Christi*; Hornus, *It Is Not Lawful for me to Fight*; Zampaglione, *The Idea of Peace in Antiquity*.

253. Yoder, "The Constantinian Sources of Western Social Ethics," 135.

254. Yoder, *Discipleship as Political Responsibility*, 18. I will unfold this further in my exposition of Yoder's eschatology. See 3.5.3 below.

255. Yoder, "If Christ Is Truly Lord," 76.

256. To read about this, see, for example, Yoder, *When War Is Unjust*; Yoder, *The War of the Lamb*, chapters 6–9.

that can be called pacifism. There are many, sometimes even substantially, very different sorts of pacifism. He has in one book developed a typology including more than two dozen different types. His own view is (. . .) *messianic* and related to the messianic *community*."[257] As we have seen, his pacifism is rooted in his Christology, and the Christian community makes up the shape of this messianic pacifism.

3.4.7 Social Ethics and Ecclesiology

In conclusion, Constantinianism fused together the church and the world, and this led to the church being filled with people in whom the presuppositions of discipleship and the ethical requirements set by the church were absent. As Christian ethics were applied to the whole society, a distinction between church and society could no longer be maintained. Against this, Yoder argues that the church will oftentimes in one way or another differ from society.[258] Following Christ will lead the church to reemerge as a distinctive community in society. Christology is an important *source* for Yoder's social ethics and, furthermore, it is crucial for Yoder that ecclesiology make up the *shape* of this Christological ethic.[259] He believes that "Christian ethics is for Christians" within the context of the distinct community called "the church," which seeks to embody faithfulness to God.[260] Further, the church is "a visible body comprised of believers who join voluntarily to pursue together discipleship in a manner distinct from the ways of the larger society."[261] Thus, Yoder envisions a visibly communal church as the social locus of Christian morality.[262] As he describes it: "The church is herself a society. Her very existence, the fraternal relations of her members, their ways of dealing with their differences and their needs are, or rather should be, a demonstration of what love means in social relations. This demonstration cannot be transposed directly into non-Christian society, for in the church it functions only on the basis of repentance and faith; yet by analogy certain of its aspects may

---

257. Rasmusson, "Revolutionary Subordination," 49; italics original. The book by Yoder that Rasmusson refers to is *Nevertheless: Varieties of Religious Pacifism*.

258. A good example is found in Yoder, *He Came Preaching Peace*, 27.

259. Cf. Carter, *The Politics of the Cross*, 7.

260. Yoder, "The Otherness of the Church," 62.

261. LeMasters, *The Import of Eschatology*, 73.

262. Ibid., 8. Yoder, *The Christian Witness to the State*, 73.

be instructive as stimuli to the conscience of society."[263] Hence, Christian ethics is for Christians.[264] As Yoder states, "there will therefore be a Christian message addressed to the State; there will not be a Christian ethic for the State."[265] Hauerwas has often stated that the church does not *have* a social ethic but it *is* a social ethic.[266] This also applies to Yoder's understanding of the church.

3.5 Eschatology

3.5.1 The Two Ages

The starting point for Yoder's eschatology is that the New Testament sees the age of the church, from Pentecost to the *Parousia*, as a period of two overlapping aeons; these two aeons are not distinct periods of time, because they exist simultaneously.[267] They differ rather in nature and in direction as the one aeon points backward to human history outside of or before Christ, and as "the other aeon points forward to the fullness of the kingdom of God, of which it is a foretaste."[268] The New Testament's message is that the promise of the awaited age is now fulfilled. The awaited age has now come "into history in a decisive way with the incarnation and the entire work of Christ."[269] Yoder describes the two aeons in this way:

> The present aeon is characterized by sin and centered on man; the coming aeon is the redemptive reality which entered history in an ultimate way in Christ. The present age, by rejecting obedience, has rejected the only possible ground for man's own well-being; the coming age is characterized by God's will being done. The seal of the possibility of His will's being done is the presence of the Holy Spirit, given to the church as a foretaste of the eventual consummation of God's kingdom. Thus, although the new aeon is described as coming, it is not only a future quantity. The old has already begun to be superseded

263. Ibid., 17.
264. Yoder, "The Otherness of the Church," 62.
265. Yoder, "The Pacifism of Karl Barth," 116–17.
266. See, for example, Hauerwas, *Truthfulness and Tragedy*, 142–43; see also Hauerwas, *A Community of Character*, 11.
267. Yoder, "If Christ Is Truly Lord," 55.
268. Ibid.
269. Ibid.

by the new, and the focus of that victory is the body of Christ, first the man Christ Jesus, and then derivatively the fellowship of obedient believers.[270]

These aeons are spiritual orders with concrete and real expressions. Hence, Yoder argues that each aeon has a social manifestation, with the former in the world and the latter in the church.[271]

3.5.2 The Creation of the World

Yoder believes that God created the world with structures, rulers and principalities. He says: "It is the divine purpose that within human existence there should be a network of norms and regularities to stretch out the canvas upon which the tableau of life can be painted."[272] Arguing that these structures are created, he refers to Paul, who says, "for in him were created all things, those in heaven and those on earth, visible and invisible; whether thrones or dominions or principalities or powers; all was created through him and by him. And he is before all things, and things subsist in him" (cf. Col 1:16–17).[273] Yoder believes that all that subsists—the world powers, the reign of order among creatures, the order of the world—is held together by Christ. This order is willed by God, and is meant to facilitate life in the world. Yoder adds that the powers "were part of the good creation of God. Society and history, even nature, would be impossible without regularity, system, order—and God has provided for this need. The universe (. . .) was made in an ordered form and 'it was good.' The creative power worked in a mediated form, by means of the Powers that regularized all visible reality."[274]

3.5.3 The Rebellion Against God

The powers, rulers, and principalities have, however, rebelled against God. Yoder points out that "world" (*aion houtos* in Paul and *kosmos* in John) does not signify the creation or the nature or the universe, but the

---

270. Yoder, *The Christian Witness to the State*, 9.
271. Yoder, "If Christ Is Truly Lord," 55.
272. Yoder, *The Politics of Jesus*, 142.
273. Quoted in ibid., 140; see also Yoder, *He Came Preaching Peace*, 83.
274. Yoder, *The Politics of Jesus*, 141.

fallen structures of the world that no longer conform to the creative intent.[275] This signifies that Yoder does not understand the fall as an ontological change in the nature of creation, but instead that the fall changed the intent of the structures of the world. These structure should have enabled "humanity to live a genuine free, loving life,"[276] but instead these created orders which dislodged them from God, made themselves idols, and bound humans to them in absolute loyalty as if they were absolute value.[277] In this way, they now harm and enslave humans. Yoder refers to several texts in the New Testament, which he believes confirm this:

> They are no longer active only as mediators of the saving creative purpose of God; now we find them seeking to separate us from the love of God (Rom. 8:38); we find them ruling over the lives of those who live far from the love of God (Eph. 2:2); we find them holding us in servitude to their rules (Col. 2:20); we find them holding us under their tutelage (Gal. 4:3). These structures which were supposed to be our servants have become our masters and our guardians.[278]

In describing these rebellious structures, Paul uses various expressions. He uses political categories such as "principalities and powers" and "thrones and dominions." He uses cosmological language such as "angels and archangels" and "heights and depths." He uses religious language such as "law" and "knowledge." At times one senses a correlation between these expressions, but at times not.

Yoder refers to Hendrik Berkhof, who believes that each of these expressions had their own precise and technical meaning to Paul. Yoder chooses to use "power" and "structure" in order to grasp this complexity of language found in the writings of Paul.[279] He believes that the bibli-

---

275. Yoder, "The Otherness of the Church," 55–56; Yoder, *The Christian Witness to the State*, 8–9.

276. Yoder, *The Politics of Jesus*, 143, see also 144–45.

277. Ibid., 142.

278. Ibid., 141.

279. Ibid., 137 fn. 2. Yoder translated Berkhof's book *Christ and the Powers* to English and he is clearly inspired by Berkhof in his understanding of Paul's writings about "the powers and principalities." Berkhof was, like Yoder, inspired by Oscar Cullmann. See, for example, Berkhof, *Christ and the Powers*, 74. However, the view of the powers and principalities in the New Testament concurred upon by Cullmann, Berkhof and Yoder and others is not commonly accepted by researchers but has been debated for years. Also, Yoder is not only inspired by Berkhof in his understanding of the precept of powers and principalities. He refers, for example, to a three volume work by Walter

cal language of powers is equivalent to the modern term "structures, by which psychological and sociological analysts refer to the dimensions of cohesiveness and purposefulness which hold together human affairs beyond the strictly personal level, especially in such realms as that of the state or certain areas of culture."[280] In this way, Yoder describes the old aeon in a very concrete, physical way.

This analysis of powers and principalities is closely tied to the old aeon for Yoder, and he claims that the state is a manifestation of the old aeon.[281] Yoder explains that we do not, in the New Testament, find a systematic or comprehensive doctrine of the state. For example, Jesus did not unfold any substantial ideas about the nature and function of the state. He just seemed to accept that there existed a state or a regime. Yet, Yoder believes that the early Christian communities offered a "New Testament realism about the nature of governmental power."[282]

It is often stated that there exist two fundamentally different understandings of the state in the New Testament. The first view of the state is expressed in Romans 13, where the state is described as an institution approved by God. The other view of the state is expressed in Revelation 13, where the state is described as a diabolic beast. Some use this to contend that the early church had an inconsistent understanding of the state. Yoder denies this. On the contrary, he believes that the early church had a clear and marked view of the state. We see this sporadically expressed in the New Testament. Yoder believes that Romans 13 and Revelation 13 express "two dimensions of the life of any state."[283]

The first dimension of the New Testament's understanding of the state makes clear that the state is derived from, and is a part of, the world, which is in rebellion against God. Therefore, the understanding of the fallen powers and the state cannot be clearly separated. Many modern

---

Wink as an important contribution to the establishment of the thesis that "a solid and consistent world view underlies" these Pauline concepts. See Yoder, "How H. Richard Niebuhr Reasoned," 85.

280. Quoted in Fitz-Gibbon, *In the World, but Not of the World*, 71.

281. Yoder's understanding of the state is in many ways similar to that of Cullmann. Cullmann also describes the state from an eschatological perspective and insists that Christians must recognize both the necessity and the limitations of the state. The state is neither the kingdom of God nor God's chief agent in history, but is has a place "in God's economy of salvation" for the ordering of human existence in between the times of Pentecost and *Parousia*. See Cullmann, *The State in the New Testament*, 87–90.

282. Yoder, "The Christian Case for Democracy," 153.

283. Yoder, *The Christian Witness to the State*, 77.

exegetes find it problematic that the spiritual and the secular powers are hold together like this. Yoder believes, nonetheless, that Paul connects the fallen powers and the state. As an example of this, he refers to Paul, who, in 1 Corinthians 2:8, says that it was the rulers of this age or the powers and principalities that crucified Jesus.[284] The state can never avoid being part of the world, which is in rebellion against God. The state, however, neglects this. This, according to Yoder, is a part of the nature of the state: "The real error of this religious criterion for the apostasy of any state is not the most extreme evil it would identify, but the implication that there can be an exercise of violent dominion which is *not* intrinsically self-glorifying, that there can be a nationalism which is *not* idolatry or a total war which is *not* intrinsic evidence of state's absolutizing itself; i.e. that the sword is itself not a part of the Fall."[285] One may naturally ask whether Yoder does not express an overly negative view of human society. To this he says,

> One mistake we need to avoid is placing the blame on some evil people. Most people within 'the system' are not nasty. They do not beat wives and children. A few of them are brutal; some are selfish or venal, profiteers or racketeers; but most of them are not. They may lack imagination or courage, just as I do. Most of the people who ran Hitler's Reich were decent people. They were gentle with their children, and they kept their files in order. They followed the rules and worked hard. They were more hostages than villains.[286]

The second dimension of the New Testament's understanding of the state makes clear that God uses the state to maintain order in society. For example, Paul says to the Christians in Rome that they "should not rebel even against a government which threatened to mistreat them."[287] Hence,

---

284. Ibid., 12.

285. Ibid., 38; italics original.

286. Yoder, *He Came Preaching Peace*, 32–33. One could add that the Gospels also picture Jesus partaking in parties to the degree that he was referred to as a waster and drinker. While the disciples of John fasted, the disciples of Jesus did not. Jesus and his disciples ate and drank perhaps as a foretaste of the joy they should one day fully enjoy. Jesus may have believed that joy should be embraced in the present as a foretaste of what was going to be fulfilled in the future (Matt 9:14–17). Hence, the kingdom of God is about victory and joy. Jesus' fellowship with the disciples may have been joyful because the bridegroom now was with them. Therefore, they should celebrate and not fast. See Højlund, *Men han gav afkald*, 191.

287. Yoder, *The Christian Witness to the State*, 75.

Christians know even better than the state itself why the state exists.[288] Christians should obey and affirm the state as long as it does not compromise their obedience to Christ, but this does not imply that Christians may use the sword. The sword is given to the authorities, not to the Christians. The Christians have other weapons (cf. Eph 6:10–20; 2 Cor 6:7).

Even though the world is fallen and is in rebellion against God, this does not mean that Christians should avoid going into politics and accepting political responsibility. Christians should not, however, go into politics with the intent to manage and control the world. They should go into politics because they want to contribute to the maintaining of order in society. Furthermore, they should not impose Christian ethics on society. As we have seen, Christian discipleship is for disciples, and Christian ethics is for Christians.

3.5.4 The Salvation of Christ

In order for God's salvation to come, the sovereignty of the powers of the old aeon had to be broken. This happened with Christ. As I have shown, Yoder believes that order and structures in the world are part of God's creational intention for human life. Yoder argues: "If God is going to save his creatures *in their humanity*, the Powers cannot simply be destroyed or set aside or ignored. Their sovereignty must be broken. This is what Jesus did, concretely and historically."[289]

Yoder believes that Jesus "accepted his own status of submission" to these powers.[290] As with everyone else, he was subject to these powers, but Jesus was, however, subject to the powers by his own free will. Yoder says: "Here we have for the first time to do with someone who is not the slave of any power, of any law or custom, community or institution, value or theory. Not even to save his own life will he let himself be made a slave of these Powers."[291]

Even though Jesus was subject to the powers of this world, he broke their rules "by refusing to support them in their self-glorification," and this is the reason why they killed him.[292] Interpreting the death of Jesus,

---

288. Ibid., 16.
289. Yoder, *The Politics of Jesus*, 144; italics original.
290. Ibid., 145.
291. Ibid.
292. Ibid.

Yoder refers to Paul, who says, "and you, who were dead, God made alive together with him, having forgiven us all our trespasses, having cancelled the bond which stood against us with its legal demands; this he set aside, nailing it to the cross. He disarmed the principalities and powers and made a public example of them, triumphing over them in him" (Col 2:13–15).[293] Yoder believes that Paul here uses three complementary verbs when interpreting the death of Jesus. He agrees with Berkhof in his interpretation of this text, and quotes him as follows:

> He 'made a public example of them.' It is precisely in the crucifixion that the true nature of the Powers has come to light. Previously they were accepted as the most basic and ultimate realities, as the gods of the world. Never had it been perceived, nor could it have been perceived, that this belief was founded on deception. Now that the true God appears on earth in Christ, it becomes apparent that the Powers are inimical to Him, acting not as His instruments but as His adversaries (. . .).
>
> Thus, Christ has 'triumphed over them.' The unmasking is actually already their defeat. Yet this is only humanly visible when they know that God Himself has appeared on earth in Christ. Therefore we must think of the resurrection as well as of the cross. The resurrection manifests what was already accomplished at the cross: that in Christ God has challenged the Powers, has penetrated into their territory, and has displayed that He is stronger than they.
>
> The concrete evidence of this triumph is that at the cross Christ has 'disarmed' the Powers. The weapon from which they heretofore derived their strength is struck out of their hands. This weapon was the power of illusion, their ability to convince us that they were the divine regents of the world, ultimate certainty and ultimate direction, ultimate happiness and the ultimate duty for small, dependent humanity. Since Christ we know that this is illusion. We are called to a higher destiny: we have higher orders to follow and we stand under a greater protector.[294]

This quotation clearly demonstrates that Yoder interprets the death and life of Jesus as a victory over these powers. His life and obedience, until death, were the first fruits of an authentic restored humanity. In this way,

---

293. Quoted in ibid.

294. Quoted in ibid., 146–47. The quote is originally from Berkhof, *Christ and the Powers*, 30–31.

God broke the sovereignty of the powers; but not only did he break their sovereignty, he also made himself lord over them.[295]

3.5.5 The Lordship of Christ

Yoder believes that despite the continued rebellion of the powers, Christ is Lord over them. In the article "But We Do See Jesus," Yoder analyzes five texts from the New Testament: a passage from the Prologue of John, a passage from the letter to the Hebrews, a passage from the letter to the Colossians, a passage from the letter to the Philippians, and a passage from the Book of Revelation.[296] These texts are addressed to five different contexts, each with its own cosmological presuppositions. The authors of these texts use concepts drawn from the historical contexts in which the texts are set, but at the same time express that Christ is above the cosmos, in charge of it and Lord of it. The victory of Christ is a cosmic victory, and therefore, "Christ is not only the Head of the church; He is at the same time Lord of history, reigning at the right hand of God over the principalities and powers. The old aeon, representative of human history under the mark of sin, has also been brought under the reign of Christ."[297] The whole old aeon has been brought under the reign of Christ.[298]

Yoder admits that what lordship means can be questioned thoughtfully as long as the powers of this world are still in rebellion. Here, Yoder first compares the lordship of Christ with the lordship of this world's earthly rulers. As he points out, "many a political sovereign, whose authority no one challenges legally, is still not effectively in total control of all the actions of all the persons and organizations in the territory over

---

295. Yoder is one-sided in his interpretation of Jesus' death on the cross. He clearly favors a "classic" view of the atonement; as a social ethicist he repeatedly emphasizes its social consequences.

296. More explicitly, Yoder refers to John 1:1–14; Hebr 2:8–9; Phil 2:9; Rev 4:1–5:4. Yoder does not present any precise references to Colossians. See Yoder, "But We Do See Jesus," 50–55.

297. Yoder, "If Christ Is Truly Lord," 58.

298. Yoder follows Cullmann "in describing present history as realistically located between Pentecost and Parousia, in the segment of time over which Christ is lord, but which is not yet God's fulfilled kingdom." See LeMasters, *The Import of Eschatology*, 44. In *The Christian Witness to the State*, Yoder acknowledges his indebtedness to Cullmann's understanding of eschatology of the New Testament; see 9.

which he claims dominion and cannot force total and unconditional obedience even in realms where his sovereignty is confessed."²⁹⁹

Second, Yoder states that Christ's lordship over the powers is not redemptive but conservative in purpose. Thus, he suggests that Christ is using the powers against their will to serve the good, given that they provide an ordering function in the world. In this way, the powers, despite their fallen state, "remain a sign of the preserving patience of God toward a world that has not yet heard of its redemption (Acts 17:22–28)."³⁰⁰ Therefore, Christians must obey the authorities because they provide order in society, which is better than chaos (Rom 13:1–7). However, the powers still have destructive capacity.

Third, referring to 1 Corinthians 15:20–28, Yoder points out that "it is possible and not essentially irrational for the New Testament to tell us both that Christ has triumphed and is reigning" over the powers, and that the powers of evil are still rampant.³⁰¹ Jesus inaugurated the new age of the kingdom of God, which will find fulfillment in the *eschaton*.³⁰² Jesus proclaimed the kingdom to be present in this world, but not yet fulfilled. As Yoder asserts: "The rebellious but already (in principle) defeated cosmos is being brought to its knees by the Lamb."³⁰³ Yoder states, furthermore: "To follow the picture suggested by Cullmann, the enemies of Christ are in the situation of a warring nation whose defeat is sure because of the overwhelming forces brought to bear by the adversary, but which continues to resist for some time before the final surrender."³⁰⁴ Yoder applies an image suggested by Cullmann describing the present age as a period between D-Day and V-Day.³⁰⁵ Carter explains this well-known event during the Second World War well: "After successfully land-

---

299. Yoder, *The Christian Witness to the State*, 11.
300. Yoder, *The Politics of Jesus*, 141–42.
301. Yoder, *The Christian Witness to the State*, 9.
302. LeMasters, *The Import of Eschatology*, 62.
303. Yoder, "But We Do See Jesus," 54.
304. Yoder, *The Christian Witness to the State*, 9.
305. Yoder, "If Christ Is Truly Lord," 60; Yoder, *The Christian Witness to the State*, 9. Cullmann's influence on Yoder is also obvious here. Cullmann believes that salvation history is an important part of what the New Testament proclaims. God's salvific involvement in history is not a dispensable husk to be removed from the kernel of the gospel. The midpoint of history for Cullmann is the death and resurrection of Jesus as a victory over the powers. It will not serve the purpose of this dissertation to clarify the relation between Cullmann and Yoder. Cullmann's *The State in the New Testament* provides a good background of how Yoder unfolds his eschatology.

ing on the beaches of Normandy, the Allied forces steadily moved toward the heart of Germany. The issue of final victory was no longer in doubt, but the war was not over yet. Soldiers still died, and individual battles could be won or lost. This is the situation in which the world finds itself now, between Pentecost and *parousia*. The final victory of Jesus Christ is now assured because of the resurrection, but the war is not over yet."[306] As Yoder states: "He [Christ] *is now* Lord. The time will come when every knee will bow and every tongue will *confess him* as Lord."[307] The lordship of Christ is independent of whether his creatures like it or whether they confess it. In the end they all will.[308]

Yoder argues that the New Testament makes a differentiation between the kingdom of the Son and the kingdom of the Father. Carter says: "The reign of the Son is now going on, as we have seen above, but the rule of the Father is still future. In the words of Paul: 'Then the end will come, when he hands over the kingdom to God the Father after he has destroyed all dominion, authority and power. For he must reign until he has put all his enemies under his feet' (1 Corinthians 15:24–25). The message of the church is that the kingdoms of this world *have become* the kingdoms of Christ *and are destined to become* the kingdom of God."[309] The church shall proclaim the kingdom of the Son, and await the kingdom of the Father.

3.5.6 Eschatology and Ecclesiology

With the New Testament, Yoder states that the church is a people whom Christ has freed from the powers of this world.[310] In this called-out community, the Jews and the gentiles are reconciled. To Yoder, justification

---

306. Carter, *The Politics of the Cross*, 145–46. However, to regard the Allied forces' landing on the beaches of Normandy during the Second World War as successful, to me, lacks nuance.

307. Yoder, *Preface to Theology*, 85; italics original.

308. Ibid., 86.

309. Carter, *The Politics of the Cross*, 147; italics original; cf. Yoder, *The Christian Witness to the State*, 9–10.

310. Paul says that Christians are drawn out of the world and into God's kingdom. He also says that Christ "gave himself for our sins to set us free from the present evil age, according to the will of our God and Father" (Gal 1:4). He freed those who slaved under the law and the powers of this world (Gal 4:1-11). He freed Christians out of the power of the darkness (Col 1:13).

has a clear social dimension and meaning. Reconciliation between Jews and Gentiles serves as a witness to the world. This reconciliation serves as an eschatological sign of the reconciliation of humanity from all nations and people, which will be established when the kingdom of God is fulfilled. In this way, "[t]he church is the unique foretaste of God's age through the power of the Spirit," which seeks to embody obedience to the way of the crucified and risen Lord in opposition to the world.[311] As LeMasters states, "the church is to embody Christ's victory over the rebellious powers, and is, thereby, to present a stark alternative of socially realized love to the corrupt ways of the world."[312] In the church, Christ's victory over the powers and action in history is most directly evident.[313] The evidence of that victory "is the body of Christ, first the man Christ Jesus, and then derivatively the fellowship of obedient believers."[314] Hence, understanding the identity of the church in light of eschatology is crucial for Yoder.[315] The church is an eschatological reality, as the new age has broken into the world, and as the church is the place where people can experience the realized eschaton within present history. The church gives people a foretaste of the kingdom that God shall one day fully establish, and the awareness of this gives hope to the church. Even though the church exists in a fallen world, it carries "a hope which, defying present frustration, defines the present position in terms of the yet unseen goal which gives it meaning."[316]

Yoder believes that Christ is Lord over both the church and the world, but whereas the lordship of Christ is visible in the church, the lordship of Christ over the world is hidden until the last day.[317] According to Yoder, this fundamental understanding of eschatology was radically changed with the Constantinian shift. He says: "Previously Christians had known as a fact of experience that the church existed, but had to believe against appearances that Christ ruled over the world. After

---

311. LeMasters, *The Import of Eschatology*, 36.

312. Ibid., 75.

313. Again, Yoder follows Cullmann, who believes that the church is the earthly center from which the lordship of Christ becomes visible. The church is the place where the Spirit, the feature of the eschatological period, is already at work as first fruits. See Cullmann, *Christus und die Zeit*, 169–74.

314. Yoder, *The Christian Witness to the State*, 9.

315. Cartwright, "Radical Reform, Radical Catholicity," 8.

316. Yoder, "If Christ Is Truly Lord," 53.

317. Ibid., 58–60.

Constantine one knew as a fact of experience that Christ was ruling over the world but had to believe against the evidence that there existed 'a believing Church.'"[318] Yoder believes that Eusebius and Augustine worked out an alternative to the eschatological understanding of the authors of the New Testament. Instead of God's lordship over the world being hidden, they now understood God to be governing history through Constantine. Rather than seeing the church as living during the overlapping of two aeons, where God's lordship over the world is unconsummated and hidden, Constantinianism sees the new aeon as clearly victorious in the dominant social order.[319] Now, the state was drawn into the realm of redemption and became a manifestation of God's reign.[320] As Rasmusson, in an article on Yoder's theology, states frankly, "one of the great tragedies of history is the fact that the church, instead of exposing the Powers (for example, the state and the nation), has sacralized them and made them into God's direct and primary instruments in history."[321] Similarly, Yoder claims, "the ultimate meaning of history will not be found in the course of earthly empires of the development of proud cultures, but in the calling together of the 'chosen race, royal priesthood, holy nation', which is the church of Christ."[322] According to Timothy, when Christians are supposed to pray for the state and for kings, it is because "God desires that all men should be brought to the knowledge of the truth—but not that the State is going to bring men to the knowledge of the truth."[323]

According to Yoder, Jesus very clearly showed that his kingdom did not have national character: "Jesus made it clear that the nationalized hope of Israel had been a misunderstanding, and that God's true purpose was the creation of a new society, unidentifiable with any of the local, national, or ethnic solidarities of any time."[324] The Jews, anachronistically, expressed Constantinian expectations and Jesus rejected these expectations. Therefore, the Jews considered his kingdom useless: "Christ had been awaited eagerly by Judaism for centuries; but when He came He

---

318. Yoder, "The Otherness of the Church," 57; see also Yoder, "The Constantinian Sources of Western Social Ethics," 136–37.

319. Yoder, "The Meaning of the Constantinian Shift," 62; see also LeMasters, *The Import of Eschatology*, 109; Yoder, "The Otherness of the Church," 59.

320. Yoder, "The Otherness of the Church," 59.

321. Rasmusson, "Revolutionary Subordination," 48.

322. Quoted in LeMasters, *Discipleship between Creation and Redemption*, 13.

323. Yoder, "The Theological Basis of the Christian Witness to the State," 141.

324. Yoder, *The Christian Witness to the State*, 10.

was rejected, for the new aeon He revealed was not what men wanted. The Jews were awaiting a new age, a bringing to fulfillment of God's plan; but they expected it to confirm and to vindicate all their national hopes, prides, and solidarities. Thus Christ's claims and His kingdom were to them scandalous."[325] Yoder points out that Jesus was confronted with this "Constantinian" temptation in the desert after he had begun his ministry, and again at his last trial in Gethsemane, where his ministry would finally be accomplished. But Jesus was also tempted throughout his entire ministry, because "[m]ore of His disciples came from the Zealot group than from any other part of the Palestinian society."[326] This represented a real temptation for Jesus: "He used their language, took sides with the poor as they did, condemned the same evils they did, created a disciplined community of committed followers as they did, prepared as they did to die for the divine cause. Yet Jesus did not take the path of the Zealots."[327] Jesus chose another way than that of "Constantinianism." Instead of imposing his ethic on society and trying to control it, he created a new distinct community, where the kingdom of God should break through and where people were invited to join voluntarily. The very existence of this community "demonstrates that the powers' rebellion has been vanquished."[328]

This leads to a fundamentally different conception of the church than that of Constantinianism.[329] This shows how misleading it is to claim that a whole society can be regarded as Christian. The church cannot be the moral teacher or the soul of society when society does not acknowledge Christ as Lord and when society is not obedient to or does not want to follow him. The church cannot be the soul of society when society fundamentally is in rebellion against God.[330] The church must respect that society does not want to follow Christ. Therefore, the church must embrace her identity as a distinct social entity, and witness to society about Christ as Lord of all that exists.

---

325. Yoder, "If Christ Is Truly Lord," 55.

326. Yoder, "The Original Revolution," 22; here Yoder is most likely again inspired by Cullmann. See Cullmann, *Jesus und die Revolutionären seiner Zeit*.

327. Yoder, "The Original Revolution," 22–23.

328. Yoder, *The Politics of Jesus*, 150.

329. Zimmerman, *Practicing the Politics of Jesus*, 190–91.

330. Ibid., 192.

3.6 Conclusion

3.6.1 The Distinctive Identity of the Church

This chapter has shown that Yoder's writings represent a fundamental theological critique of Constantinianism. We may even say that his critique of Constantinianism makes up the background for important aspects of his theological project.[331] All significant perspectives of this critique can in one way or another be related to the distinctive identity of the church. For Yoder, Constantinianism is "a metaphor for a shift in the relationship between church and world that has had, and continues to have," ramifications which profoundly corrupt the Christian church and Christian theology.[332]

In each of the past three sections, I have shed light on important aspects of what Yoder believes to be the distinctive identity of the church. It is important for me to say that the analysis I have presented does not exhaustively capture the church's distinctive identity, an analysis which I do not believe is possible to present. It is also important to note that the analysis I have presented does not exhaustively capture the distinctive identity of the church in the writings of Yoder. Instead, I have tried to identify and focus on three important themes that shed light on the distinctive identity of the church. Furthermore, I have at the end of each of these sections briefly pointed out that Christology plays a central role in Yoder's theology.[333] Taking into consideration that Yoder disclaimed being a systematic theologian, and that he preferred to write when asked to, the consistency of Yoder's writings is impressive. His theology appears as a well-integrated, consistent whole. If one disagrees with Yoder on one aspect of his theology, it seems to affect the whole system of thought. I will now sum up his understanding of the distinctive identity of the church.

The church as a distinct people: Constantinianism led to all citizens being baptized and considered Christians, and the entire social order subsequently being declared Christian.[334] This, ultimately, led to the church severely compromising its identity as a distinct community of faith.[335] The distinctiveness of the church permeates every aspect of

---

331. See 3.2.1 above.
332. LeMasters, *The Import of Eschatology*, 101.
333. See 3.3.7, 3.4.7 and 3.5.6 above.
334. Yoder, "The Meaning of the Constantinian Shift," 62.
335. Yoder, "The Otherness of the Church," 57; LeMasters, *The Import of Eschatology*, 93.

Yoder's ecclesiology. As we have seen, he argues that the normal existence for the church is existence in exile.[336] Thus, the church gathers around baptism and communion. Baptism initiates persons into a new people, which profoundly transcend all social and cultural barriers. He asserts that the "distinguishing mark of this people is that all prior given or chosen identity definitions are transcended."[337] Belonging to Christ Communion embodies an act of "economic sharing among the members of the messianic community."[338] It expresses responsibility for each other, not symbolically but concretely.[339]

The church as a distinct way of living: Constantinianism fused the church and the world, and this led to the church being filled with people in whom the presuppositions of discipleship and the ethical requirements set by the church were absent. As the Christian ethic was applied to the whole society, a distinction between church and society could no longer be maintained. Yoder envisions a visibly communal church as the social locus of Christian morality.[340] This means that Christian ethics is for Christians, and discipleship is for disciples. As Yoder states: "There will therefore be a Christian message addressed to the State; there will not be a Christian ethic for the State."[341] The church does not have a social ethic; the church *is* a social ethic.[342]

The church as an eschatological reality: After Constantine, one had to believe that there existed an invisible community of believers within the nominally Christian mass, "but one knew for a fact that God was in control of history" through the dominion of the Empire.[343] This understanding presupposes that "the *state* was unequivocally in the realm of redemption" and a manifestation of God's reign.[344] To Yoder, "[t]he church is the unique foretaste of God's age through the power of the Spirit," which seeks to embody obedience to the way of the crucified and risen Lord in opposition to the world.[345] This shows how misleading it is to claim that

---

336. See 3.3.1 above.
337. Yoder, *Body Politics*, 28.
338. Ibid., 21.
339. See 3.3.3 above.
340. LeMasters, *The Import of Eschatology*, 8.
341. Yoder, "The Pacifism of Karl Barth," 116–17.
342. See 3.5 above.
343. Yoder, "The Constantinian Sources of Western Social Ethics," 137.
344. Yoder, "The Otherness of the Church," 59; italics mine.
345. LeMasters, *The Import of Eschatology*, 36.

a whole society can be regarded as Christian. The church cannot be the moral teacher or the soul of society when society does not acknowledge Christ as Lord, and when society is not obedient to him or following him. The church cannot be the soul of society when society is fundamentally in rebellion against God.[346] Understanding the identity of the church in light of eschatology is crucial for Yoder.[347] With Christ, the new age has broken into the world and the church is the place where people can experience the realized eschaton within present history. The church is a foretaste of the kingdom that God shall one day fully establish.[348]

As we have seen, the church is a distinct people, the church is a social ethic and the church is an eschatological reality. Yoder would also say that the church should be a social embodiment of God's mission in the world. Yoder taught quite a few courses in missiology, and was a consultant on the research process that came before the publication of the influential book, *Missional Church*.[349] He certainly presents thoughts on church and mission, however, and I have tried to integrate these reflections in particular into my exposition of his ecclesiology.[350] As we have seen, the church is, like Israel, scattered for mission and called to exist for the world. The church is a community called to go out into the world, into the diaspora.[351] God has called a community into existence who must serve instead of rule, suffer instead of inflict suffering, and cross social lines instead of reinforcing them.[352] This community "is not merely the agent of mission or the constituency of a mission agency. *This is the mission.*"[353] It is, however, notable that Yoder never emphasized how the church in medieval Christendom lost sight of mission. This has been mentioned by

---

346. Zimmerman, *Practicing the Politics of Jesus*, 192.

347. Cartwright, "Radical Reform, Radical Catholicity," 8.

348. See 3.6 above.

349. See Guder, *Missional Church*. Just to mention a few courses on mission which I know of, in the spring of 1970 and 1973 Yoder taught a course on "Theology of the Christian World Mission" and in the fall of 1983 he taught a course on "Ecclesiology in Missional Perspective." The syllabi to these courses are available at the John Howard Yoder Archive in Goshen, Indiana, box 181 and 182. Here it is also possible to find correspondences between Yoder and various missiologists.

350. See especially 3.3.6 but also 3.3.1 above.

351. Weaver states this with reference to Yoder. See his "On Exile," 146.

352. Yoder, "A People in the World," 91.

353. Ibid.; italics mine.

many missiologists, but Yoder does not pay much attention to this, and it never became an important part of his critique of Christendom.[354]

Yoder, indeed, understands the church as a social embodiment of a special way of seeing the world, but this is an integrated part of his social ethic and eschatology; in fact, epistemology cannot be separated from social ethics and eschatology. I have also tried to integrate some of these epistemological aspects into my exposition of Yoder's understanding of how Scripture ought to be read.[355] He believes that the consequences of Constantinianism are not only ecclesiological, ethical, and eschatological, but epistemological as well. With the rise of Western Christendom, secular philosophy and biblical wisdom merged, and common sense and natural law became important sources for moral knowledge.[356] Yoder believes that Christ offers insight into God's nature, person and intentions for his creation. Christ is divine revelation and Scripture testifies to this revelation. The meaning of history and the world are revealed in Jesus Christ and not in the powers and principalities of society. According to Huebner, "Yoder claims that the concrete body of the church precedes any methodology or epistemology, since there is no non-neutral or non-particular place from which to produce a general method or system."[357] Thus, the church gathers to interpret reality in light of the revelation of Christ. Huebner also says: "The faith of the church becomes unintelligible when it is expressed in abstraction from a life of disciplined imitation of Christ. The church does not develop and seek to sustain a stable, settled body of knowledge but engages in an agonizing and ongoing conversational exchange."[358] Hence, the Christian community forms and nurtures a common way of seeing the world, which is determined by the revelation in Christ. Yoder calls this "a congregational epistemology."[359]

As we have seen, Yoder presents an extensive and fundamental theological critique of the fusion of church and society, which is designated as *corpus Christianum*. Against this, Yoder argues that the church, *corpus Christi*, must be a distinct social entity, which oftentimes differs from society. To Yoder, particularity is an integral part of ecclesiology,

354. I have, for example, referred to Shenk who frankly states, "Christendom is Christianity without mission." See Guder, "Walking Worthily," 252; cf. 3.3.6 above.
355. See 3.2 above.
356. Yoder, "The Meaning of the Constantinian Shift," 63–74.
357. Huebner, *A Precarious Peace*, 59.
358. Ibid., 143–44.
359. Yoder, "The Forms of a Possible Obedience," 125.

social ethics, and eschatology, which qualifies important aspects of the distinctive identity of the church.

3.6.2 The Role of the Church in a Post-Christendom Society

The Church as Minority in a Post-Christendom Society

Yoder believes that the normal existence of the church is that of a minority that represents a special way of life and viewing the world. He argues that the normal existence for the Jewish people is existence in exile, and that the notion of exile preconfigured the Christian understanding of the church's existence in the world. Hence, he argues that the normal existence for the church is also existence in exile.[360] The church does not, however, exist in exile because it wants to, but because the world does not acknowledge Christ as Lord and follow him.[361] Yoder clearly understands the life of the church from a subservient perspective, and his notion of peoplehood is clearly non-sovereign. The church should not serve society as a part of the prevailing establishment. As he suggests, "there are other more useful ways to contribute to the course of society than attempting to 'rule.'"[362] In connection with this, Yoder argues that social creativity often is a minority function.[363] He states,

> More often, the way in which 'not in charge' minorities contribute to social process is backhanded. By denouncing the veneration of the national flag as idolatrous, the Jehovah's Witnesses in the US enlarged the notion of religious liberty. By conscientiously declaring themselves unavailable for military service, the 'objectors' widen the notion of religious liberty to include not only ideas but also behaviour, not only cultic but also political behaviour. By conscientiously claiming responsibility for their children's education the Old Order Amish break the stranglehold of homogeneous state education (. . .). Non-co-operation, when empowered by a level of conviction that is willing to suffer, is a more powerful way to move a society than is the ballot box.[364]

---

360. See 3.4.1 above.
361. Yoder, "Let the Church Be the Church," 116. See also 3.5.3 above.
362. Yoder, "Christ, the Hope of the World," 164.
363. Ibid., 171–74.
364. Yoder, "On Not Being in Charge," 174.

Hence, he argues that the powerless are often very powerful. In two articles, Rasmusson has, along the same lines as Yoder, expanded on the theme of how Christian minorities have impacted the wider society.[365] Among several examples, Rasmusson argues that an important inspiration of modern democracy came from the Independents, the Anabaptists, and the Quakers. He also argues that the modern struggle against slavery in England and the English colonies was driven by Mennonites, Quakers, and evangelical Christians. Rasmusson says, "most of these Christians did not think that they were part of an historical democratic project, or the Enlightenment project. They just practiced what they thought was a truthful Christian practice. But it did influence the 'wider' society; the practice was taken up by others, and it has shaped how we now think."[366]

The Church in a Diverse Post-Christendom Society

The modern, Western post-Christendom society is a highly diverse society. We find important theological sources in the writings of Yoder, which help us to understand how the church should exist in such a society. He goes back to the story of the Tower of Babel in Genesis 11 to argue that a diasporic existence, the normal way of existence for the people of God, is an original, divine intent. Consequently, diverse identities, languages and cultures are divinely intentional.[367] Hence, it seems obvious that the church should become present in various segments and subcultures of a post-Christendom society. As Yoder suggests,

> This community does not live into itself. It is scattered amidst a world full of other systems (. . .). There is the world of the arts, the world of sports, the world of science (. . .). No one of these—no more the state than any other—is identical either with the believing community or with the rebellious and fallen world. In the midst of each, in ways varying infinitely according to location and vocation, the presence of the confessing community will raise up signs of the kingdoms.[368]

---

365. Rasmusson, "The Church as a 'Creative Minority,'" 72–88.

366. Ibid.

367. Yoder, "'See How They Go with Their Face to the Sun,'" 64; see also Yoder, "Meaning After Babble," 132.

368. Yoder, "The Spirit of God and the Politics of Men," 234.

He believes that God's chosen people "might be called an underground movement, or a political party, or an infiltration team, or a cell movement. The sociologist would call it an intentional community."[369]

The Church and State in a Post-Christendom Society

Even though we, in the past three centuries, have left the era of Christendom behind and have moved into a new situation, the church is still challenged by Constantinianism.[370] According to Yoder, a faithful church obtains a separationist stance with respect to the state. This church does not attempt to Christianize society. This church respects the freedom to say no. But in the midst of society, the church is "a demonstration of what love means in social relations. This demonstration cannot be transposed directly into non-Christian society, for in the church it functions only on the basis of repentance and faith; yet by analogy certain of its aspects may be instructive as stimuli to the conscience of society."[371] Yoder believes that "there will therefore be a Christian message addressed to the State; there will not be a Christian ethic for the State."[372] The church should not impose Christian legislation on society, he believes, for God's chosen people will always be called to be "a distinct community with its own deviant set of values and its coherent way of incarnating them."[373]

Hereby I have given an introduction to Yoder's life and work, identified the background of major parts of his writings, and suggested that Yoder's ecclesiology, social ethics, and eschatology all shed light on the distinctive identity of the church and its role in a post-Christendom society.

---

369. Yoder, "The Original Revolution," 28.
370. See 3.2.3 above.
371. Yoder, *The Christian Witness to the State*, 17.
372. Yoder, "The Pacifism of Karl Barth," 116–17.
373. Yoder, "The Original Revolution," 28.

PART IV

Toward a Post-Christendom Ecclesiology

4
Beyond Sectarianism

4.1 Introduction

AS WE HAVE SEEN, this book engages a theological debate which has emerged due to important cultural and religious changes in the Western world since the time of the Enlightenment. Thus, during the past three centuries, the church has gradually lost its central and influential role in Western society and, therefore, an increasing number of theologians state that the Western world has moved from, or is in transition from, an era of Christendom to one of post-Christendom. I have presented an analysis of the work of two theologians who respond to this development, arguing that Lesslie Newbigin's critique of Christendom essentially is that the church ceased to understand itself as a missionary community, whereas John Howard Yoder's critique of Christendom first and foremost is that the church ceased to understand itself as a distinct community. Hence, for Newbigin, it is decisive to re-envision the missional identity of the church, whereas, for Yoder, it is decisive to re-envisage the distinctive identity of the church. I have, however, also demonstrated that not only Yoder, but also Newbigin, can help us to qualify our understanding of the distinctive identity of the church.[1]

Thus, both Newbigin and Yoder present a strong notion of the distinctive identity of the church and, consequently, both of them have been charged with developing an ecclesiology with sectarian tendencies with respect to society.[2] The charge of sectarianism has played a central role

---

1. Major parts of this chapter have been published in my article "Missional kirke i et pluralistisk samfund", which has also been publish in English as "Beyond Sectarianism."

2. See n38 in chapter 1; see Bevans, *Models of Contextual Theology*, 124–27. Newbigin's theology has also been charged with being anticultural. See Graham and Walton, "A Walk on the Wild Side," 2.

in ecclesiological debates, especially in North America, for several years.[3] However, the term is not only used in an ecclesiological context, but also in an ethical and an epistemological context. At times, the concept is used fairly neutrally to designate a relatively small, distinct group in society.[4] More often than not, however, the term is used negatively to designate a relatively small group of persons who are "withdrawing from culture" and "abnegating responsibility for the world."[5] This concern may be expressed as such: If one so strongly affirms the distinctive identity of the church, is the church, then, not in danger of isolating itself from society? Is the church, then, not in danger of abnegating its responsibility for society? Is the church, then, not in danger of becoming a closed replica of its own tradition?

Newbigin has been accused of developing an ecclesiology with sectarian tendencies, which may be due to the fact that his theology represents a strong emphasis on the distinctive identity of the church, and that his theology contains clear countercultural traits. A classification of Newbigin's ecclesiology as sectarian can, however, be questioned.[6] A strong notion of the distinctive identity of the church also plays an important role in the theology of Yoder, as he presents an even more emphatic distinction between the church and the world than does Newbigin. Consequently, Daniel Izuzquiza states that mainline theologians often regard Yoder as sectarian.[7] Yet, Rodney J. Sawatsky states, "Yoder is but a sign of the Mennonite recovery from a sectarian retreat to an open

---

3. Kenneson, *Beyond Sectarianism*, 15. In theology, the term *sect* was originally used in reference to a group of believers who rejected "orthodox" doctrines, practice or leadership. With Max Weber and Ernst Troeltsch the term came to be used primarily in a sociological sense with respect to the relation of the church to its surrounding society. See Rasmusson, *Church as Polis*, 233–42. In this chapter, I use the term with respect to the relationship between church and society.

4. Cf. Kelsey, "Church Discourse and Public Realm," 12.

5. Kenneson, *Beyond Sectarianism*, 13.

6. We have seen that Newbigin strongly emphasizes the missionary nature of the church, and a missionary encounter with Western culture, and moreover, his theology also represents aspects that seem almost imperialistic. See 2.8.2 above.

7. Izuzquiza, *Rooted in Jesus Christ*, 67. On Yoder's reaction on being labeled "sectarian," see Yoder, *For the Nations*, 3–7. See also Dorrien, *Social Ethics in the Making*, 469–70, 473–74.

witness to the nonresistant Gospel."[8] Yoder certainly takes steps in this direction, but, as I will argue, further steps can be taken.[9]

I will not demonstrate this by presenting a comparative analysis of the theologies of Newbigin and Yoder, or by mediating between them.[10] Rather, by employing a synthetic-constructive method, I will utilize a missional position to compose the framework for an understanding of central aspects of the church, with the purpose of arguing that a strong notion of the distinctive identity of the church must not lead to an abandonment of its engagement in society. I will mainly keep within a complementary framework of Newbigin and Yoder's thinking, but I will also draw upon other sources. In the two preceding chapters, I have argued that an inescapable particularity is an integral part of five important theological themes, which is further rooted in the church. In this chapter, my goal is to argue that embracing this particularity must not lead to sectarianism.

I will structure this in a specific way: first, I will demonstrate that mission should determine the existence of the church in the world; second and consequently, the inescapable particularistic character of ecclesiology, social ethics and epistemology must therefore be outwardly

---

8. Sawatsky, "John Howard Yoder," 240. McClendon states that Yoder "is the scion of old-line Mennonites, and within that community has sometimes been perceived as a troublemaker exactly because he has been so deeply committed to responsible social action." See McClendon, *Ethics*, 74.

9. Some believe that Hauerwas, by making use of the theology of Yoder, has taken up a sectarian position. As an example of this, many refer to Hauerwas publishing a book with the title *Against the Nations*, whereas Yoder published a book with the title *For the Nations*. It is not my intention to discuss this point of view. I just want to point out that my intention is the opposite. Even though I disagree with many theologians' use of the concept of sectarianism, I do not plan on explaining why I do not believe Newbigin and Yoder's ecclesiologies can reasonably be classified as sectarian. Neither do I plan on presenting an historical analysis of the background of the concept of sectarianism, as I do not plan on explaining how I believe the concept ought to be deliberated from its modernistic presumptions and reconceptualized for today.

10. Both Newbigin and Yoder were a part of the ecumenical movement in the twentieth century and there is a chance that they might have met. I have found no examples of Newbigin referring to Yoder, whereas Newbigin's name appears in Yoder's introductory theology course. See Yoder, *Preface to Theology*, 43. Yoder also refers to Newbigin in his *The Ecumenical Movement and the Faithful Church*, 34. Also, Woodard-Lehmann mentions: "Wilbert Shank [sic] once asked Newbigin about Yoder. Newbigin replied, 'John wrote the most penetrating critique of *The Household of God* that I received. And I still haven't answered him.'" See Woodard-Lehmann, "Being and Bearing the Witness of the Spirit," 438.

focused to serve the world;[11] and third, I will expound upon how the final goal of the *missio Dei* is not the church, but the coming establishment of God's kingdom.[12] Thus, I argue that the church must always be oriented toward the coming kingdom of God. In this way, missiology and eschatology make up a framework for ecclesiology, social ethics and epistemology, which might correspond with the three central marks of the church *koinonia, diakonia* and *kerygma*.[13]

4.2 Sent by a Missionary God

According to the Christian faith, God is Triune. God is God the Father, God the Son, and God the Holy Spirit. God is three and yet one. Further, the origination of mission is not the fall, nor creation, but the Triune God himself. Thus, the Triune God is by nature missionary.

Trinitarian theology has, in recent decades, experienced a renaissance within theological research.[14] One could say that God's existence in community enables an existence in love, or expressed the other way around, because God's essence is love, God cannot exist in isolated loneliness. For this reason, the Triune God is by nature missionary. Brad Harper and Paul Louis Metzger affirm that, "Genesis reveals a God who desires to create. God does not need to create, for God is content as the divine communion of persons. As the Triune God, the Lord Almighty freely fashions a world and a people as an overflowing expression of that holy love experienced in the communion of the divine life. God creates the world through the Word and the Spirit."[15] God is love and must by

---

11. Thus, the church must have, by its very constitution, an outward focus to the world.

12. Andersen, "Further Toward a Theology of Mission," 304.

13. The inspiration stems from Guder's book *The Continuing Conversion of the Church*, where he, in a modest footnote, mentions that the mark of the church, *martyria*, can serve as an "overarching term," drawing together community (*koinonia*), service (*diakonia*) and proclamation (*kerygma*). Ibid., 53. Guder also presents this thesis in the book *Be My Witnesses*, 48–54. I do not claim that these three marks of the church comprehensively capture or fully express the identity of the church. Other marks of the church such as *didache* and *leitourgia* could also have been drawn into the analysis.

14. Some of the theologians who have contributed to this development are Karl Barth, Colin Gunton, Paul Louis Metzger, Karl Rahner, Joseph Ratzinger, Miroslav Volf, and John D. Zizioulas.

15. Harper and Metzger, *Exploring Ecclesiology*, 21.

nature give of or share himself. This happens internally in the communal life of the Trinity, but also externally, for example, in the act of creating the world. Thus, if we, with Christ, gain insight into God's nature and person, and if *kenosis* characterizes God's nature, *kenosis* may also characterize the creational act. Hence, not only the incarnation and the atonement, but also the creation expresses God's *kenosis*. It has been said that the creation of the world expresses a *creatio ex amore Dei*.[16] Accordingly, we may also say that the creation of the world expresses a *creatio ex missione Dei*. The creation of the world expresses, thus, the mission of God.[17] Thus, both God's creational work (*missio Dei generalis*) and his redemptive activities (*missio Dei specialis*) must be regarded as expressions of God's mission. For this reason, the overall framework of divine action can be designated as mission.[18]

Creation, however, should not be ignored, nor referred to merely by way of introduction.[19] The mission of the church should not only be understood in light of the mission of Christ, but also in light of the creation of the world. John P. Brennan explains: "God is the Lord of *creation*, and the only one with the absolute right to be called 'King.' It is not surprising then that Jesus should utilize a phrase as the 'Kingdom of God.'"[20]

However, as we read in Genesis, God's good creation became fundamentally corrupted with the fall. Therefore, God set a rescue plan in motion with Abraham and the creation of a people. The decisive starting point for the creation of Israel is God's promise to Abraham—that he

---

16. See, for example, Torrance, "*Creatio ex Nihilo* and the Spatio-Temporal Dimensions," 84.

17. God created the world as an expression of *shalom*; a good world with good orders and structures that facilitates the good life for humans. This is God's mission.

18. One also finds such a point of view in Bevans and Schroeder's book *Constants in Context*, 288. This does not correspond with Newbigin's understanding of mission, which is strictly connected to Israel, Christ, the Holy Spirit, and the church. For Newbigin the mission of God emerges into view in the Old Testament with the election of Israel as God's people. See 2.3.1 and 2.4.3 above. I believe that we already, with the creation of the world, gain insight into the mission of God. This corresponds with Bosch's use of the term, *missio Dei*, which he also uses with respect to God's creational work: "In creation God was already the God of mission, with his Word and Spirit as 'Missionaries' (cf. Gen. 1:2–3)." See Bosch, *Witness to the World*, 239.

19. Lohfink states that it is not a coincidence that "the Bible does not begin with the election of the people of God, but with the creation of the world" and that its first figure is not Abraham, but Adam. See Lohfink, *Does God Need the Church?*, 21.

20. Brennan, *Christ, the One Sent*, 74; italics mine.

shall one day be a great nation and that all should be blessed through him. As we read in Genesis:

> I will make you into a great nation
> and I will bless you;
> I will make your name great,
> So that all the people on earth may be blessed through you.
> In order that you may be a blessing;
> I will bless those who bless you,
> And whoever curses you I will curse.
> *So that all the people on earth may be blessed through you.*[21]

The very creation of the people of God is accordingly bound to a missional vocation.[22] God wants to bless all people through his chosen people. Walter Brueggemann affirms, "The address to Abraham gives a subsequent community a peculiar identity and vocation in the world."[23] Hence, it is with good reason that Newbigin states, "the centre of God's plan for salvation is an actual community of men and women called by God for this purpose (. . .) that through them God's love may reach others, and all men be drawn together into one reconciled fellowship."[24]

Deuteronomy makes it particularly clear that the divine choice of Israel as God's people, through whom all other people shall be blessed, was not based on its size or virtue.[25] This leads Brueggemann to conclude: "It is impossible to overstate the significance of the divine choice of Israel for Old Testament theology. That choice places a 'scandal of particularity' at the center of faith. That choice places YHWH by implication in the midst of the vagaries of history, for the chosen people are an identifiable people in history who will not be explained away as a theological idea."[26] It is solely due to God's gracious election that God and Israel have a special relationship. Again, Brueggemann explains this: "Israel is known among the nations as *the people of YHWH*; it is equally the case that YHWH is known among the nations first and foremost as *the God of Israel*."[27] This does not, however, imply a rejection of all other people, but rather that

---

21. Gen 12:2–3; italics mine.

22. Kaiser believes that "if an Old Testament 'Great Commission' must be identified, then it will be Genesis 12:3." See Kaiser, *Mission in the Old Testament*, 7.

23. Brueggemann, *Old Testament Theology*, 200.

24. Newbigin, *Sin and Salvation*, 46.

25. Brueggemann, *Old Testament Theology*, 198; see Deut. 7:6–10; 9:4–5; 10:14–15.

26. Ibid., 199.

27. Brueggemann, *Old Testament Theology*, 199; italics original.

the God of Israel is the creator of the whole earth. Therefore all nations, should worship the God of Israel as the one true God.[28]

Historically, Israel exists among other nations who are both a political threat and a religious temptation, yet Israel has a common consciousness that they should trust Yahweh as their king and deliverer.[29] It seems accepted among many Old Testament scholars that Israel was "self-consciously distinctive from the surrounding nations."[30] Accounting for this distinction is a wide-scale task, I turn to now to Christopher J. H. Wright, who argues that Israel "formed a living society with its own customs, institutions, laws and culture. Its social system lies before us as a legitimate subject for the attention of sociology."[31] In the book *Walking in the Ways of the Lord*, Wright analyzes the distinctive social, economic, political, and cultic structures of Israel.[32] For example, he claims that with the implementation of the monarchy, "Israel was now a nation state (. . .). But it was consciously a nation unlike those around."[33] They were to be a kingdom but a priestly one; they were a nation but a holy one. "Priestliness and holiness both denote separateness, but not an inward-looking, isolationist kind of existence. Rather, their distinctiveness was to be for the sake of the very nations they were different from."[34] Thus, Wright concludes: "This distinctiveness was deliberately a part of what it was to be 'Israel.'"[35]

Along the same lines, Johannes Blauw asserts: "The sharp distinction from other nations cannot be rationalized out of the Old Testament."[36] Thus, he states that, according to the Old Testament, God made the

28. Cf. Blauw, *The Missionary Nature of the Church*, 25–26.

29. Ibid., 25; Wright, *Walking in the Ways of the Lord*, 150.

30. Ibid., 161. This seems at least to be accepted by Old Testament researchers such as Walther C. Kaiser, Walther Brueggemann, Christopher J. H. Wright, N. K. Gottwald, and also by theologians such as Johannes Blauw and Gerhard Lohfink.

31. Ibid., 147.

32. Wright is heavily dependent on N. K. Gottwald. One can meaningfully ask if it is possible to identify such features of the Israelite society, since it changed dramatically, for example, by the emergence of the monarchy. Hence, an important presumption for Wright's argumentation is that "a basic infrastructure of characteristically Israelite arrangements of social, economic and political life remained which were sufficiently coherent and enduring to be worthy of systematic study." See ibid., 149.

33. Ibid., 158.

34. Ibid.

35. Ibid., 161.

36. Blauw, *The Missionary Nature of the Church*, 37.

nations as his nations (Pss 86:9; 87). These nations, however, lie in darkness, worshipping other gods and refusing to acknowledge Yahweh as the one true God (Isa 60:2–3).[37] Several texts from the New Testament view the nations in the same dark colors: The world exists in darkness (Col 1:13); it can act only contrary to God (Mark 10:33); it does not know God (Matt 6:32); it refuses to acknowledge Jesus as Lord and to worship God (John 7:7).[38] These viewpoints lie in continuation of Newbigin and Yoder's understanding of Paul's perception of the powers and principalities in the New Testament.[39]

God chooses Israel to stand as a light before the nations who lie in darkness.[40] Thus, as Newbigin notes, the election of Israel is not a call to privilege, but responsibility.[41] Arguing a similar point of view, Kaiser states: "Almost a dozen and a half times in Scripture the reason that is given for the plagues and the crossing of the Red Sea is that they are not simply to eradicate the Egyptians or their king, but so that 'the Egyptians will know that I am the LORD' (Exod. 7:5, 17; 8:22; 14:4, 18)."[42] Especially in the book of Isaiah, for example, we read about Israel's missionary calling, where God says about Israel: "I will give you as a light to the nations, that my salvation may reach to the end of the earth" (Isa 49:6). Still, the missionary function of Israel is first and foremost centripetal.[43]

In the Old Testament, however, we also read about "the centrifugal missionary task of the Servant of the Lord," which is a part of an eschatological expectation of Israel (Isa 42:4).[44] The task and mission of the

---

37. Ibid.

38. See also John 14:17, 15:19, 16:33, 18:36; Rom 12:2; 1 Cor 1:20; Eph 2:2; 2 Tim 4:10; Jas 4:4; cf. ibid., 67.

39. See 2.5 and 3.5 above.

40. Deut 7:6–11; Isa 43:10; Isa 42:1–7; 48:1–9a; 50:4–9; 52:13—53:12.

41. See 2.3 above.

42. Kaiser, *Mission in the Old Testament*, 21. See also Exod 9:29.

43. I find it difficult to argue that the missionary function of Israel is entirely centripetal. Kaiser, for example, refers to several Psalms that call for "active and centrifugal outreach on the part of Israel." He refers to Ps 57:9, which states, "I will make confession about you, O Lord. I will sing to you among the nations," and to Ps 96:2–3, which states: "Declare his glory among the nations, his marvelous deeds among all peoples." See ibid., 34–35.

44. Blauw, *The Missionary Nature of the Church*, 41. However, Blauw admits that "scholarship is divided between those who believe that Isaiah teaches that Israel offers no salvation for the Gentiles and those who believe that Isaiah picks up the informing and antecedent theology of the Abrahamic promise and the message of Ex. 19:4–6 to remind the nation of her duty to be a witness." See ibid., xx.

Servant of the Lord takes on the antecedent theology of the Abrahamic promise and in two songs of the Servant of the Lord, three central tasks for the Messiah are outlined (Isa 42:1-7; 49:1-7; 53): first, he shall establish a new covenant with the people of God; second, he shall form a new social order; and third, he shall be a light to the nations.[45] Here, we find a fundamental missionary vocation of the Messiah. The Christian church believes that Jesus was *sent* by the Father to fulfill exactly this.

Several texts in the New Testament express that Jesus is sent.[46] This leads Brennan to suggest that the whole life of Jesus "is total, complete, dedication to the mission given to him by his Father. It is the guiding principle of all his words, all his actions, all his prayers."[47] Jesus is the Messiah who fulfills the eschatological expectation of Israel, who inaugurates a peaceable kingdom, who forms a new social order, who gathers the twelve tribes of Israel, and who establishes a new covenant with the people of God (Isa 49:5-6; Jer 31:27-28). Jesus is the Lord returning to Zion (Isa 60:2-3). After his death and resurrection, Jesus sends his disciples to the ends of the world (cf. Acts 1:8; Matt 28:16-20).[48] The Father sent Jesus to the world, and just as Jesus was sent, the church is now sent to the world (John 20:21). Thus, the people of God are decentered, and spread out over the entire world in order to continue the mission of Christ.[49]

So, the *missio Dei* is the starting point from which the *missio Christi* and the *missio ecclesiae* derive. The *missio Dei* leads to the sending of Jesus, and with the sending of the Holy Spirit, a *missio continuata* is set in motion.[50] Therefore, Newbigin states with good reason that the *raison d'être* of the church is its mission to the world. I find it difficult to find

---

45. Cf. ibid., 31.

46. Rom 8:3; Matt 10:40; Luke 10:16; Mark 9:37; Luke 9:48; Luke 4:18-19; John 13:20; Mark 10:40; Luke 10:16; Luke 15:24; cf. ibid., 34-35.

47. Brennan, *Christ, the One Sent*, 43.

48. However, in his early ministry, Jesus was only sent to the Jewish people; he was sent only to the lost sheep of the house of Israel (cf. Matt 15:24).

49. Newbigin, *Presiding at the Lord's Supper*, paragraph six.

50. This might shed new light on the great credal tradition of the church if the First Article (the creation of the world), the Second Article (the sending of the Son), and the Third Article (the sending of the Holy Spirit and the church), are all understood in light of mission. Cf. Guder, *The Incarnation and the Church's Witness*, 9. Also, Christ establishes the *eschaton*, and the Holy Spirit is sent to the church on the Day of Pentecost as God's gift to his people in the last days, realizing the end-time reign of God in the world. The mission of the church must be understood in relation to eschatology, as I shall return to later. See also 4.6 below.

a motive that more fundamentally epitomizes the calling of the church than this. Yoder also states that the church is spread out over the whole world to witness to God. Still, this does not change the fact that Yoder's understanding of the mission of the church is, to a great extent, centripetal. He more often than not emphasizes that the church should live its life in obedience to Christ *before the watching world*.[51] This centripetal understanding of the mission of the church is legitimate. Yet, this one-sided emphasis expresses a limitation in the theology of Yoder. It is, after all, not the world which is sent to the church, but the church that is sent to the world. Thus, Yoder could profitably have developed a stronger notion of the sending of the church to the world.

So far I have argued that God is missionary by nature and that the very creation of the people of God expresses a fundamental, missional vocation of this people. Thus, I believe it is fair to state that the sending of the church to the world must determine the self-understanding and existence of the church in the world.[52] But what is implied in this sending to the world? As I will argue below, it essentially implies that the church must exist *for* the world as Christ existed *for* the world.[53] I believe this can be qualified as a communal witness, a diaconal witness and a kerygmatic witness to the world. Given that this is a fundamental vocation for the church, it has consequences that are anything but sectarian.[54]

4.3 The Church as Community

The church is a people that confess Christ as Lord, who embody loyalty and obedience to Christ in this world. Baptism initiates persons into this people, who meet to discern their way in the world, worship and "break bread" in remembrance of their Lord.

51. Cf. the title of Yoder's book *Body Politics*.

52. Aagaard also argues for "eine sendungsbestimmte Ekklesiogie." As she states, "die Sendung ist es, die die Kirche bestimmt, und nicht umgekehrt. Mission ist nicht bloß etwas, was die Kirche *hat*. Kirche *ist* Mission, weil sie konstituiert wird durch die Gottesgegenwart der Sendungen in der Welt." See Aagaard, "Missio Dei in katholischer Sicht," 423; italics original.

53. Newbigin, *Your Kingdom Come*, 27. Cf. Goheen, "Is Lesslie Newbigin's Model of Contextualization Anticultural?," 138–41. See also 2.6.2 above.

54. Kjell Nordstokke has made me aware of the mission document, *Mission in Context*, produced by the Lutheran World Federation, which holds many similar points of view to those I have presented here. See Lutheran World Federation, *Mission in Context*.

The biblical term, *koinonia*, is not an expression of the church as such, but rather an aspect of the church. For example, in the New Testament, the term, *koinonia*, expresses fellowship with Christ (1 Cor 1:9), fellowship with others in the local church (1 John 1:3.6–7) and fellowship with other churches (2 Cor 8:4). *Koinonia* implies mutual love (John 13:34–35), a sharing of joy and sorrow (1 Cor 12:26) and a sharing of financial resources (Rom 15:26).[55] I believe this *koinonia* aspect of the church should be understood as a part of the mission of the church—that is, when Christians experience communal blessings through *koinonia*, they also serve as a missional witness to society. Thus, mission is not only about giving, but also about receiving.

This concept of the church as a distinct people in the world has often been accused of expressing a sort of ecclesial sectarianism, which will only lead the church to isolate itself from society.[56] However, the distinctiveness of the church is not to be understood spatially. Even though the church is a called-out community, it is not called to leave the world. On the contrary, the church is sent to the world. Christ embodies and incarnates a true existence in the world and, hence, as Zimmerman says: "Discipleship is not just a matter of imitating Jesus' actions but of being fully present in the world in the same way that Jesus was."[57]

Thus, Christ informs the church about its presence in the world. As we have seen, Yoder outlines several possible options for Jesus to react to the Palestinian society of his time. One option was that of violent revolution as represented by the Zealots. But, as Yoder argues, when Jesus refrained from violent revolution, it was not because it would cause too much change, but rather that it would change too little. An order created by the sword was, at the heart, not the sort of new community that Jesus had in mind.[58] Thus, Jesus could have used violence to bring his kingdom forth by force. But he did not. Another option was to escape to the desert like the Qumranites. They withdrew from the tension and conflicts of society and escaped to the desert where they believed they could be pure and perfectly faithful.[59] Jesus rejected both of these options and

---

55. Hegstad, *Den virkelige kirke*, 87–90. Hence, Sandnes argues that the early churches in many ways had several traits in common with a family. Cf. ibid., 90. See Sandnes, *A New Family*.

56. Cf. Kenneson, *Beyond Sectarianism*, 3, 14–16.

57. Zimmerman, *Practicing the Politics of Jesus*, 142.

58. Yoder, "If Christ is Truly Lord," 23–24.

59. See Yoder, "The Original Revolution," 18–33. Here Yoder lists four options for

instead created a new people who, on the one hand, were not to isolate themselves from society by taking refuge in the desert and who, on the other hand, were not to assimilate to society but should live an alternative way of life.[60] This is how Jesus found his way and thus, the church must now discern its way in a complex, modern world.

The road between isolation and assimilation is a *via dolorosa*. Jesus could have isolated himself from society and thereby have eschewed the death on the cross. But he did not. Jesus could also have assimilated with society and thereby have eschewed the death on the cross. But he did not. It is noteworthy, as Newbigin also points out, that Jesus rode directly into the center of the powers and principalities, and confronted Pontius Pilate with the fact that his kingdom was not of this world.[61] So, to follow Jesus is to follow him into the world. Suffering is, thus, a sign of the church existing between isolation and assimilation, a sign of a church not conforming to society, and proof of a church not withdrawing from society.

Interestingly, Jesus' warning of the salt losing its power, and of the lamp put under a basket, corresponds with the fundamental challenge for the church finding its way between isolation and assimilation. On the one hand, the church must not lose its saltiness; that is, the church must not assimilate with society. On the other hand, the church must not put

---

Jesus reacting to the Palestinian society of his time.

60. Here and later in this chapter I make use of the contrast between isolationism and assimilation. However, I ought to present a clarification. Yoder critiqued Richard Niebuhr for assuming culture "to be a single bloc, which an honest and consistent approach would either reject entirely or accept without qualification; you must either withdraw from it *all*, transform it *all*, or keep it *all* in paradox." See Yoder, "How H. Richard Niebuhr Reasoned," 54; italics original. Along the same lines, I do not understand "society" to be a monolithic entity which the church can fully isolate itself from or assimilate with. Rather, the dialectic interaction between the church and other communities and cultures in society is far more complex. Therefore, it is not possible to fully isolate ourselves, since we are cultural creatures by our very constitution, or to assimilate fully with all the different cultures and communities in the society in which the church lives. Still, I believe the contrast between isolation and assimilation is helpful when understood respectively as a posture of perpetual rejection and restless absorption of all kinds of cultures in society.

61. Newbigin, *Your Kingdom Come*, 33. Here, Newbigin also mentions the violent option represented by the Zealots, and the option of escaping to the desert represented by the Essenes. Newbigin says that Jesus rode into the center of the political power, whereas Yoder states that Jesus voluntarily submitted himself to these powers. See 3.4.4 above.

the lamp under the basket; that is the church must not isolate itself from society (Matt 5:13–16).[62]

Concerning this, Georg Vandervelde interestingly remarks, "for Newbigin, however, the Christian community is properly *counter-cultural* only to the extent that it is *engaged in culture*; conversely, the church is properly engaged in culture only to the extent that it is counter-cultural."[63] Newbigin expresses the tension in this difficult balancing act with the concept of "challenging relevance."[64] He warns the church against both challenging society without becoming a part of the culture and becoming conformed to culture without challenging it.[65] One might also say that Newbigin challenges the church to find its way between isolation and assimilation.

Furthermore, the church's existence between isolation and assimilation can never be defined in static terms. I have argued that the foreignness of the church is an aspect of its very ontology and should deliberately be a part of being church.[66] However, the distinctiveness of the church cannot be predetermined once and for all, and must instead be discerned in each new situation. Yoder rightly states that the church is not always different, or in every way different, since others will often act in the same way because it is normal, humane, or democratic.[67] Thus, the church's distinctiveness is a "dynamic distinctiveness" or a "variable distinctiveness."

The church is sent to the world and, therefore, must be present in society, in various segments of society. Therefore, the church must develop new, flexible structures so that it may become present in these various segments of Western society. Engaging new subcultures will inevitably shape the church, which is a natural consequence of the church being sent into the world, and thus the life of the church in the world. All human life is embedded in culture and so, too, was Jesus' life embedded in culture. The church's sending into the world will, thus, raise new questions that may give new insight to the gospel.

62. Both metaphors imply a minority status of the church.

63. Vandervelde, *The Church as Missionary Community*, 6; italics original.

64. See, for example, Newbigin, "Christ and the Cultures," 12; Newbigin, "Mission in the 1980s," 154–55.

65. Newbigin, *Foolishness to the Greeks*, 7; see also Newbigin, "The Cultural Captivity of Western Christianity as a Challenge to a Missionary Church," 67–68.

66. Cf. Wright, *Walking in the Ways of the Lord*, 161.

67. Yoder, "The Believers' Church and the Arms Race," 156.

In conclusion, even though the church is a called-out community, this should not lead to isolationism. The church is sent to the world, and therefore must not divorce itself from society, but should make present in the world what would otherwise be absent: a people confessing Christ as Lord.[68] Therefore, being *not of this world* and being *in the world* do not necessarily contradict each other.

4.4 The Church as Servant

As we have seen, the very creation of the people of God is bound to a missional vocation.[69] Thus, the mission of the church must determine the self-understanding and existence of the church in the world. In relation to this, I will now qualify the mission of the church as a diaconal witness to the world.

Jesus in fact gave a "social structure to the group of those who followed him."[70] Yoder has clearly demonstrated this. Jesus incarnated and embodied obedience to God, and his life is a paradigm for how Christians are to exist in the world. As Yoder says, "Christ was exactly what God meant man to be; man in free communion with God, obeying God and loving mankind, even his enemies with God's love."[71] Thus, Christian ethics is located for Christians within the context of the distinct community called the church, which seeks to embody faithfulness to God. Thus, the Christian community constitutes a common ethical commitment and reasoning which differs from society. Such points of views have often been accused of promoting a sort of ethical sectarianism: If Christian ethics is only for Christians, does not the church then lose an outward focus? Should the church then stop advising on matters of public policy?[72] Will this not then lead to an abnegation of responsibility for society? As we shall now see, I believe this critique is mistaken. Christian ethics is for Christians, but this does not necessarily lead to the church cutting itself

---

68. Cf. Hauerwas, *Christian Existence Today*, 195.
69. See 4.2 above.
70. Lohfink, *Does God Need the Church?*, 157.
71. Quoted in LeMasters, *The Import of Eschatology*, 59.
72. For example, Nelson says that, if Stanley Hauerwas "were to be consistent, he would relinquish the possibility of advising (however generally) on matters of public policy." See Nelson, *Narrative and Morality*, 138.

off from the society in which the church exists. Christian ethics simply shows how *Christians* should take responsibility for society.

This becomes clear when we draw our attention to *diakonia* as an important mark of the social life of the church. As Newbigin points out, God has sent Jesus to the world (cf. John 20:21) in order to serve and give his life for many (Mark 10:45).[73] Moreover, Paul characterizes Jesus as *diakonos* (Rom 15:8) and even as *doulos* (Phil 2:7). Christ's healing of the sick and the disabled (Matt 4:23–25) and his fellowship with sinners and tax collectors (Matt 11:19) may, in this way, be viewed as a part of his servant ministry. For this reason, the disciples are sent out to heal the sick and preach the gospel (Luke 9:2). Thus, the church is now incorporated in the mission of Jesus: it is sent to serve, and when it serves the naked, the sick, the hungry, and the stranger, it in fact serves Christ (Matt 25:31–46; see also Acts 5:12–16). We therefore can say that serving the world is a *nota Christi* and should also be a *nota corporis Christi*.[74] Hence, as Newbigin says, the "fundamental form"[75] or "authentic nature"[76] of the church must be the form of a servant. Here, Yoder would likely say that the servant nature of the church is not something new, as the people of God were told to pray for and seek the welfare of the people they were living among, as seen already in the Old Testament (Jer 29:7).[77]

As we have seen, Newbigin refers to the early church as an example of how the church must let this servant nature impact its liturgy and way of life.[78] If this is also to be the case for the church in a post-Christendom society, the church is confronted with several major challenges. First, as

---

73. See 2.3.1 above.

74. This would be a natural consequence of Yoder's theological methodology. Also, I have here stressed the service of the church to people outside the church. However, in the New Testament, *diakonia* is most often used to designate how Christians should serve each other. See, for example, Phil 2:5–7; 1 Pet 4:10; Heb 6:10.

75. Newbigin, "Bible Studies Given at the National Christian Council Triennial Assembly, Shillong," 131; cf. Goheen, *As the Father Has Sent Me*, 303.

76. Newbigin, "The Church as a Servant Community," 261.

77. Cf. 3.4.3 above. On the close connection between Israel and the church, Lindbeck says, "Christians identified themselves as the same people of God of which the Old Testament speaks (. . .). Their churches simply were Israel—Israel in the New Age, to be sure, and Israel as including the uncircumcised who believed in the Jewish Messiah, but nonetheless Israel. This conviction is reflected in the New Testament. The ecclesiology of the Apostolic writings is, one might say, Israelo-logy." See Lindbeck, "The Gospel's Uniqueness," 435. This is of course related to the debate concerning "supersession," which I cannot discuss here.

78. See 2.6.2 above.

Newbigin also argues, the church has often been so entrenched in the established order, that it has neglected to take the side of the weak, marginalized and oppressed. It has sought prestige, rather than humble service. It has indulged in the advantages of fraternizing with elite, rather than serving the poor. Second, Newbigin also rightly states that powerful denominational structures and nationwide agencies for social action have led to an understanding of social responsibility "no longer [being] seen as the direct responsibility of the local congregation except insofar as they are called upon to support them financially."[79] Third, due to the close connection between church and state, the church has in many countries, especially in Northern Europe, entrusted some of its most important tasks to the state. This has occurred to such an extent that many Christians do not know how the church should exercise diaconal ministry in a welfare society. The church should not, however, rely on the state in this. It must be true to its own nature, and thus engage itself in the diaconal service of society.[80] This is also true since all states are limited. Along the same lines, Gerhard Lohfink frankly states, "[the church] must not surrender more and more of its tasks to the state so that, in the end, it is reduced to a watered-down separate department of society responsible only for the rites of passage and marginal situations, or acts as guarantor of the hope for life beyond."[81]

A rediscovering of the church's distinctive identity implies a rediscovering of the church's diaconal ministry as an essential aspect of its own nature and identity. While the church considers itself as part of the protected chaplaincy[82] and spiritual arm of society,[83] this can in actual fact lead to the church losing itself, that is, its diaconal engagement and responsibility for society. This is not to say that the church cannot learn from the world about how to act in service of the world. For example, the church can learn much about social justice from the world. Hence, it is not only the world that can learn from the church, but also the church that can learn from the world. Therefore, the church may occasionally cooperate with organizations and other communities that have the same intent as the church.

---

79. Newbigin, *The Gospel in a Pluralist Society*, 229.
80. Cf. Cavanaugh, "Separation and Wholeness," 28.
81. Lohfink, *Does God Need the Church?*, 290.
82. Newbigin, "Christ, Kingdom, and Church," 4.
83. Newbigin, *Your Kingdom Come*, 28.

However, a rediscovering of the distinctive identity of the church also implies that the church must rediscover a renewed acceptance of those who live differently than them. Christianity is no longer the ideological foundation for contemporary Western society, and in many Western countries Christians are now a minority. Almost everywhere in Western society, church and state today parallel each other as two independent institutions with their own ideological foundation in a way that was unthinkable at the time of the Reformation.[84] Still, if the church is convinced that it knows the true way of living, then why should the church not advise society how to follow this way of life? I believe the answer to this question is three-fold.

First, it should advise society how to follow the way of Christ. But the task for the church is not to impose Christian legislation on a post-Christendom society, but to invite people to become a part of a distinct community that follows the example of Christ called the church. Everything else would be imperialism. Second, however, the church should not complain if society adopts Christian practices. That has happened often in history. Thus, we have seen how Yoder demonstrates that minorities often have contributed to society by way of social creativity.[85] Along the same lines, Arne Rasmusson has demonstrated how Christian minorities have impacted the wider society; pointing out several examples, he argues that an important inspiration of modern democracy came from the Independents, the Anabaptists, and the Quakers, and that the modern struggle against slavery in England and the English colonies was driven by Mennonites, Quakers and evangelical Christians.[86] Thus, history shows that minorities can and often have contributed constructively to society. Third, with Yoder, we may also say that even though the church should not impose Christian legislation on society, it can still in its critique of the state encourage the state to live up to its own ideals. Thus, the church cannot refer to Christ as the authority or use Christian language, but must use worldly terms like "liberty," "equality," "democracy" and "human rights" when asking society or the state to live up to its own principles.[87] Hence, the church should not appeal to *agape*, but "to the

84. Lyby, "Luthers øvrighedsskrift i historisk perspektiv," 16.

85. Yoder, "Christ, the Hope of the World," 171–74. See also Yoder, "On Not Being in Charge," 174.

86. Rasmusson, "The Church as a 'Creative Minority,'" 72-88. See also 3.6.2 above.

87. Yoder, *The Christian Witness to the State*, 73. Yoder calls these translated concepts for "middle axioms." In his book *The Christian Witness to the State*, he presents

state's concept of *justitia*."[88] Often, the church is forced to participate in society in this relatively indirect manner, as it will rarely help to argue "But Christ said . . . "[89] in public debates.

In conclusion, since Christianity is no longer the moral foundation of society, the church can no longer speak on behalf of the whole of society. The Christian ethic is for Christians, but this does not mean that Christians cannot take responsibility for society. Thus, a part of the church's distinctive identity is that it serves the world or at least should do so. Hence, the church can only serve society on its own terms, and can by no means compromise its loyalty to Christ. To do so, some would say, may limit the service of the church in society. Yet this may in fact promote creative contributions to society. Hence, it is evident that being *not of this world* and being *for this world* are not mutually exclusive.

4.5 The Church as Prophet

I have argued that the mission of the church must determine its very existence in the world.[90] Like Israel, the church is meant to be a light to the world. It must, in its life, deeds and words, serve and witness to the world. I will now examine the mission of the church as a kerygmatic witness to the world.

The Christian church believes that God has acted throughout history to reveal himself and, as we have seen, Newbigin believes this to imply that Christianity offers a whole new *arché* or a whole new starting point for understanding reality. Thus, I agree with Newbigin when he says: "The Christian tradition of rationality takes as its starting point not any alleged self-evident truths. Its starting point is events in which God made himself known to men and women in particular circumstances (. . .) to the

---

nine examples of "middle axioms." See ibid., 35–44. Also, LeMasters believes that this expresses a Constantinian strategy. See LeMasters, *The Import of Eschatology*, 198.

88. Yoder, "The Theological Basis of the Christian Witness to the State," 143.

89. The thoughts presented in this paragraph are subject of major discussions within political philosophy. For example, Stanley Hauerwas takes up a position that promotes a view that emphasizes the specific traditions and languages of various communities in society, whereas, for example, Jürgen Habermas emphasizes a common language and rationality in the public space. Habermas's position is, however, interpreted differently. I would also say that Nigel Biggar and Jeffrey Stout, for example, hold moderate mid-positions in this debate. Above, I have limited myself to present a few perspectives inspired by Yoder.

90. See 4.2 above.

first apostles and witnesses who saw and heard and touched the incarnate Word of God himself, Jesus of Nazareth."[91] Similar to Newbigin's thought, but also inspired by Yoder, I wish to briefly consider three important factors that determine this interpretation of reality: namely, the revelation in Christ, the Christian tradition, and the Christian community.[92]

Thus, the *church* is a social embodiment of a *tradition* with a special understanding of reality, which takes *Christ* as the starting point. First, the Christian church takes God's self-revelation in Christ as the starting point for its understanding of reality.[93] Christ is an *episteme* which is a distinctive source for the church's understanding of the world. Christ is divine revelation, and Scripture testifies to this revelation. The knowledge that Scripture offers is not purely propositional, but formational, and thus shapes the life of the church by both training and helping it to live in the world. Second, the church has an obligation to its own tradition and must therefore understand reality in accordance with this tradition. However, the limits of this tradition are difficult to discern and, thus, it "is not a source of authority separate from Scripture" and the revelation in Christ.[94] This implies that new theological assertions sustain a burden of legitimization to prove their Christian authenticity.[95] Third, the church is a hermeneutic community that maintains and communicates an understanding of the gospel and the world. It is a community that participates in an open, communal process of reading Scripture, guided by the Holy Spirit and in light of confessing Christ as Lord. As Yoder states, this is how the authors of Scripture imagine Scripture being read: in the church and in light of the confession to Christ as Lord.

Both Newbigin and Yoder oppose foundationalism, thus denying a self-evident and universally accepted foundation for human knowledge.[96] This is, however, not to say that theology and the church do not have a foundation. Theology does in fact have a foundation, namely the divine revelation in Christ. Rather, the intention here is to make clear that this foundation is only acknowledged within a distinct community called "the church." However, such a stance has often been accused of ex-

---

91. Newbigin, *The Gospel in a Pluralist Society*, 63.
92. See 2.7.3 and 2.7.5 above.
93. Newbigin, *Truth and Authority in Modernity*, 38.
94. Ibid., 49.
95. Gregersen, *Teologi og kultur*, 237. See also 1.3 above.
96. Cf. Nikolajsen, "Lesslie Newbigins postfundamentistiske epistemologi."

pressing a sort of epistemological sectarianism.[97] As Philip D. Kenneson asserts: "Those charged with being epistemological sectarians argue that knowledge claims and their justifications are always rooted in particular, tradition-dependent assumptions, rather than in universal, tradition-independent ones. Most so-called epistemological sectarians presuppose and endorse the contemporary critique of foundationalism."[98] In other words, if the church is a social embodiment of a distinct understanding of reality, this would apparently lead to sectarianism, tribalism and a closed replica of the Christian tradition. I disagree.

The flaw in this argument becomes clear when we draw our attention to the proclamation of the gospel to the world as an important mark of the identity of the church.[99] An important mark of the ministry of Jesus was that he proclaimed the gospel, which he did for more than just his disciples (Matt 4:23–25). So should it also be for the church. As proclaiming the gospel to the world is a *nota Christi*, it should also be a *nota corporis Christi*. Let me here refer to Niels Henrik Gregersen, who says,

> If the motivation of theology only is that there should be preaching on Sundays and if the function of theology only is constituted by the needs of the church, then it is at least possible to claim that the only truth demand that is required of theology is that its truth claims should correspond with the confession of the church. If, on the contrary, society in its totality makes up the context of theology, then, theology is forced to acknowledge that its truth claims must be made intelligible within this context.[100]

However, this is not to say that the church should make the gospel acceptable to the modern world, or that it should explain the gospel on the basis of Western culture. The church must refer to Christ as a new starting point for the understanding of human existence, or as Newbigin

---

97. Cf. Kenneson, *Beyond Sectarianism*, 20–24.

98. Ibid., 20.

99. Dodd summarizes the *kerygma* of Peter's speeches in Acts like this: "First, the age of fulfillment has dawned," "Second, this has taken place through the birth, life, ministry, death and resurrection of Jesus Christ," "Third, by virtue of the resurrection Jesus has been exalted at the right hand of God as Messianic head of the new Israel," "Fourth, the Holy Spirit in the Church is the sign of Christ's present power and glory," "Fifth, the Messianic Age will reach its consummation in the return of Christ," "Six, an appeal is made for repentance with the offer of forgiveness, the Holy Spirit, and salvation." See *Apostolic Preaching and Its Developments*, 21–24. Dodd also identifies a Pauline *kerygma*. See ibid., 24–26.

100. Gregersen, *Teologi og kultur*, 41; my translation.

puts it, as an alternative foundation for a new plausibility structure. Thus, it is not the task of the church to make the gospel acceptable to modern thought, but to refer to it as a new starting point for seeing the world.[101] This implies that Christian truth claims may often be affirmed in conflict with society.[102] However, this must not lead the church to withdraw from society. The church is sent to the world to proclaim the gospel to *the whole of creation* (Mark 16:15), demonstrating, for example, a better alternative to the origin of the world than simple coincidence, and a better explanation of the meaning of life than just materialism. As Newbigin explains:

> [The church] is called to be that community in which a tradition of rational discourse is developed which leads to a true understanding of reality, because it takes as its starting point and as its permanent criterion of truth the self-revelation of God in Jesus Christ. It is necessarily a *particular* community among all the human communities. It cannot pretend to be otherwise. But it has a *universal* mission, for it is the community chosen and sent by God for this purpose.[103]

Johannes Aagaard elaborates on this theme as follows,

> [The proclamation] is the decisive task of the church in its mission, because—in this understanding—the church is first of all understood as the community of those who know the truth about this world. The world does not know about itself, it is blind and walks in darkness. In the proclaiming acts of the church, in its witness too, the world receives the knowledge about itself and about its God. There has been in Protestant missiology since the Barthian influence began, a strong emphasis on the cognitive function of the church in its mission.[104]

In regards to this, Gregersen notes that there exist two fundamental dangers for the church. On the one hand, "the constitutional self-reference of Christianity" may lead the church to become an isolated replica of its own tradition, while on the other hand, "the constitutional openness of Christianity" may lead the church to assimilate with the surrounding society.[105] Thus, the church must find its way in this complex world,

---

101. Newbigin, "Gospel and Culture."
102. Newbigin, *On the Gospel as Public Truth*, paragraph 3.
103. Newbigin, *The Gospel in a Pluralist Society*, 87–88; italics mine.
104. Aagaard, "Some Main Trends in Modern Protestant Missiology," 242.
105. Gregersen, *Teologi og kultur*, 25; my translation.

becoming present in various segments of society, serving the world "by giving the world the means to see itself truthfully."[106]

The church must explore the meaning of the gospel in relation to new circumstances as it shares the gospel with the world. Doing this, the church may make use of the language of society as did Jesus: "[He] translated the message of the kingdom into a language that could be grasped by a tax collector and a prostitute, a leper and a Samaritan, a learned Pharisee and an uneducated fisherman."[107] Thus, even though the divine revelation in Christ is only acknowledged within the church, this does not mean that the church cannot claim universal validity. This epistemological particularity does not lead away from universality, but into it. Again, this is not to say that the church should explain the gospel based on the premises of Western culture, but the church may have to make use of concepts and imagery other than its own in order to proclaim what is true for all.

All of these reflections could, indeed, have been unfolded far more comprehensively. Here my intention has been to emphasize that if mission is to determine the existence of the church in the world, then the church cannot leave the world or keep the gospel to itself. It should also be emphasized that I am not suggesting that the Christian faith offers a theoretical interpretation by which we can understand every detail of reality. In contrast to this, the church can, in fact, learn much about the world from sources other than the divine revelation in Christ. However, the church will be increasingly challenged on its way of viewing the world in a post-Christendom society, and yet, the church has too often sought the acceptance of society, while its task should rather be to question fundamental assumptions of society. Thus, the collapse of the Old Christendom calls for a change in the role of the church in society, as the church can no longer be the baptizer of the whole society, but must now act as a prophet or a herald proclaiming the gospel to the world.[108]

---

106. Hauerwas, *The Peaceable Kingdom*, 101–2. Lutherans would say that this is the work of the law.

107. Guder, *The Incarnation and the Church's Witness*, 51.

108. Cf. Yoder, "The Otherness of the Church," 56. See also Goldingay, "The Man of War and the Suffering Servant: The Old Testament and the Theology of Liberation," 79–113.

4.6 Oriented to the Kingdom of God

The New Testament's message is that the promised new age has dawned and that the kingdom of God has broken into the world. Even though the church does not fully establish the kingdom of God, it is still a sign of this kingdom. This fact reflects a tension between maintaining an eschatological humility on the one hand and, on the other hand, insisting that the church, in spite of its sinfulness, in fact points to the consummation of the kingdom of God. Even though the church is a result of the *missio Dei*, "the final and real goal of the *missio Dei* (. . .) is not the Church, but the establishment of God's kingdom, to which the Church as *ecclesia viatorum* is on its way."[109]

The church is inescapably part of the new eschatological reality, which has broken into the world. The awaited age came "into history in a decisive way with the incarnation and the entire work of Christ."[110] Jesus created a distinct community where the kingdom of God is meant to break through, and where individuals are invited to join voluntarily. Thus, in the midst of the world, a people exist that refuse to acknowledge worldly powers and principalities as ultimate realities, but still confess Christ as Lord. The Holy Spirit is given to this people as an eschatological sign. Even though the church is not to be identified with the kingdom, the very existence of the church still points to the coming kingdom of God.[111] Hence, the church belongs to the realm of eschatology.

The church as a distinct social order is also an inescapable part of this new eschatological reality that has broken into the world. As Newbigin rightly asserts: "The works of mercy, of healing, of liberation—all are part of the breaking in of a new reality (. . .) the deeds of healing and liberation must not be separated from the new reality of which they are a part. They are part of the overflowing of God's grace. Jesus' deeds of love were not part of a contrived program with some ulterior purpose: they were the overflowing of the love which filled his whole being. Just so, the Church's deeds of love ought to be—not contrived signs but natural and spontaneous signs of the new reality in which we have been made sharers through Christ."[112]

---

109. Andersen, "Further Toward a Theology of Mission," 304.

110. Yoder, "If Christ Is Truly Lord," 55.

111. Newbigin, *Mission in Christ's Way*, 12; Newbigin, "Does Society Still Need the Parish Church?," 62; Newbigin, "Church, World, Kingdom," 106.

112. Newbigin, *The Good Shepherd*, 93.

Just as ecclesiology and social ethics belong to the realm of eschatology, so does epistemology. Not only the hearts of Christians, but also their minds and thoughts are transformed and renewed (Titus 1:1–3). God's wisdom has been revealed for the church, a wisdom that is foreign for the rulers of this age (1 Cor 1:20–21; 2:8; 3:19). At present, Christians only know in part, but when the end is coming they shall know fully (1 Cor 1:5; 12:8–12; 2 Cor 8:7). The church has knowledge about the coming kingdom even before the world has reached its *telos*. Thus, the church has partial epistemic access to this coming kingdom.

In other words, God has chosen a people (ecclesiology), who he transforms (social ethics) and enlightens (epistemology) as a foretaste and sign of the kingdom that shall one day be established. God has infused the Holy Spirit into this community in order to make this happen. Thus, ecclesiology, social ethics, and epistemology must be understood in light of missiology as well as eschatology. Consequently, the very ontology of the church obtains a teleology. The church is, here and now, anticipating what it will be in the future. The church is not an end in itself, but rather, points to the age that is to come. The being, acting and knowing of the people of God are determined by the future it points to.

4.7 Conclusion

In this chapter, I have demonstrated that a missionary God has sent the church and, consequently, this sending must fundamentally determine its existence in the world. I have argued that even though an inescapable distinctiveness is an integral part of ecclesiology, social ethics, and epistemology, this should not lead to isolationism. I have pointed out that the church will always be oriented toward the coming kingdom. Thus, I have, in continuation of the preceding two chapters, centered an understanding of the church around five central theological themes which are inextricably linked with each other.

The primary goal in this chapter has been to argue that mission should frame and determine the existence of the church in the world, and that the distinctiveness of the church by no means should threaten an engagement in society. I have argued that this distinctiveness must not lead the church to isolate itself from society, abnegate responsibility for society or become a closed replica of its own tradition. On the contrary, I have argued that a strong emphasis on the distinctive identity of the church should be seen as an important precondition for its involvement in society.

Closing this book, I will now present a concluding summation and point to three major challenges for the church in Western society implied in the ecclesiological position I have outlined.

PART V
Conclusion

5
Corpus Christianum or *Corpus Christi*?

TO SUMMARIZE, DURING THE past three centuries, the church has gradually lost its central and influential role in Western society due to important cultural and religious changes. Therefore, an increasing number of theologians believe that the Western world has moved from, or is in transition from, an era of Christendom to one of post-Christendom. The formerly Christian West is today to a large extent multi-religious, and the formerly homogeneous West is now a highly diverse society.

This book underlines the fact that this development in the Western world raises important challenges for the church in Western culture. With the collapse of the old Christendom, the self-understanding of the church is now threatened, and a theological inquiry into the distinctive identity of the church and its role in a modern Western society has become more and more pressing. Whereas much traditional ecclesiology has been developed in a context where ecclesial hegemony could be presupposed, and where society was characterized by strong social coherence, in recent years, a number of ecclesiological contributions have been developed which no longer take this for granted.

This book goes, I believe, to the heart of this ecclesiological debate asking a decisive question: How are we to understand the distinctive identity of the church with special reference to its role in a post-Christendom society? Thus, this book presents an analysis of the work of two theologians who have responded to the new situation in which the church now finds itself, and who reflect on how we should understand the important question posed above. The analyses have not focused on these two authorships for their own sake but have had a constructive aim, namely, to construct two positions which can be related, learned from, and built upon in the ongoing development of a post-Christendom ecclesiology.[1]

---

1. This approach to theological research is quite similar to a model presented by Browning. He outlines "a fundamental practical theology," arguing that theological

What have these analyses, then, shown? They demonstrate how Lesslie Newbigin's writings present a strong theological critique of Christendom, most importantly, pointing out how the church lost sight of mission in the era of Christendom. We have also seen how Newbigin, against the fusion of church and world, which is designated as *corpus Christianum*, argues that the church, *corpus Christi*, normally and in various ways will differ from its surrounding society. It turns out that, to Newbigin, an inescapable distinctiveness is an integral part of ecclesiology, missiology, eschatology, social ethics, and epistemology, rooted in the church. Thus, the church is a chosen people (ecclesiology), meant to embody God's mission in the world (missiology), manifest the kingdom of God in the world (eschatology), be a distinct social order in the world (social ethics), and embody a tradition of a particular way of viewing the world (epistemology).

Newbigin believes, based on both historical and theological evidence, that the normal status of the church is that of a minority or at least of a functional minority. First, given that the era of Christendom is over, the church in the Western world must come to terms with new societal parameters and accept its minority status. Second, due to theological reasons, Newbigin believes that the church will often make up a minority within society.

Furthermore, for Newbigin, the idea of a neutral, secular society is a myth and, therefore, the choice between a religious and a neutral public space is really a choice between Christ and idolatry. Thus, as he argues, where Christ is not present in society, an idol takes his place. Based on this, he asserts that the task of the church is to intentionally impact and shape various areas of society (such as art, economy, science, and politics) from its Christian standpoint. As he sees it, the church under Christendom claimed an equivalent responsibility for society, which Newbigin understands in positive terms. His "particularistic" ecclesiology, however, implies that the church cannot expect society to be fully Christianized, as the church will in most cases be a minority. I have criticized Newbigin, arguing that the church is not called to Christianize society, but to

---

thought must always enter into dialogue with the practical reality of the church. He, thus, argues that the task of theology is to deal with the practical problems that the church is confronted with. The task of theology is to deal theoretically with these problems, serving and guiding the church along the way. As a result, theology must move from practice to theory and back again from theory to practice. I have no intention of reflecting on Christian theology without relating it to the real life of the church. See *A Fundamental Practical Theology*, 13–74.

make disciples of Christ, which is not the same. I do believe, however, that society may pick up Christian practices, with the church in this way becoming an important and legitimate inspiration for society.

Newbigin, in actual fact, went further in his argument, promoting a vision for a "Christian society" at the end of the 1990s. He believed that, because the Christian church preserves the freedom to dissent and to disobey, it is capable of providing a framework for a pluralistic society. In this way, the church could reflect that God is not only Lord of the church but also of the world, thus being a faithful witness of God's rightful rule over all. I have criticized Newbigin on this point, arguing that his suggestion is foreign to early Christianity, and should not be envisioned today. I have also pointed out that his vision for a Christian society contradicts his own thinking about "the powers and principalities," which he typifies as fallen structures in this world, which are rebellious against God, and act against the good intentions of God. Thus, as it appears in his later work, Newbigin came to the eventual conclusion that it was a mistake to speak of a Christian society, and therefore he completely avoided using the phrase in his last years.

John Howard Yoder's writings present a fundamental theological critique of Constantinianism, which provides the background for important aspects of his theological project, with all significant perspectives in one way or another relating to the distinctiveness of the church. Constantinianism is, in Yoder's thought, a metaphor for a shift in the relationship between church and world that has had, and continues to have, ramifications which are profoundly corrupting ecclesiology.[2] Thus, he presents a profound critique of the fusion of the church and the world, designated as *corpus Christianum*. Against this, Yoder argues that the church, *corpus Christi*, will always be a distinct social entity within the society in which it lives. To Yoder, a particularity is an integral part of ecclesiology, social ethics, and eschatology which qualify important aspects of the distinctive identity of the church: first, Constantinianism led to all citizens, and in fact the entire social order, being declared Christian, which resulted in the church severely compromising its integrity as a distinct community of faith; second, Constantinianism fused the church and the world, resulting in the church consisting of people for whom the presuppositions of discipleship, and the ethical requirements set by the church, were absent; third, to Yoder, the state cannot express the realm of redemption

---

2. LeMasters, *The Import of Eschatology*, 101.

and manifest God's reign, but the church is the unique foretaste of the new age, through the power of the Spirit.

Yoder shows how misleading it is to claim that a whole society can be regarded as Christian, and to claim that the church should be the soul or moral teacher of society, when society does not follow the way of Christ or acknowledge Christ as Lord. He believes that the normal existence for the Jewish people is existence in exile, and that the notion of exile preconfigured the Christian understanding of the church's existence in the world. Thus, in the writings of Yoder, we find important theological sources for understanding how the church must exist in a highly diverse post-Christendom society. Hence, the church must become present in various segments and subcultures of modern, Western society.

In relation to the preceding analyses, this book then discusses the charge of sectarianism, which has played a central role in ecclesiological debates for several years, especially in North America. On the background of the preceding analyses of this book, a synthetic-constructive method was employed, framing three important aspects of the church from a missiological perspective, all with the purpose of arguing that a strong notion of the distinctiveness of the church must not lead to isolationism. Thus, I have argued that mission should fundamentally determine the church's existence in the world. Subsequently, I have argued that even though an inescapable particularity is an integral part of ecclesiology, social ethics, and epistemology, this must, by no means, lead to isolationism. I have argued that this distinctiveness should not lead the church to isolate itself from society, abnegate responsibility for society, or become a closed replica of its own tradition. On the contrary, this particularity should constitute the basis for its openness and engagement in society. However, this ecclesiological position implies major challenges for the church in Western society.

First, it points to a major challenge for theologians dealing with ecclesiology. Since the Enlightenment, the ecclesial hegemony in the Western world has gradually been disestablished.[3] Yet, many theologians refuse to accept that the church now exists within a pluralistic society and that it can no longer be the task of the church to create a social cohesion within society or to be responsible for sustaining a common national identity.[4] Since the church is a distinct people, and since Christians today

---

3. Badham and Sigurdson, "The Decentered Post-Constantinian Church," 155.

4. On the notion of creating social cohesion in society, see Cavanaugh, "Separation and Wholeness," 25–26. On the notion of sustaining a common national identity, see Lodberg and Ryman, "Church and Society," 99–100.

are a minority in many Western countries, it cannot be the task of the church to create harmonious social coherence in society. However, my primary intention has not been to argue that since we cannot overcome the present societal realities, we might as well adjust.[5] More profoundly, I suggest that the Western society has gone through a historical and cultural shift that should open our eyes to a fundamental theological truth, namely that the true church will always be a distinct social entity within the society in which it lives.

Second, this also points to a major challenge for theologians dealing with social ethics. As Roger A. Badham and Ola Sigurdson assert, "it is [their] contention that Protestant social ethics, as heir to medieval and Reformation theologies and Enlightenment moral theories, have continued to function under the rubric of universality. Mainline Protestant theology has largely refused to give up its role of speaking on behalf of the whole society."[6] This expresses a sort of imperialism, and ultimately violence, which contradicts the very nature of the gospel, the kingdom of God and the church. Also, as a consequence of the close relationship between church and state, the church in many Western societies, especially in Northern Europe, has surrendered some of its most important tasks to the welfare state, to such an extent that the diaconal ministry of the church in many places has virtually disappeared. However, all states are limited, and the church cannot simply entrust the state to take over a task that belongs to the very nature of the church.

Third, this also points to a major challenge for theologians dealing with epistemology. Given that the church now exists in a post-Christendom society, it must acknowledge that the Christian worldview is no longer shared by the whole of society. Accepting Christ as Lord implies seeing the world in a new way that will in many ways, not be self-evident and reasonable for a society that does not accept Christ as divine revelation. However, the church has too often sought the acceptance of society, when its task should rather be to question fundamental assumptions of society, highlighting society's refusal to acknowledging Christ as Lord. This calls for an imperative change of role for the church today. The

---

5. Hauerwas and Willimon, *Resident Aliens*, 38–39.

6. Badham and Sigurdson, "The Decentered Post-Constantinian Church," 156. In contrast to Badham and Sigurdson, Lodberg and Ryman seem to agree with the critique of the revival movements in the Nordic countries that the theological heritage of these movements is one of individual ethics and therefore lacks "a coherent view of social ethics for all of society." See Lodberg and Ryman, "Church and Society," 109.

church can no longer be the baptizer of the whole society, but must now instead act as a herald and prophet proclaiming the gospel to the world.[7]

Not only the Christian church, but also Christian theology, is in a time of transition as a result of the collapse of the old Christendom. Consequently, theology should acknowledge its own distinctiveness by developing theological reflection in support of a church, which exists in a post-Christendom society. This calls for a reconfiguration of Western theological discourse. The task that lies before the church in the Western world is not to bypass its distinctiveness with accusations of sectarianism, but to provide constructive contributions to the ongoing ecclesiological conversation that acknowledge that the church in the Western world no longer includes everyone.

Acknowledging that mission must determine the life of the church in the world should serve as a warning that the church can never leave the world or keep the gospel to itself, and should prompt the church turn outward to the society in which it lives. The task that lies before the church in the Western world is to recapture a profound understanding of its own distinctive identity and to let this distinctiveness constitute the basis for its openness to, responsibility for, and engagement in the society in which it exists. Such an ecclesiological position holds, in my mind, significant potential for an understanding of the role of the church in pluralistic Western societies. Such a position, I believe, points to the future of the church in Western societies.

---

7. Cf. Yoder, "The Otherness of the Church," 56; Goldingay, "The Man of War and the Suffering Servant," 79–113.

Bibliography

Aagaard, Anna Marie. "Missio Dei in katholischer Sicht." *Evangelische Theologie* 34 (1974) 420–33.
Aagaard, Johannes. "Some Main Trends in Modern Protestant Missiology." *Studia Theologica* 19 (1965) 238–56.
Ahonen, Tina. "Antedating Missional Church: David Bosch's Views on the Missionary Nature of the Church and on the Missionary Structure of the Congregation." *Swedish Missiological Themes* 92 (2004) 573–89.
Andersen, Heine, and Lars Bo Kaspersen, eds. *Klassisk og moderne samfundsteori.* Copenhagen: Reitzels, 2003.
Andersen, Wilhelm. "Further toward a Theology of Mission." In *The Theology of Christian Mission*, edited by Wilhelm Andersen, 300–314. New York: McGraw-Hill, 1961.
———. *Towards a Theology of Mission: A Study of the Encounter between the Missionary Enterprise and the Church and its Theology.* IMC Research Pamphlet 2. London: SCM, 1965.
Bader-Saye, Scott. *Church and Israel after Christendom.* Boulder, CO: Westview, 1999.
Badham, Roger A., and Ola Sigurdson. "The Decentered Post-Constantinian Church: An Exchange." *Cross Currents* 47 (1997) 154–65.
Barnes, Timothy. *Constantine and Eusebius.* Cambridge, MA: Harvard University Press, 1981.
Bartley, Jonathan. *Faith and Politics after Christendom.* Carlisle, UK: Paternoster, 2006.
Baynes, Norman H. *Constantine the Great and the Christian Church.* London: Milford, 1929.
Berentsen, Jan-Martin. "Missio Dei: Nøkkelbegrep til bestemmelse av et hovedproblem i etterkrigstidens protestantiske misjonstenkning." *Norwegian Journal of Missiology* 37 (1983) 1–19.
Berger, Peter L., and Thomas Luckmann. *The Social Construction of Reality: A Treatise in the Sociology of Knowledge.* Garden City, NY: Anchor, 1966.
Berkhof, Hendrik. *Christ and the Powers.* Translated by John H. Yoder. Scottdale, PA: Herald, 1962.
———. *Christ the Meaning of History.* Richmond: Knox, 1966.
Bevans, Stephen B. *Models of Contextual Theology.* Rev. and exp. ed. Maryknoll, NY: Orbis, 2002.
Bevans, Stephen B., and Roger P. Schroeder. *Constants in Context: A Theology of Mission for Today.* Maryknoll, NY: Orbis, 2004.
Blauw, Johannes. *The Missionary Nature of the Church: A Survey of the Biblical Theology of Mission.* 2nd ed. Cambridge: Lutterworth, 2002.
Bonhoeffer, Dietrich. *The Cost of Discipleship.* London: SCM, 1995.

Bosch, David J. *Transforming Mission: Paradigm Shifts in the Theology of Mission.* Maryknoll, NY: Orbis, 1991.

———. *Witness to the World.* Atlanta: Knox, 1980.

Buber, Martin. *Ich und Du.* Berlin: Schocken, 1922.

Bredero, Adriaan H. *Christendom and Christianity in the Middle Ages.* Grand Rapids: Eerdmans, 1994.

Brennan, John P. *Christ, the One Sent.* Collegeville, MN: Liturgical, 1997.

Bretherton, Luke. "Constantinianism." In *Cambridge Dictionary of Christian Theology*, edited by David Fergusson et al., 113–14. Cambridge: Cambridge University Press, 2011.

Browning, Don S. *A Fundamental Practical Theology: Descriptive and Strategic Proposals.* Minneapolis: Fortress, 1996.

Brueggemann, Walter. *Old Testament Theology: An Introduction.* Nashville: Abingdon, 2008.

Buber, Martin. *Ich und Du.* Berlin: Schocken, 1922.

Carter, Craig A. *The Politics of the Cross: The Theology and Social Ethics of John Howard Yoder.* Grand Rapids: Brazos, 2001.

Cartwright, Michael G. "Editors' Introduction." In *The Jewish-Christian Schism Revisited*, edited by Michael G. Cartwright and Peter Ochs, 6–29. Scottdale, PA: Herald, 2008.

———. *Practices, Politics, and Performance: Toward a Communal Hermeneutic for Christian Ethics.* Eugene, OR: Wipf & Stock, 2006.

———. "Radical Reform, Radical Catholicity: John Howard Yoder's Vision of the Faithful Church." Introduction to *The Royal Priesthood: Essays Ecclesiastical and Ecumenical*, edited by Michael G. Cartwright, 1–49. Scottdale, PA: Herald, 1994.

Cavanaugh, William T. "From One City to Two: Christian Reimagining of Political Space." *Political Theology* (2006) 299–321.

———. "Separation and Wholeness: Notes on the Unsettling Political Presence of the Body of Christ." In *For the Sake of the World: Swedish Ecclesiology in Dialogue with William T. Cavanaugh*, edited by Jonas Ideström, 7–31. Eugene, OR: Pickwick, 2009.

Clapp, Rodney. *A Peculiar People: The Church as Culture in a Post-Christian Society.* Downers Grove, IL: InterVarsity, 1996.

Clapp, Rodney, and Robert E. Webber. *People of the Truth: The Power of the Worshipping Community in the Modern World.* San Francisco: Harper & Row, 1988.

Cullmann, Oscar. *Christus und die Zeit. Die urchristliche Zeit- und Geschichtsauffasung.* 3rd ed. Zürich: EVZ-Verlag, 1962.

———. *Die Christologie des Neuen Testaments.* Tübingen: Mohr-Siebeck, 1965.

———. *Heil als Geschichte. Heilsgeschichtliche Existenz im Neuen Testament.* Tübingen: Mohr-Siebeck, 1965.

———. *The State in the New Testament.* New York: Scribner's, 1956.

Daube, David. *Civil Disobedience in Antiquity.* Edinburgh: Edinburgh University Press, 1972.

Delumeau, Jean. *Le catholicisme entre Luther et Voltaire.* Paris: Presses Universitaires de France, 1971.

Dodd, C. H. *Apostolic Preaching and Its Developments.* Rev. ed. London: Hodder & Stoughton, 1963.

Doerksen, Paul G. *Beyond Suspicion: Post-Christendom Protestant Political Theology in John Howard Yoder and Oliver O'Donovan*. Carlisle, UK: Paternoster, 2009.

Dorrien, Gary. *Social Ethics in the Making: Interpreting an American Tradition*. Malden, MA: Wiley-Blackwell, 2009.

Engelsviken, Tormod. "Missio Dei: The Understanding and Misunderstanding of a Theological Concept in European Churches and Missiology." *International Review of Mission* 92 (2003) 481–97.

Engen, Charles Van. *The Growth of the True Church*. Amsterdam: Rodopi, 1981.

Fitz-Gibbon, Andrew L. *In the World, but Not of the World*. Lanham, MD: Lexington, 2000.

Flett, John G. *The Witness of God: The Trinity, Missio Dei, Karl Barth, and the Nature of Christian Community*. Grand Rapids: Eerdmans, 2010.

Frost, Michael. *Exiles: Living Missionally in a Post-Christian Culture*. Peabody, MA: Hendrickson, 2006.

Furseth, Inger and Pål Repstad. *Innføring i religionssociologi*. Oslo: Universitetsforlaget, 2003.

Graham, Elaine, and Heather Walton. "A Walk on the Wild Side: A Critique of 'The Gospel and Our Culture.'" *Modern Churchman* 33 (1991) 1–7.

Grane, Leif. *Evangeliet for folket. Drøm og virkelighed i Martin Luthers liv*. Copenhagen: Gad, 1983.

Gregersen, Niels Henrik. *Teologi og kultur. Protestantismen mellem isolation and assimilation i det 19. og 20. århundrede*. 2nd ed. Aarhus, Denmark: Aarhus University Press, 2001.

Goheen, Michael W. *As the Father Has Sent Me, I Am Sending You: J. E. Lesslie Newbigin's Missionary Ecclesiology*. Zoetermeer, Netherlands: Uitgeverij Boekencentrum, 2000.

———. "As the Father Has Sent Me, I Am Sending You: Lesslie Newbigin's Missionary Ecclesiology." *International Review of Mission* 91 (2002) 345–69.

———. "Is Lesslie Newbigin's Model of Contextualization Anticultural?" *Mission Studies* 19 (2002) 136–58.

———. "The Missional Church: Ecclesiological Discussion in the Gospel and Our Culture Network in North America." *Missiology: An International Review* 30 (2002) 480–90.

Goldingay, John. "The Man of War and the Suffering Servant: The Old Testament and the Theology of Liberation." *Tyndale Bulletin* 27 (1976) 79–113.

Goodall, Norman, ed. *Missions Under the Cross: Addresses Delivered at the Enlarged Meeting of the Committee of the International Missionary Council at Willingen, in Germany, 1952; with Statements Issued by the Meeting*. London: Edinburgh House, 1953.

Griffith-Jones, E. *The Dominion of Man*. London: Hodder & Stoughton, 1926.

Guder, Darrell L. *Be My Witnesses: The Church's Mission, Message, and Messengers*. Grand Rapids: Eerdmans, 1985.

———. *The Continuing Conversion of the Church*. Grand Rapids: Eerdmans, 1998.

———. *The Incarnation and the Church's Witness*. Eugene, OR: Wipf & Stock, 1999.

———. "Missional Hermeneutics: The Missional Authority of Scripture—Interpreting Scripture as Missional Formation." *Mission Focus: Annual Review* 15 (2007) 106–21.

———. "Walking Worthily: Missional Leadership after Christendom." *Princeton Seminary Bulletin* 28 (2007) 251–91.
Guder, Darrell L., et al., eds. *Missional Church: A Vision for the Sending of the Church in North America*. Grand Rapids: Eerdmans, 1998.
Guroian, Vigen. *Ethics After Christendom*. Grand Rapids: Eerdmans, 1994.
Hall, Douglas John. *The End of Christendom and the Future of Christianity*. Eugene, OR: Wipf & Stock, 2002.
Harnack, Adolf von. *Militia Christi: The Christian Religion and the Military in the First Three Centuries*. Philadelphia: Fortress, 1981.
Harper, Brad, and Paul Louis Metzger. *Exploring Ecclesiology: An Evangelical and Ecumenical Introduction*. Grand Rapids: Brazos, 2009.
Harvey, Barry A. *Another City: An Ecclesiological Primer for a Post-Christian World*. Harrisburg, PA: Trinity, 1999.
Hazard, Paul. *The European Mind: The Critical Years, 1680–1715*. New Haven: Yale University Press, 1953.
Hauerwas, Stanley. *Against the Nations: War and Survival in a Liberal Society*. Notre Dame: University of Notre Dame Press, 1992.
———. *Christian Existence Today: Essays on Church, World, and Living in Between*. Durham, NC: Labyrinth, 1988.
———. *A Community of Character: Toward a Constructive Christian Social Ethics*. Notre Dame: University of Notre Dame, 1981.
———. *The Peaceable Kingdom: A Primer in Christian Ethics*. 2nd ed. London: SCM, 2003.
———. "Reading Yoder Down Under." In *Faith and Freedom: Christian Ethics in a Pluralist Culture*, edited by David Neville and Philip Matthews, 170–73. Hindmarsh: ATF, 2003.
———. *Truthfulness and Tragedy*. Notre Dame: Notre Dame University Press, 1977.
Hauerwas, Stanley, and Mark Sherwindt. "The Kingdom of God: An Ecclesial Space for Peace." *Word and World* 2 (1982) 127–36.
Hauerwas, Stanley, and William H. Willimon. *Resident Aliens: Life in the Christian Colony*. Nashville: Abingdon, 1989.
Hegstad, Harald. *Den virkelige kirke. Bidrag til ekklesiologien*. Trondheim, Norway: Tapir Akademisk Trondheim, 2009.
Helgeland, John, Robert J. Daly, and J. Patout Burns. *Christians and the Military: The Early Experience*. Philadelphia: Fortress, 1985.
Herrin, Judith. *The Formation of Christendom*. London: Fontana, 1989.
Hooft, Willem A. Visser 't. *The Pressure of Our Common Calling*. London: SCM, 1959.
Hogg, Alfred G. *The Christian Message to the Hindu: Being the Duff Missionary Lectures for Nineteen Forty-Five on the Challenge of the Gospel in India*. London: SCM, 1945.
———. *Karma and Redemption: An Essay toward the Interpretation of Hinduism and the Re-statement of Christianity*. London: Christian Literature Society, 1909.
Hornus, Jean-Michel. *It Is Not Lawful for Me to Fight: Early Christian Attitudes toward War, Violence, and the State*. Translated by Alan Kreider. Scottdale, PA: Herald, 1980.
Hovey, Craig R. "The Public Ethics of John Howard Yoder and Stanley Hauerwas: Difference or Disagreement?" In *A Mind Patient and Untamed: Assessing John Howard Yoder's Contributions to Theology, Ethics, and Peacemaking*, edited by Ben C. Ollenburger and Gayle G. Koontz, 205–20. Telford, PA: Cascadia, 2004.

Huebner, Christ K. *A Precarious Peace: Yoderian Explorations on Theology, Knowledge, and Identity*. Waterloo, ON: Herald, 2006.

———. "Unhandling History: Anti-Theory, Ethics, and the Practice of Witness." PhD diss., Duke University, 2002.

Hunsberger, George R. *Bearing the Witness of the Spirit: Lesslie Newbigin's Theology of Cultural Plurality*. Grand Rapids: Eerdmans, 1998.

———. "Biography as Missiology: The Case of Lesslie Newbigin." *Missiology* 27 (1999) 523–31.

———. "The Missionary Significance of the Biblical Doctrine of Election as a Foundation for a Theology of Cultural Plurality in the Missiology of J. E. Lesslie Newbigin." PhD diss., Princeton Theological Seminary, 1987.

———. "The Newbigin Gauntlet." In *The Church between Gospel and Culture: The Emerging Mission in North America*, edited by George R. Hunsberger and Craig Van Gelder, 3–25. Grand Rapids: Eerdmans, 1996.

Højlund, Asger Chr. *Men han gav afkald. Bidrag til kristologien*. Fredericia, Denmark: Kolon, 2007.

International Missionary Council (IMC). *Tambaram Madras Series I–VII*. London: Oxford University Press, 1938.

Izuzquiza, Daniel. *Rooted in Jesus Christ: Toward a Radical Ecclesiology*. Grand Rapids: Eerdmans, 2009.

Kaiser, Christopher. *Creation and the History of Science*. Grand Rapids: Eerdmans, 1991.

Kaiser, Walther C., Jr. *Mission in the Old Testament: Israel as a Light to the Nations*. Grand Rapids: Baker, 2000.

Kant, Immanuel. *Die Religion innerhalb der Grenzen der blossen Vernunft*. Königsberg, 1794.

———. *Religion within the Limits of Reason Alone*. New York: HarperCollins, 1988.

Kee, Alistair. *Constantine versus Christ*. London: SCM, 1982.

Kelsey, David. "Church Discourse and Public Realm." In *Theology and Dialogue: Essays in Honor of George Lindbeck*, edited Bruce Marshall, 7–34. Notre Dame: University of Notre Dame Press, 1990.

Kenneson, Philip D. *Beyond Sectarianism: Re-imagining Church and World*. Harrisburg, PA: Trinity, 1999.

Kerr, Nathan K. *Christ, History and Apocalyptic: The Politics of Christian Mission*. London: SCM, 2008.

Kimball, Robert R., and Paul Tillich. *Theology of Culture*. New York: Oxford University Press, 1959.

Kraft, Charles H. *Christianity in Culture*. Maryknoll, NY: Orbis, 1979.

Kreider, Alan. "Beyond Bosch: The Early Church and the Christendom Shift." *International Bulletin of Missionary Research* 29 (2005) 59–68.

Kuhn, Thomas. *The Structure of Scientific Revolutions*. Chicago: University of Chicago Press, 1962.

Laing, Mark. "The Calling of the Church to Mission and to Unity: Bishop Lesslie Newbigin and the Integration of the International Missionary Council with the World Council of Churches." PhD diss., University of Edinburgh, 2009.

Lausten, Martin S. *Danmarks kirkehistorie*. Copenhagen: Gyldendal, 2004.

Lehmann, Paul. "Willingen and Lund: The Church on the Way to Unity." *Theology Today* 9 (1953) 431–41.

LeMasters, Philip. *Discipleship between Creation and Redemption: Towards a Believers' Church*. Lanham, MD: University Press of America, 1997.

———. *The Import of Eschatology in John Howard Yoder's Critique of Constantinianism*. San Francisco: Mellen Research University Press, 1992.

Leithart, Peter J. *Defending Constantine: The Twilight of an Empire and the Dawn of Christendom*. Downers Grove, IL: InterVarsity, 2012.

Lindbeck, George A. "Confession and Community: An Israel-like View of the Church." *Christian Century* 107 (1990) 492–96.

———. "The Gospel's Uniqueness: Election and Untranslatability." In *Modern Theology* 13 (1990) 423–50.

———. *The Nature of Doctrine: Religion and Theology in a Postliberal Age*. Chicago: University of Chicago Press, 1984.

Lodberg, Peter, and Björn Ryman. "Church and Society." In *Nordic Folk Churches: A Contemporary Church History*, edited by Gunnar Heiene et al., 99–121. Grand Rapids: Eerdmans, 2005.

Lohfink, Gerhard. *Does God Need the Church? Towards a Theology of the People of God*. Translated by Linda M. Maloney. Collegeville, MN: Liturgical, 1999.

———. *Jesus and Community: The Social Dimension of Christian Faith*. Translated by John P. Calvin. Philadelphia: Fortress, 1984.

Lutheran World Federation. "Mission in Context: Transformation, Reconciliation, Empowerment." Geneva: Lutheran World Federation, 2004.

Lyby, Thodkild C. "Luthers øvrighedsskrift i historisk perspektiv." In *Martin Luther om verdslig øvrighed*, edited by Svend Andersen, 7–31. Aarhus, Denmark: Aarhus University Press, 2006.

MacIntyre, Alasdair. *After Virtue: A Study in Moral Theory*. Notre Dame: University of Notre Dame Press, 1981.

———. *Whose Justice? Which Rationality?* Notre Dame: University of Notre Dame Press, 1988.

Markus, R. A. *The End of Ancient Christianity*. Cambridge: Cambridge University Press, 1990.

Martin-Achard, Robert. *A Light to the Nations*. London: Oliver and Boyd, 1962.

McClendon, James William. *Ethics*. Vol. 1 of *Systematic Theology*. Nashville: Abingdon, 1986.

McLeod, Hugh, and Werner Ustorf, eds. *The Decline of Christendom in Western Europe, 1750–2000*. Cambridge: Cambridge University Press, 2003.

Murphy, Nancey. "John Howard Yoder's Systematic Defense of Christian Pacifism." In *The New Yoder*, edited by Peter Dula and Chris K. Huebner, 42–69. Eugene, OR: Cascade, 2010.

Murray, Stuart. *Post-Christendom: Church and Mission in a Strange New World*. Carlisle, UK: Paternoster, 2004.

Nation, Mark Theissen. *A Comprehensive Bibliography of the Writings of John Howard Yoder*. Goshen, IN: Mennonite Historical Society, Goshen College, 1997.

———. *John Howard Yoder: Mennonite Patience, Evangelical Witness, Catholic Convictions*. Grand Rapids: Eerdmans, 2006.

Neill, Stephen. *The Unfinished Task*. London: Edinburgh House Press and Lutterworth Press, 1957.

Nelson, Paul. *Narrative and Morality: A Theological Inquiry*. University Park: Pennsylvania State University Press, 1987.

Newbigin, J. E. Lesslie. "Baptism, the Church and Koinonia: Three Letters and a Comment." In *Some Theological Dialogues*, edited by M. M. Thomas, 110-44. Madras: CLS, 1977.

———. "The Basis, Purpose and Manner of Inter-Faith Dialogue." *Scottish Journal of Theology* 30 (1977) 253-70.

———. "The Bible and Our Contemporary Mission." *Clergy Review* 69 (1984) 9-17.

———. "Bible Studies Given at the National Christian Council Triennial Assembly, Shillong." *National Christian Council Review* 88 (1968) 9-14, 73-78, 125-31, 177-85.

———. "The Bishop and the Ministry of Mission." In *Today's Church and Today's World*, edited by J. Howe, 242-47. London: CIO, 1977.

———. "Can a Modern Society Be Christian?" In *Christian Witness in Society*, edited by K. C. Abraham, 95-108. Bangalore: BTE-SSC, 1998.

———. "Can the Churches Give a Common Message to the World?" *Theology Today* 9 (1953) 512-18.

———. "The Centrality of Jesus for History." In *Incarnation and Myth: The Debate Continued*, edited by Michael Goulder, 197-210. Grand Rapids: Eerdmans, 1979.

———. "Christ and the Cultures." *Scottish Journal of Theology* 31 (1978) 1-22.

———. "Christ, Kingdom, and Church: A Reflection on the Papers of George Yule and Andrew Kirk." Unpublished paper, 1983.

———. *Christian Freedom in a Modern World*. London: SCM, 1937.

———. *Christian Witness in a Plural Society*. London: British Council of Churches, 1977.

———. "The Church as a Servant Community." *National Christian Council Review* 91 (1971) 256-64.

———. "Church, World, Kingdom." In *Signs Amid the Rubble: The Purposes of God in Human History*, edited by Geoffrey Wainwright, 95-109. Grand Rapids: Eerdmans, 2003.

———. "The Cultural Captivity of Western Christianity as a Challenge to a Missionary Church." In *A Word in Season: Perspectives on Christian World Missions*, 66-79. Grand Rapids: Eerdmans, 1994.

———. "Developments During 1962: An Editorial Survey." *International Review of Mission* 52 (1963) 3-14.

———. "Does Society Still Need the Parish Church?" In *A Word in Season: Perspectives on Christian World Missions*, 48-65. Grand Rapids: Eerdmans, 1994.

———. "The Duty and Authority of the Church to Preach the Gospel." In *The Church's Witness to God's Design*, edited by Lesslie Newbigin and Hendrik Kraemer, 19-35. Amsterdam Assembly Series 2. New York: Harper, 1948.

———. "Evangelism in the City." *Reformed Review* 41 (1987) 3-8.

———. "Evangelism in the Context of Secularization." In *A Word in Season: Perspectives on Christian World Missions*, 148-57. Grand Rapids: Eerdmans, 1994.

———. *A Faith for This One World?* London: SCM, 1961.

———. *The Finality of Christ*. London: SCM, 1969.

———. *Foolishness to the Greeks: The Gospel and Western Culture*. Grand Rapids: Eerdmans, 1986.

———. "The Future of Missions and Missionaries." *Review and Expositor* 74 (1977) 209-18.

———. *The Good Shepherd: Meditations on Christian Ministry in Today's World.* Leighton Buzzard, UK: Faith, 1977.

———. "Gospel and Culture." Unpublished paper given to a conference organized by Danish Mission Council and the Danish Churches' Ecumenical Council in Denmark, 1995.

———. *The Gospel in a Pluralist Society.* Grand Rapids: Eerdmans, 1989.

———. *The Holy Spirit and the Church.* Madras: CLS, 1972.

———. *Honest Religion for Secular Man.* London: SCM, 1966.

———. *The Household of God: Lectures on the Nature of the Church.* London: SCM, 1953.

———. "How Should We Understand Sacraments and Ministry?" Unpublished paper written for an Anglican-Reformed International Commission, London, 1983.

———. *Is There Still a Missionary Job Today?* Glasgow: Iona Community, 1963.

———. "Jesus, Saviour of the World." *South India Churchman* (1972).

———. *Mission in Christ's Way: Bible Studies.* WCC Missions Series 8. Geneva: WCC, 1987.

———. "Mission in the 1980s." *Occasional Bulletin of Missionary Research* 4 (1980) 154-55.

———. *Den missionerende kirke i dag.* Copenhagen: Duplex-trykkeriet, 1965.

———. "On the Gospel as Public Truth: Response to the Colloquium." Unpublished response to the Leeds Colloquium, 1996.

———. *One Body, One Gospel, One World: The Christian Mission Today.* London: International Missionary Council, 1958.

———. *The Open Secret: Sketches for a Missionary Theology.* London: SPCK, 1978.

———. *The Other Side of 1984: Questions for the Churches.* Geneva: WCC, 1983.

———. "The Present Crisis and the Coming Christ." *Ecumenical Review* 6 (1954) 118-23.

———. "Presiding at the Lord's Supper." Unpublished paper, 1979.

———. *Priorities for a New Decade.* Birmingham: National Student Christian Press and Resource Centre, 1980.

———. *Proper Confidence: Faith, Doubt and Certainty in Christian Discipleship.* Grand Rapids: Eerdmans, 1995.

———. "The Prophetical Task of Pastoral Ministry: The Gospels." In *The Pastor as Prophet*, edited by Earl E. Shelp and Ronald H. Sunderland, 78-98. New York: Pilgrim, 1985.

———. "Recent Thinking on Christian Beliefs: VIII. Mission and Missions." *Expository Times* 88 (1977) 260-64.

———. *The Relevance of Trinitarian Doctrine for Today's Mission.* CWME Study Pamphlet 2. London: Edinburgh House, 1963.

———. "Religious Pluralism: A Missiological Approach." *Studia Missionalia* 42 (1993) 227-44.

———. "Religious Pluralism and the Uniqueness of Jesus Christ." *International Bulletin of Missionary Research* 13 (1989) 50-54.

———. "Reply to Konrad Raiser." *International Bulletin of Missionary Research* 18 (1994) 51-52.

———. *The Reunion of the Church: A Defence of the South India Scheme.* Rev. ed. London: SCM, 1960.

———. "Review of God's Order: The Ephesian Letter and This Present Time." *Theology Today* 10 (1954) 543–47.

———. *Signs amid the Rubble: The Purposes of God in Human History*. Edited by Geoffrey Wainwright. Grand Rapids: Eerdmans, 2003.

———. *Sin and Salvation*. London: SCM, 1956.

———. *Trinitarian Faith and Today's Mission*. American ed. of *The Relevance of Trinitarian Doctrine for Today's Mission*. Richmond: Knox, 1964.

———. *Truth and Authority in Modernity*. Philadelphia: Trinity, 1996.

———. *Truth to Tell: The Gospel as Public Truth*. Grand Rapids: Eerdmans, 1991.

———. *Unfinished Agenda: An Autobiography*. Grand Rapids: Eerdmans, 1985.

———. *Unfinished Agenda: An Updated Autobiography*. Grand Rapids: Eerdmans, 1993.

———. "Why Study the Old Testament?" *National Christian Council Review* 74 (1954) 71–76.

———. "Will God Dwell on the Earth?" *National Christian Council Review* 79 (1959) 99–102.

———. *A Word in Season: Perspectives on Christian World Missions*. Grand Rapids: Eerdmans, 1994.

———. *Your Kingdom Come*. Leeds, UK: John Paul the Preacher's, 1980.

Niebuhr, H. Richard. *Christ and Culture*. New York: Harper & Row, 1951.

Nikolajsen, Jeppe B. "Beyond Christendom: Lesslie Newbigin as a Post-Christendom Theologian." *Exchange: A Journal of Missiological and Ecumenical Research* 41 (2012) 364–80.

———. "Beyond Sectarianism: The Missional Church in a Post-Christendom Society." *Missiology: An International Review* 41 (2013) 462–75.

———. "The Formative Power of Liturgy: The Church as a Liturgical Community in a Post-Christendom Society." *European Journal of Theology* 23 (2014) 161–68.

———. "Kirkens konstantinske fangenskab: Aktuel problemstilling og kritisk begrebsudvikling." In *National kristendom til debat*, edited by Jeppe Bach Nikolajsen, 9–19. Fredericia, Denmark: Kolon, 2015.

———. "Lesslie Newbigins postfundamentistiske epistemologi. Om følgerne af opgøret med oplysningstidens epistemologi." *Dansk Tidsskrift for Teologi og Kirke* 34 (2007) 26–34.

———. "Lesslie Newbigins udfordringer til den vestlige kirke." *Kristeligt Dagblad*, December 8, 2009 (feature on the occasion of the centennial of Lesslie Newbigin).

———. "Missional Church: An Historical and Theological Analysis of an Ecclesiological Tradition." *International Review of Mission* 102 (2013): 249–61.

———. "Missional ekklesiologi: En teologihistorisk analyse af en ekklesiologisk tradition." *Norwegian Journal of Missiology* 63 (2009) 19–34.

———. "Missional Folk Church? A Discussion of Hans Raun Iversen's Understanding of the Danish Folk Church as a Missional Church." *Swedish Missiological Themes* 100 (2012) 23–36.

———. "Missional kirke i et pluralistisk samfund." In *Missional kirke—en introduktion*, edited by Jeppe Bach Nikolajsen, 127–44. Fredericia, Denmark: Kolon, 2012.

———. "Kirkens mulighed for at genvinde sig selv: John Howard Yoders antikonstantinske teologi." In *National kristendom til debat*, edited by Jeppe Bach Nikolajsen, 154–181. Fredericia, Denmark: Kolon, 2015.

———. *Udfordringer til den vestlige kirke. En studie af Lesslie Newbigins sene forfatterskab*. Aarhus, Denmark: Teoltryk, 2007.

Nissen, Karsten. *En gammel folkekirke i en ny tid: Evangeliet og vores kultur*. Frederiksberg, Denmark: Aros, 2008.

———. "Folkekirken—sendt til det danske folk." In *Missional kirke—en introduktion*, edited by Jeppe B. Nikolajsen, 89–110. Fredericia, Denmark: Kolon, 2012.

———. "Mission og enhed." Thesis, Aarhus University, 1973.

———. "Missional kirke. Ens kirke sendt til det danske folk." *Dansk Tidsskrift for Teologi og Kirke* 36 (2009) 97–111.

Nugent, John C. *Radical Ecumenicity: Pursuing Unity and Continuity after John Howard Yoder*. Abilene, TX: Abilene Christian University Press, 2010.

Ochs, Peter. "Editors' Introduction." In *The Jewish-Christian Schism Revisited*, edited by Michael G. Cartwright and Peter Ochs, 2–6. Scottdale, PA: Herald, 2008.

Ollenburger, Ben C., and Gayle G. Koontz, eds. *A Mind Patient and Untamed: Assessing John Howard Yoder's Contributions to Theology, Ethics, and Peacemaking*. Telford, PA: Cascadia, 2004.

Pannenberg, Wolfhart. *Systematische Theologie I–III*. Göttingen: Vandenhoeck and Ruprecht, 1991.

———. *Wissenschaftstheorie und Theologie*. Frankfurt: Suhrkamp, 1973.

Parham, Robert M. "An Ethical Analysis of the Christian Social Strategies in the Writings of John C. Bennett, Jacques Ellul, and John Howard Yoder." PhD diss., Baylor University, 1984.

Park, Joon-Sik. *Missional Ecclesiologies in Creative Tension: H. Richard Niebuhr and John Howard Yoder*. New York: Lang, 2007.

Ramachandra, Vinoth. *The Recovery of Mission*. Carlisle, UK: Paternoster, 1996.

Ramsey, Paul. *Speak Up for Just War or Pacifism*. University Park: Pennsylvania State University Press, 1988.

Rasmusson, Arne. "The Church as a 'Creative Minority': On Being Church in Today's Europe." In *Religions and Churches in a Common Europe*, edited by János Wildmann, 72–88. Bremen, Germany: Europäischer Hochschuleverlag.

———. *Church as Polis: From Political Theology to Theological Politics as Exemplified by Jürgen Moltmann and Stanley Hauerwas*. Notre Dame: University of Notre Dame Press, 1995.

———. "Christendom." In *The Cambridge Dictionary of Christian Theology*, edited by Ian McFarland et al., 97–98. Cambridge: Cambridge University Press, 2011.

———. "The Politics of Diaspora: The Post-Christendom Theologies of Karl Barth and John Howard Yoder." In *God, Truth, and Witness: Essays in Conversation with Stanley Hauerwas*, edited by L. Gregory Jones et al., 88–111. Grand Rapids: Brazos, 2005.

———. "Revolutionary Subordination: A Biblical Concept of Resistance in the Theology of John Howard Yoder." In *Peace in Europe, Peace in the World: Conflict Resolution and the Use of Violence*, 35–67. Iustita et Pax Dokumentation 3. Vienna: Südwind, 2002.

———. "Sacrament as Social Process: Some Historical Footnotes." In *For the Sake of the World: Swedish Ecclesiology in Dialogue with William T. Cavanaugh*, edited by Jonas Ideström, 32–48. Eugene, OR: Pickwick, 2009.

Rescher, Nicolas. *Philosophical Reasoning: A Study in the Methodology of Philosophizing*. Malden, MA: Blackwell, 2001.

Ricoeur, Paul. *Oneself as Another*. Translated by Kathleen Blamey. Chicago: University of Chicago Press, 1992.
Pohlsander, Hans A. *The Emperor Constantine*. New York: Routledge, 1996.
Polanyi, Michael. *Personal Knowledge: Toward a Post-Critical Philosophy*. Chicago: University of Chicago Press, 1958.
———. *Science, Faith, and Society*. Oxford: Oxford University Press, 1946.
———. *The Tacit Dimension*. Garden City, NY: Doubleday, 1966.
Roth, John D. *Constantine Revisited: Leithart, Yoder, and the Constantinian Debate*. Eugene, OR: Pickwick, 2013.
Rowell, Andrew D. "The Ecclesiology of John Howard Yoder: Scripture, Five Practices of the Christian Community, and Mission." Personal blog of Andy Rowell, http://www.andyrowell.net/andy_rowell/files/the_ecclesiology_of_john_howard_yoderpdf.pdf (accessed January 29, 2015).
Roxburgh, Alan. *What Is Missional Church? An Introduction to the Missional Church Conversation*. Eagle, ID: Allelon, 2007.
Sandnes, Karl Olav. *A New Family: Conversion and Ecclesiology in the Early Church with Cross-Cultural Comparisons*. New York: Lang, 1994.
Sawatsky, Rodney J. "John Howard Yoder." In *Non-Violence: Central to Christian Spirituality*, edited by Joseph T. Culliton, 239–69. New York: Mellen, 1982.
Schlabach, Gerald. "Deuteronomic or Constantinian: What Is the Most Basic Problem for Christian Social Ethics?" In *The Wisdom of the Cross: Essays in Honor of John Howard Yoder*, edited by Stanley Hauerwas et al., 449–71. Grand Rapids: Eerdmans, 1999.
Schuster, Jürgen. *Christian Mission in Eschatological Perspective: Lesslie Newbigin's Contribution*. Nürnberg: VTR, 2009.
Schuurman, Douglas J. *Vocation after Christendom*. Grand Rapids: Eerdmans, 2004.
Shenk, Wilbert R. "Lesslie Newbigin's Contribution to Mission Theology." *International Bulletin of Missionary Research* 24 (2000) 59–64.
Sherman, Steven B. *Revitalizing Theological Epistemology: Holistic Evangelical Approaches to the Knowledge of God*. Eugene, OR: Wipf & Stock, 2008.
Shin, Won Ha. "Two Models of Social Transformation: A Critical Analysis of the Theological Ethics of John H. Yoder and Richard J. Mouw." PhD diss., Boston University, 1997.
Sider, J. Alexander. *To See History Doxologically: History and Holiness in John Howard Yoder's Ecclesiology*. Grand Rapids: Eerdmans, 2011.
Simons, Menno. "Reply to Gellius Faber." Translated by Leonard Verduin. In *The Compele Writings of Menno Simons, c. 1496–1561*, edited by John Christian Wenger, 739–44. Scottdale, PA: Herald, 1956.
Smith, David. *Mission after Christendom*. London: Darton, Longman & Todd, 2003.
Stoltzfus, Philip E. "Nonviolent Jesus, Violent God? A Critique of John Howard Yoder's Approch to Theological Construction." In *Power and Practices: Engaging the Work of John Howard Yoder*, edited by Jeremy M. Bergen and Anthony G. Siegrist, 29–46. Scottdale, PA: Herald, 2009.
Stone, Bryan. *Evangelism after Christendom: The Theology and Practice of Christian Witness*. Grand Rapids: Brazos, 2007.
Stults, Donald Le Roy. *Grasping Truth and Reality: Lesslie Newbigin's Theology of Mission to the Western World*. Eugene, OR: Wipf & Stock, 2008.
Søvik, Atle O. *The Power of God and the Problem of Evil*. Leiden: Brill, 2011.

Thiemann, Ronald F. *Revelation and Theology: The Gospel as Narrated Promise*. Notre Dame: University of Notre Dame Press, 1985.

Torrance, Alan J. "*Creatio ex Nihilo* and the Spatio-Temporal Dimensions, with Special Reference to Jürgen Moltmann and D. C. Williams." In *The Doctrine of Creation: Essays in Dogmatics, History and Philosophy*, edited by Colin E. Gunton, 83–103. London: T. & T. Clark, 2004.

Vandervelde, George. "The Church as Missionary Community: The Church as Central Disclosure Point of the Kingdom." Unpublished paper given at a colloquium on the theme "A Christian Society? Witnessing to the Gospel of the Kingdom in the Public Life of Western Culture," Leeds, England, 1996.

Veldhorst, Berend J. "A Christian Voice in a World without God." PhD diss., State University of Utrecht, 1990.

Vicedom, Georg F. *Missio Dei: Einführung in eine Theologie der Mission*. Münich: Kaiser, 1958.

Volf, Miroslav. *After Our Likeness: The Church as the Image of the Trinity*. Grand Rapids: Eerdmans, 1998.

Wainwright, Geoffrey. *Lesslie Newbigin: A Theological Life*. New York: Oxford University Press, 2000.

Weaver, Alain E. "On Exile: Yoder, Said, and a Theology of Land and Return." In *The New Yoder*, edited by Peter Dula and Chris K. Huebner, 142–65. Eugene, OR: Cascade, 2010. Reprinted from *Cross Currents* 52 (2003) 439–61.

Wessels, Anton. *Europe: Was It Ever Really Christian?* London: SCM, 1994.

Weston, Paul, compiler. *Lesslie Newbigin: Missionary Theologian: A Reader*. Grand Rapids: Eerdmans, 2006.

———. "Mission and Cultural Change: Critical Engagement with the Writings of Lesslie Newbigin." PhD diss., University of London, 2001.

Wolterstorff, Nicholas. *Reason within the Bounds of Religion*. Grand Rapids: Eerdmans, 1984.

Woodard-Lehmann, Derek Alan. "Being and Bearing the Witness of the Spirit: Toward a Postcolonial Missional Politics." *Pro Ecclesia* 18 (2009) 437–58.

Wright, Christopher J. H. *Walking in the Ways of the Lord: The Ethical Authority of the Old Testament*. Downers Grove, IL: InterVarsity, 1995.

Wright, Nigel G. *Disavowing Constantine: Mission, Church and the Social Order in the Theologies of John Howard Yoder and Jürgen Moltmann*. Eugene, OR: Wipf & Stock, 2007.

Yoder, John H. "The Authority of Tradition." In *The Priestly Kingdom: Social Ethics as Gospel*, 63–79. Notre Dame: University of Notre Dame Press, 1984. Reprinted from *Foundations of Ethics*, edited by Leroy S. Rouner, 57–75. Notre Dame: Notre Dame University Press, 1983.

———. "The Believers Church and the Arms Race." In *For the Nations: Essays Public and Evangelical*, 148–61. Grand Rapids: Eerdmans, 1997.

———. *Body Politics: Five Practices of the Christian Community before the Watching World*. Scottdale, PA: Herald, 1992.

———. "'But We Do See Jesus': The Particularity of Incarnation and the Universality of Truth." In *The Priestly Kingdom: Social Ethics as Gospel*, 46–62. Notre Dame: University of Notre Dame Press, 1984. Reprinted from *Foundations of Ethics*, edited by Leroy S. Rounder, 57–75. Notre Dame: University of Notre Dame Press, 1983.

———. "Christ, the Hope of the World." In *The Original Revolution*, 140–76. Scottdale, PA: Herald, 1971.

———. *Christian Attitudes to War, Peace, and Revolution*. Edited by Theodore J. Koontz and Andy Alexis-Baker. Grand Rapids: Brazos, 2009.

———. "The Christian Case for Democracy." In *The Priestly Kingdom: Social Ethics as Gospel*, 151–71. Notre Dame: University of Notre Dame Press, 1984. Substantially rewritten edition of an article with the same title from *Journal of Religious Ethics* 5 (1977) 209–23.

———. *The Christian Witness to the State*. 1964. Newton, KS: Faith and Life, 2002.

———. "Church and State according to a Free Church Tradition." In *On Earth Peace*, edited by Donald F. Durnbaugh, 279–88. Elgin, IL: Brethren, 1978.

———. "Church Growth Issues in Theological Perspective." In *The Challenge of Church Growth: A Symposium*, edited by Wilbert R. Shenk, 25–48. Scottdale, PA: Herald, 1973.

———. "The 'Constantinian' Sources of Western Social Ethics." In *The Priestly Kingdom: Social Ethics as Gospel*, 135–47. Notre Dame: University of Notre Dame Press, 1984. Reprinted from *Missionalia* 4 (1976) 98–108.

———. "Discerning the Kingdom of God in the Struggles of the World." *International Review of Mission* 68 (1979) 366–72.

———. *The Ecumenical Movement and the Faithful Church*. Scottdale, PA: Mennonite, 1958.

———. *For the Nations: Essays Public and Evangelical*. Grand Rapids: Eerdmans, 1997.

———. "From the Wars of Joshua to Jewish Pacifism." In *Nonviolence—A Brief History: The Warsaw Lectures*, edited by Paul Martens, Matthew Porter, and Myles Werntz, 73–84. Waco, TX: Baylor University Press, 2010.

———. *The Fullness of Christ: Paul's Vision of Universal Ministry*. Elgin, IL: Brethren, 1987.

———. *He Came Preaching Peace*. Scottdale, PA: Herald, 1985.

———. "Hoekendijk and Evangelism." Unpublished letter to Theron Schlabach, December 10, 1973. Available at the John Howard Yoder Archives in Goshen, Indiana, box 181.

———. "If Abraham Is Our Father." In *The Original Revolution*, 85–104. Scottdale, PA: Herald, 1971.

———. "If Christ Is Truly Lord." In *The Original Revolution*, 52–84. Scottdale, PA: Herald, 1971.

———. "Introduction." In *For the Nations: Essays Public and Evangelical*, 1–11. Grand Rapids: Eerdmans, 1997.

———. "It Did Not Have to Be." In *The Jewish-Christian Schism Revisited*, edited by Michael G. Cartwright and Peter Ochs, 43–66. Scottdale, PA: Herald, 2008.

———. "Jesus' Life-Style Sermon and Prayer." In *Social Themes of the Christian Year: A Commentary on the Lectionary*, edited by Dieter T. Hessel, 87–96. Philadelphia: Geneva, 1983.

———. "Jesus the Jewish Pacifist." In *The Jewish-Christian Schism Revisited*, edited by Michael G. Cartwright and Peter Ochs, 69–89. Scottdale, PA: Herald, 2008.

———. *The Jewish-Christian Schism Revisited*, edited by Michael G. Cartwright and Peter Ochs. Scottdale, PA: Herald, 2008.

———. *Karl Barth and the Problem of War and Other Essays on Barth*. Edited by Mark Thiessen Nation. Eugene, OR: Cascade, 2003.

———. "Let the Church Be the Church." In *The Original Revolution*, 107–24. Scottdale, PA: Herald, 1971.

———. "Meaning after Babble: With Jeffrey Stout beyond Relativism." *Journal of Religious Ethics* 24 (1996) 125–39.

———. "The Meaning of the Constantinian Shift." In *Christian Attitudes to War, Peace, and Revolution*, edited by Theodore J. Koontz and Andy Alexis-Baker, 57–74. Grand Rapids: Brazos, 2009.

———. *Nevertheless: Varieties of Religious Pacifism*. Rev. and exp. ed. Scottdale, PA: Herald, 1992.

———. "The New Humanity as Pulpit and Paradigm." In *For the Nations: Essays Public and Evangelical*, 37–50. Grand Rapids: Eerdmans, 1997.

———. *Nonviolence: A Brief History; The Warsaw Lectures*. Edited by Paul Martens, Matthew Porter and Myles Werntz. Waco, TX: Baylor University Press, 2010.

———. "The Nonviolence of Rabbinic Judaism." In *Christian Attitudes to War, Peace, and Revolution*, edited by Theodore J. Koontz and Andy Alexis-Baker, 137–43. Grand Rapids: Brazos, 2009.

———. "On Not Being in Charge." In *The Jewish-Christian Schism Revisited*, edited by Michael G. Cartwright and Peter Ochs, 168–79. Scottdale, PA: Herald, 2008. Reprinted from *War and Its Discontents*, edited by J. Patout Burns, 74–90. Washington, DC: Georgetown University Press, 1996.

———. "The Original Revolution." In *The Original Revolution*, 13–33. Scottdale, PA: Herald, 1971.

———. "The Otherness of the Church." In *The Royal Priesthood: Essays Ecclesiastical and Ecumenical*, edited by Michael G. Cartwright, 53–64. Scottdale, PA: Herald, 1998. Reprinted from *The Drew Gateway* 30 (1960) 151–60.

———. "Outline Commentary on Matthew 28:16ff. and Acts 1:8." Unpublished paper presented to a conference of missionary leaders in Lake Forest, Illinois, in August 1961. Available at the John Howard Yoder Archives in Goshen, Indiana.

———. "The Pacifism of Karl Barth." In *Karl Barth and the Problem of War and Other Essays on Barth*, edited by Mark Thiessen Nation, 109–32. Eugene, OR: Cascade, 2003.

———. "The Pacifism of Pre-Constantinian Christianity." In *Christian Attitudes to War, Peace, and Revolution*, edited by Theodore J. Koontz and Andy Alexis-Baker, 42–56. Grand Rapids: Brazos, 2009.

———. "The Peace Testimony and Conscientious Objection." *Gospel Herald* (1958) 57–58.

———. "A People in the World." In *The Royal Priesthood: Essays Ecclesiastical and Ecumenical*, edited by Michael G. Cartwright, 65–101. Scottdale, PA: Herald, 1998. Reprinted from *The Concept of the Believers' Church*, edited by James Leo Garrett, 250–83. Scottdale, PA: Herald, 1969.

———. *The Politics of Jesus: Vicit Agnus Noster*. 2nd ed. Grand Rapids: Eerdmans, 1994.

———. *Preface to Theology: Christology and Theological Method*. Grand Rapids: Brazos, 2007.

———. *The Priestly Kingdom: Social Ethics as Gospel*. Notre Dame: University of Notre Dame Press, 1984.

———. "The Prophetical Task of Pastoral Ministry: The Gospels." In *The Pastor as Prophet*, edited by Earl E. Shelp and Ronald H. Sunderland, 78–98. New York: Pilgrim, 1985.

Bibliography

———. "Radical Reformation Ethics in Ecumenical Perspective." In *The Priestly Kingdom: Social Ethics as Gospel*, 105–22. Notre Dame: University of Notre Dame Press, 1984. Reprinted from *Journal of Ecumenical Studies* 15 (1978).

———. *The Royal Priesthood: Essays Ecclesiastical and Ecumenical*. Edited by Michael G. Cartwright. Scottdale, PA: Herald, 1998.

———. "Sacrament as Social Process: Christ the Transformer of Culture." In *The Royal Priesthood: Essays Ecclesiastical and Ecumenical*, edited by Michael G. Cartwright, 359–73. Scottdale, PA: Herald, 1998.

———. "'See How They Go with Their Face to the Sun.'" In *The Jewish-Christian Schism Revisited*, edited by Michael G. Cartwright and Peter Ochs, 183–202. Scottdale, PA: Herald, 2008.

———. *Täufertum und Reformation in der Schweiz: I. Die Gespräche zwischen Täufern und Reformatoren 1523–1538*. Karlsruhe: H. Schneider, 1962.

———. "The Theological Basis of the Christian Witness to the State." In *On Earth Peace*, edited by Donald Durnbaugh, 136–43. Elgin, IL: Brethren, 1978.

———. "A Theological Critique of Violence." In *The War of the Lamb: The Ethics of Nonviolence and Peacemaking*, edited by Glen H. Stassen, Mark Thiessen Nation, and Matt Hamsher, 27–41. Grand Rapids: Brazos, 2009.

———. "The Theology of the Church's Mission." *Mennonite Life* (1966) 30–33.

———. *The War of the Lamb: The Ethics of Nonviolence and Peacemaking*. Edited by Glen H. Stassen, Mark Thiessen Nation, and Matt Hamsher. Grand Rapids: Brazos, 2009.

———. "What Do Ye More than They?" *Gospel Herald* (1973) 72–75.

———. *When War Is Unjust: Being Honest in Just-War Thinking*. 2nd ed. Eugene, OR: Wipf & Stock, 2001.

———. "Why Ecclesiology Is Social Ethics: Gospel Ethics versus the Wider Wisdom." In *The Royal Priesthood: Essays Ecclesiastical and Ecumenical*, edited by Michael G. Cartwright, 102–26. Scottdale, PA: Herald, 1998.

Zampaglione, Gerardo. *The Idea of Peace in Antiquity*. Translated by Richard Dunn. Notre Dame: University of Notre Dame Press, 1973.

Zimmerman, Earl. *Practicing the Politics of Jesus: The Origin and Significance of John Howard Yoder's Social Ethics*. Telford, PA: Cascadia, 2007.

Index

Aagaard, Anna Marie, 172
Aagaard, Johannes, 183
Adam, 36, 38, 167
Abraham, 34–35, 73, 107, 119, 133, 167–68, 170–71
Accra, 47
Ahonen, Tina, 45
Anabaptist(s), Anabaptism, 12–14, 96, 98, 118, 120, 159, 179
Andersen, Wilhelm, 42, 166, 185
Anglican, 14, 73
Anselm, 126
Anticultural, 11, 18, 163, 172
Apocalyptic, apocalypse, 3, 107
Aquinas, Thomas, 69–70
Arché, 69, 73, 180
Aristotle, 69
Assimilate, assimilation, 174–75, 183
Athanasius, 69
Atonement, 78, 148, 167
Augustine, 69, 72, 116, 152
Authority, authorities, 7–8, 27, 56, 71, 77/79, 89, 104–5, 124, 129, 146, 148–50, 179, 181
Babylon, 107, 109–10
Bacon, Francis, 70
Bader-Saye, Scott, 10
Badham, Roger A., 194–95
Baptism, 6, 27–30, 115–16, 136, 155, 172
Barnes, Timothy, 5
Barth, Karl, 12, 14, 24, 35, 70, 78, 96–98, 166,
Barthian, 183
Bartley, Jonathan, 10
Baumgartner, Walther, 96
Baynes, Norman H., 5
Bender, Harold S., 96
Berentsen, Jan-Martin, 45, 50

Berger, Peter L., 75
Berkhof, Hendrik, 56, 143, 147
Bevans, Stephen B., 10–11, 82, 163, 167
Bible, 4, 7, 16, 33–35, 54–55, 68, 74, 87, 91, 100, 132, 167
Blauw, Johannes, 169–70
Body of Christ, 36–37, 53, 60, 82, 142, 151, 157
Bonhoeffer, Dietrich, 14, 68,
Bosch, David J., 44, 47, 49–50, 167
Bredero, Adriaan H., 6
Brennan, John P., 167, 171
Bretherton, Luke, 26
Brueggemann, Walther, 168–69
Buber, Martin, 78

Calvin, John, 113
Carey, William, 42
Carter, Craig A., 97–98, 100, 105, 113, 114, 123–24, 126, 140, 149–50
Cartwright, Michael G., 108, 111, 151, 156
Catholic(ity/ism), 73, 98, 117, 125
Cavanaugh, William, ix, 178, 194
Clapp, Rodney, 9, 13, 98
Chandran, Russell, 44
Chaplaincy, 27, 30, 84, 178
Christendom, 3–11, 13–14, 23, 25–33, 40, 62, 66, 80, 84, 86, 89, 91, 99, 102–3, 105, 115–17, 120, 131, 156–57, 163, 184, 191–92, 196
Christian ethic(s), 63, 66, 83, 98, 101–2, 122, 124, 140–41, 146, 155, 160, 176–77, 180
Christocentric, 48, 52, 57
Christology, Christological(ly), 3–4, 14, 52, 65–67, 80–83, 97, 122, 124–25, 140, 154

213

Index

Church,
  and accomodation to society, 3
  and baptism, 28–29, 115–16, 155, 172
  and Bible, 4
  and eschatology, 102, 105, 150–53, 155–58, 166, 171, 185–86, 192–93
  and the Holy Spirit, 4, 46, 49, 51–52, 59, 74, 141, 171, 181–82, 185–86
  as a chosen people, 10–11, 33, 41, 82, 107, 109, 121, 134, 160, 168, 192
  as minority, 84, 89–90, 101, 107, 158, 175, 179, 192, 195
  as missionary, 25–31, 40, 43–44, 85, 119–20, 129, 163–64
  as prototype, 53, 82, 119
Citizenship, 111
Coercion, 89
Commission for World Mission and Evangelism, 24
Communion, 28, 114, 118, 126, 155, 166, 176
Congregation(al/s), 63, 65–66, 76, 96, 114–15, 117–19, 129, 157, 178
Conversion, 5, 27, 51, 70, 98–99
Consistency, 17, 123, 131, 154
Constantine, 4–5, 27, 30, 98–103, 109, 111, 121, 123, 138, 152, 155
Constantinian(ism), 5, 13, 26, 31–32, 88, 98–105, 111, 116, 122, 138, 140, 151–55, 157, 160, 180, 193
Contextualization, 11, 86, 122
Cornelius, 51–52
Corpus Christi, 157, 191–93
Corpus Christianum, 7, 28, 31, 80, 157, 191–93
Cosmos, 36, 78–79, 148–49
Countercultural, 11, 82, 164, 175
Creatio ex amore Dei, 167
Creatio ex missione Dei, 167
Creation(al), 34–36, 41, 49–50, 53–54, 79, 83, 96, 100, 105, 122, 126–27, 142–43, 146, 152, 157, 166–68, 171–72, 176, 183
Creator, 33, 49, 54–55, 60, 169

Cross, 37, 59–60, 62, 76, 89, 122, 126, 129–31, 137, 147, 148, 156, 174
Crucifixion, 36, 58, 147
Cullmann, Oscar, 55, 96–98, 136, 138, 143–44, 148–49, 151, 153
Cyprian, 138

Daube, David, 139
Delumeau, Jean, 8–9
Democracy, democratic, 88, 120, 122, 128, 159, 175, 179
Descartes, René, 70,
Diaspora, 106, 110–11, 119, 121, 156
Discipleship, 58, 78, 98, 125, 127, 130, 140, 146, 155, 173, 193
Disunity, disunities, 29, 37
Distinct(ive/ness)
  and church, 5–6, 9–19, 23, 25, 30, 32–33, 37, 40–41, 52–54, 61–64, 66–67, 79–84, 87, 91, 95, 101–2, 105, 111, 113, 116, 119–21, 127–28, 140, 153–54, 158, 160, 163–65, 169, 173, 175–76, 178–82, 185–86, 191–96
Dodd, C. H., 182
Doerksen, Paul G., 13, 103, 106–8, 124
Dorrien, Gary, 164

Early church, 24, 26, 28–29, 40, 65, 69, 87, 113, 114, 115–116, 125, 128–29, 139, 144, 173, 177,
Ecclesia, 26, 46, 87, 116, 171, 185
Ecclesia invisibilis, 116
Ecclesial, ecclesiology, ecclesiological, 3–4, 10, 12–14, 18–19, 23–28, 31–33, 37, 40, 46, 48, 52, 61, 66, 72, 79–82, 86, 89, 91, 95, 98, 101, 105, 110, 112–13, 121, 129, 140, 150, 155–57, 160, 163–66, 173, 177, 186–87, 191–94, 196
Ecumenical movement, 13–14, 28, 37, 41–42, 46, 48, 104, 165
Ecumenism, 24, 27, 30–31, 98
Election, 12, 33–40, 52, 54–55, 81, 167–68, 170
Engelsviken, Tormod, ix, 45
Engen, Charles Van, 53

Index

Enlightenment, 9, 32, 70–72, 84, 103–4, 159, 163, 186, 194–95
Epistemology, epistemologies, epistemological(ly), 67, 71, 72, 74, 77, 79–81, 83, 102, 157, 164–66, 182, 184, 186
Eschatology, eschatological, 3–4, 12–13, 23, 27, 32, 51, 54–55, 58, 61, 63–64, 66, 70, 80–82, 91, 95, 101–2, 105, 124, 125, 139, 141, 144, 148–52, 155–58, 160, 166, 170–71, 185–86, 192–93
Ethic(al/ist/ists/s), 12–13, 23, 32, 62–63, 66–67, 80–81, 83, 91, 95–96, 98, 101–3, 105, 122–28, 133, 140–41, 146, 148, 153, 155–58, 160, 164–66, 176–77, 180, 186, 192–95
Eucharist, 114–15
Eusebius, 152
Evangelical, evangelicalism, 98, 159, 179
Evangelism, 24, 66, 96
Evangelization, 53
Excommunicated, 114
Exile(d), exilic, 107–11, 121, 155, 158, 194

Flett, John G., 45
Free church tradition, 13
Freedom, 48, 59, 90, 105, 160, 193
Frost, Michael, 9
Furseth, Inger, 75

Gentile(s), 40, 51, 106, 115, 136, 150–51, 170
Goheen, Michael W., ix, 6, 12–13, 25, 27–32, 44, 46, 48–49, 51–52, 60, 63, 65, 78, 85–89, 172, 177
Goodall, Norman, 44
Gospel, 75–77, 79, 81–82, 84–86, 88–89, 105–6, 118, 120–21, 124–26, 138, 145, 149, 165, 175, 177, 181–84, 195–96
Gospel and Our Culture movement, 13, 25
Grane, Leif, 7
Great Commission, 36, 42, 119

Gregersen, Niels Henrik, 17, 181–83
Guder, Darrell L., 3–4, 120, 156–57, 166, 171, 184
Guroian, Vigen, 10

Hall, Douglas John, 7, 9–10
Harnack, Adolf von, 139
Harper, Brad, 166
Hartenstein, Karl, 44
Harvey, Barry A., 7, 9–10
Hauerwas, Stanley, 10, 14, 131, 141, 165, 176, 180, 184, 195
Hegstad, Harald, 173
Helgeland, John Robert J., 99
Hermeneutic(al/s), 15–16, 18, 63, 67, 76, 79, 181
Herrin, Judith, 5–6
Holy Spirit, 4, 17, 29, 46, 48–49, 51–52, 55, 59, 74, 141, 166–67, 171, 181–82, 185–86
Holy war(s), 6, 103, 131–34
Hooft, Willem A. Visser 't, 117–18
Hogg, Alfred G., 85
Hope(s), 3, 57, 59, 70, 77, 110, 112, 132, 151–53, 178
Hornus, Jean-Michel, 139
Hospitality, 127–28
Hovey, Craig R., 14
Huebner, Chris K., 100, 157
Hunsberger, George R., 12, 33, 35, 37, 39, 53, 72, 81–83
Højlund, Asger Chr., 127, 145

Imago Dei, 54
Imperialism, imprerialistic, 89, 164, 179, 195
Incarnation, 52, 82, 102, 122, 141, 167, 185
Individual(ism/ ly /s), 3, 17, 29, 34, 38, 54, 86–87, 113, 133, 150, 185, 195
International Mission Council, 24, 43, 47
Irrelevant/irrelevance, 85, 123, 125,–26
Isolation(ism/ist), 39, 55, 169, 174–76, 186, 194

Israel(ite), 31, 33–36, 41, 50, 52–53, 55, 68–69, 106–10, 121, 131–36, 152, 156, 167–71, 177, 180, 182
Izuzquiza, Daniel, 164

Jaspers, Karl, 96
Jeremian shift/turn, 109
Jerusalem, 43, 69, 97, 106, 109–10, 134
Jews, 7, 34, 40, 68, 101, 106, 108, 110, 115, 132, 136, 150–53
Jewish, 68, 105–6, 109–10, 119, 129, 132, 135–36, 158, 171, 177, 194
Jewish people, 106, 109–10, 119, 158, 171, 194
Jewry, 106–7
Judaism(s), 105–6, 109–11, 135–36, 152

Kaiser, Walther C., Jr., 168–70
Kant, Immanuel, 74
Kee, Alistair, 5, 99
Kelsey, David, 164
Kenneson, Philip D., 10, 19, 164, 173, 182
Kenosis, 138, 167
Kerr, Nathan K., 100
Kingdom of God, 50–51, 56–59, 61, 64–65, 81–82, 141, 144–45, 149–51, 153, 166–67, 185, 192, 195
Knowledge, 67, 69–73, 78, 97, 102, 132, 143, 152, 157, 181–83, 186
Kraemer, Hendrick, 86
Kraft, Charles H., 3
Kuhn, Thomas, 72

Laing, Mark, 47
Lausten, Martin S., 7
Lehmann, Paul, 44
Lindbeck, George A., 17, 177
Lodberg, Peter, 194–95
Lohfink, Gerhard, 167, 169, 176, 178

MacIntyre, Alasdaire, 67
Markus, R. A., 6
Martin-Achard, Robert, 53
McClendon, James William, 165
Missio Dei generalis, 45, 167
Missio Christi, 46, 171

Missio ecclesiae, 46, 171
Missiology, 3–4, 12, 23–25, 32–33, 37, 40–41, 46, 48, 52–53, 66, 80–82, 91, 120, 156, 166, 183, 186, 192
Missional, 4, 13, 24–26, 28, 42, 76, 80, 156, 163, 165, 168, 172–73, 176
Missional church, 13, 156
Missional ecclesiology, 24–26, 28
Modernity, 72
Monocultural, 11, 18
Moses, 73, 107, 131–32, 136
Murphy, Nancey, 95
Murray, Stuart, 4–5, 8–10, 31

Nation(s/al/alism), 7, 16, 32, 35–36, 40, 49, 66, 82, 88, 103–4, 106–8, 110–12, 119, 134, 136, 145, 149, 151–53, 158, 168–71, 194
Nation, Mark T., 95–98
Natural law, 97, 102, 157
Neill, Stephen, 118
New Delhi, 47–48
New Testament, 27, 29, 37, 54–58, 68–69, 90, 96–97, 100, 107, 109–10, 112, 124–25, 128, 130, 132–33, 135, 137, 141, 143–45, 148–50, 152, 170–71, 173, 177, 185

Newbigin, J. E. Lesslie,
  life and work of, 12, 14, 23–24
  on baptism, 28–29
  on Christendom, 28–32, 40, 62, 66, 80, 84, 86, 89, 91, 192
  on Christian society, 89–91, 193
  on Christian tradition, 60, 68–69, 71–74, 77–79, 180
  on communion, 28
  on election, 11
  on ecumenism, 14, 28, 30, 37, 48, 86
  on *missio Dei*, 46, 49–50, 52
  on plausibility structure, 75–77, 87
  on powers and principalities, 56–58, 62, 90, 97
Newton, Isaac, 70
Niebuhr, H. Richard, 3, 144, 174
Nissen, Karsten, 5–7, 43–45
Nonviolence, nonviolent, 133

Index

Obedience, 68, 87, 101, 121, 126–27, 130, 141, 146–47, 149, 151, 155, 172, 176
Ochs, Peter, 106, 111
Old Testament, 34, 56, 96, 103, 106, 108, 126, 131–35, 167–70, 177
Origen, 69, 138

Pacifism, pacifist(s), 97, 99, 102, 128, 131, 135–36, 138–40
Pannenberg, Wolfhart, 17
Parham, Robert M., 130–31
Parousia, 55, 141, 144, 148, 150
Particularity, 12, 35, 37, 40, 52, 157, 165, 168, 184, 193–94
Paul(ine), 100, 105–7, 115, 124, 129, 131, 138, 142–45, 147, 150, 170, 177, 182
Peace(able), 60, 96, 110, 119, 131, 139, 171,
Pentecost, 35, 51, 141, 148, 150, 171
Peoplehood, 158
Persecuted, persecution, 4–5, 31, 90, 104, 107, 130–31, 135, 138
Plausibility structure(s), 72, 75–77, 87, 183
Pneumatology, 3–4, 82
Politic(s/al/ally), 86–87, 89, 99, 104, 110–11, 115, 120–22, 125–26, 130, 136–37, 143, 146, 148, 158, 160, 169, 174, 180, 192
Polanyi, Michael, 67, 71–72, 74
Post-Christendom, 3–4, 8–10, 12–19, 23, 26, 62, 83–85, 87, 91, 95, 158–60, 163, 177, 179, 184, 191, 194–96
Post-Christian, 9
Powers and principalities, 56, 58, 62, 90, 97, 110, 143–45, 157, 170, 174, 185, 193
Practical theology, 4, 191–92
Pre-Constantinian(ism), 26, 99, 102, 138
Pre-Christendom, 4–5, 27–30, 32
Presence, 41, 50–51, 53, 57–58, 60, 121, 130, 141, 159, 173
Private, 26, 55, 87, 114
Privatization, 88

Protestant(ism), 13–14, 45, 90, 98, 183, 195
Public(ly), 14, 26, 32, 61, 64, 75, 84, 87–90, 112, 120, 122, 147, 176, 180, 192
Pluralistic, x, 9, 33, 90, 193–94, 196

Quakers, 159, 179

Rabbinic Judaism, 111, 136
Ramachandra, Vinoth, 12, 24
Ramsey, Paul, 124–25
Rationality, 60, 70–71, 73, 74, 78–79, 83, 180
Rasmusson, Arne, ix, 7–8, 11, 98, 125, 130, 139–40, 152, 159, 164, 179
Reason(ing), 61, 70–75, 78–79, 128, 176, 195
Redemption, 54, 79, 102, 116, 135, 149, 152, 155, 193
Reformation, 6–8, 28, 103, 118, 120, 179, 195
Reformed, 7, 14, 22, 24, 96
Repentance, 88–89, 101, 140, 160, 182
Repstad, Pål, 75
Rescher, Nicolas, 17
Responsibility, 30–32, 36, 66, 88, 90, 102, 114, 123, 146, 155, 158, 164, 170, 176–78, 180, 186, 192, 194, 196
Resurrection, 35, 51, 55, 126, 147, 149–50, 171, 182
Revelation, 16, 59, 70–74, 79, 97, 122, 126, 144, 148, 157, 181, 183–84, 195
Relevance, 12, 85–86, 134, 175
Revolution(ary), 69, 104, 128–30, 137, 173
Ricoeur, Paul, 15–16
Rome, 107, 129, 145
Roman Empire, 4–6, 26, 121
Rowell, Andrew D., 113–15
Roxburgh, Alan, 13

Sacrament(s), 27–29, 31, 76, 81, 117, 134

Salvation, 3, 26, 28, 33–35, 37–40, 47, 50–51, 55, 63, 66, 119, 134, 144, 146, 149, 168, 170, 182
Salvation history, 33, 50, 55, 149
Sandnes, Karl Olav, 173
Sawatsky, Rodney J., 164–65
Secular(ization), 7, 9, 33, 55, 62, 82, 84, 86–88, 90, 102–3, 145, 157, 192
Sectarian(ism), 11, 18, 163–65, 172–73, 176, 182, 194, 196
Scripture(s), 4, 31, 73, 79, 105, 107–10, 113, 122, 125, 139, 157, 170, 181
Schlabach, Gerald, 108
Schuster, Jürgen, 12, 31–32, 54, 57–58, 61, 63–64
Schuurman, Douglas J., 10
Shalom, 55, 61, 108, 119, 167
Shenk, Wilbert R., 12, 24, 120, 157
Shin, Won Ha, 97, 125, 128
Simons, Menno, 118
Slavery, 159, 179
Smith, David, 10
Soteriology, 3–4
Spener, Philipp Jakob, 113
Stoltzfus, Philip E., 95
Stone, Bryan, 10, 100, 105
Suffer(ing), 50, 58, 61, 90, 118, 120–21, 127–28, 130–31, 136–38, 156, 158, 174, 184
Synagogue(s), 106, 109
Syncretism, 8, 85–86
Søvik, Atle O., 17

Talmud, 109, 135
Tambaram, 43–44, 46
Tertullian, 69, 138
Temple, 36, 106, 109, 111, 139
Theocratic, 90, 112–13
Thiemann, Ronald F., 17
Tillich, Paul, 3
Torah, 108–9, 135–36
Torrance, Alan J., 167
Tower of Babel, 159
Trinity, 8, 46, 55, 167
Trinitarian, 41, 46, 48–49, 52, 58, 166

Uppsala, 45

Ustorf, Werner, 9

Vandervelde, George, 23, 175
Vicedom, Georg F., 45
Violence, 102, 127, 131–33, 139, 173, 195
Visibility and church, 116, 118, 121
Volf, Miroslav, 112, 166

Wainwright, Geoffrey, 12, 24, 63, 65
Weaver, Alain Epp, 108, 110, 119, 156
Webber, Robert E., 13, 98
Wessels, Anton, 8–9
Weston, Paul D. A., 71
Whitby, 44
Willingen, 44–47
Williams, Rowan, 14
Witness(ed/es/ing), 3–4, 24–25, 28, 32–34, 36–37, 40–42, 50, 58–59, 73, 82, 84–86, 90, 102, 114, 118–21, 151, 153, 158, 165, 170, 172–73, 176, 180–81, 183, 193
Wolterstorff, Nicholas, 74
Woodard-Lehmann, Derek Alan, 165
World Council of Churches, x, 24, 47, 96
Wright, Christopher J. H., 169, 175

Yoder, John H.
  life and work of, 11–14, 95–97
  on baptism, 115–16, 136, 155
  on Christology, 97, 122, 124–25, 140, 154
  on Constantinianism, 98–105, 111, 116, 122, 138, 140, 151–55, 157, 160, 193
  on diaspora, 106, 110–111, 119, 121, 156
  on holy wars, 103, 131–34
  on marks of the church, 117–18
  on method, 157, 177
  on pacifism, 97, 128, 131, 135–36, 140
  on powers and principalities, 97, 110, 142–45, 147–48, 157
  on suffering, 118, 120–21, 127–28, 130–31, 136–38, 156, 158

on subordination, 128–30
on the visibility of the church, 116, 118

Zampaglione, Gerardo, 139
Zealot(s), 136–37, 153, 173–74
Zimmerman, Earl, 96, 98, 130, 136, 153, 156, 173

www.ingramcontent.com/pod-product-compliance
Lightning Source LLC
Chambersburg PA
CBHW062024220426
43662CB00010B/1469